College English for Art Majors

An Integrated Course

艺术类大学英语综合教程

1

主　编　张云鹤　杨　莉
副主编　陈　为　李　颖　王　芳
编　委　王晓宇　杨　平　牛晓平　陈文雅
　　　　王秀芹　吴　楠　王少逸　庞　淼
　　　　王　芳　李　颖　谷童宇　陈　为
　　　　杨　莉　张云鹤

清华大学出版社
北　京

版权所有，侵权必究。举报：010-62782989，beiqinquan@tup.tsinghua.edu.cn。

图书在版编目（CIP）数据

艺术类大学英语综合教程. 1 / 张云鹤, 杨莉主编. —北京：清华大学出版社，2016（2022.7重印）
（高校英语选修课系列教材）
ISBN 978-7-302-43478-8

Ⅰ.①艺⋯　Ⅱ.①张⋯②杨⋯　Ⅲ.①艺术—英语—高等学校—教材　Ⅳ.①H31

中国版本图书馆 CIP 数据核字（2016）第 078299 号

责任编辑：朱　琳
封面设计：平　原
责任校对：王凤芝
责任印制：杨　艳

出版发行：清华大学出版社
　　　　　网　　址：http://www.tup.com.cn, http://www.wqbook.com
　　　　　地　　址：北京清华大学学研大厦 A 座　　邮　编：100084
　　　　　社 总 机：010-83470000　　　　　　　　　邮　购：010-62786544
　　　　　投稿与读者服务：010-62776969, c-service@tup.tsinghua.edu.cn
　　　　　质量反馈：010-62772015, zhiliang@tup.tsinghua.edu.cn
印　刷　者：北京富博印刷有限公司
装　订　者：北京市密云县京文制本装订厂
经　　　销：全国新华书店
开　　　本：185mm×260mm　　印　张：15.5　　字　数：329 千字
版　　　次：2016 年 9 月第 1 版　　　　　　　　印　次：2022 年 7 月第 8 次印刷
定　　　价：65.00 元

产品编号：066041-06

前　言

当今时代，艺术文化内涵不断丰富，国际艺术、文化交流活动日益频繁，艺术人才走向国际的机会也越来越多。因此，熟练掌握英语成为艺术专业人才踏上国际艺术舞台、接触其他文化艺术形式的重要条件。在这样的背景下，提高艺术类大学的英语教学质量，推动教学模式的改革与发展，是艺术类高校面临的重要任务之一。《艺术类大学英语综合教程》编写组从艺术类学生的专业特点及实际英语水平出发，借鉴国内外优秀教材编写经验，以书面问卷、学生座谈和教师座谈形式进行了广泛的调查研究，历经两年编写完成。本套教材将英语教学和艺术通识教育紧密结合，充分调动学生的学习积极性，从而达到提高学生艺术英语实际运用能力的目的。

本套教材共两册，每册包括十个单元，供艺术类本科生两学年的公共英语课使用。

本套教材的编写主要遵循以下原则：

1. 坚持人文主义教育观。按照《大学英语课程教学要求》中对艺术类本科生的"一般要求"的教学目标，即"大学英语不仅是一门语言基础课"，更"兼具工具性与人文性"。从艺术类学生基础薄弱、对英语学习兴趣淡薄的实际出发，以夯实基础英语为目标，同时将英语学习、人文素养与艺术熏陶融合为一体。学生在学习的过程中，不仅提高了语言技能，也同时提高了综合文化素养。

2. 强调大学英语教学目标。即"培养学生具有一定的英语综合应用能力，特别是听说能力，使他们在今后工作和社会交往中能较熟练地用英语行口头和书面的信息交流，同时不断增强学生自主学习能力，提高综合文化素养，以适应培养应用型、高层次技能型人才及社会发展和经济建设的需要"。本套教材在选材方面，充分挖掘艺术领域多样化的题材，为学生提供真实的艺术场景模拟，使学生的英语学习与今后的实际工作紧密结合。

3. 体现教学模式改革。改变以教师为主体、学生被动接受的教学模式，凸显自主学习和个性化学习理念，注重调动学生的积极性，发挥学生在学习中的能动作用和教师在教学中的引导作用。在教材练习的设计上，学生能够充分发挥自己的专业优势和艺术创造力，激发学生对英语学习的兴趣和想象力。

教材特色：

1. 完整的知识体系：本套教材把听、说、读、写四个模块有机融合为一体。本套教材的编写从教学实际出发，各单元设计了听说、阅读、语法、写作相结合的板块。听说板块帮助学生强化巩固基本语音和听力技能，培养真实情境下的交际能力；阅读板块注重通识与专业素养培养相结合，每单元的阅读板块由三篇文章构成，包括精读和快速阅读两部分；语法板块通过简明扼要的方式对语法知识进行系统梳理和讲解，帮助学生巩固语法基础；写作板块由造句到一段话，依次递进，逐步提高学生写作水平，打好写作基本功。

2. 丰富的主题内容：本套教材充分考虑艺术类专业学生的学习兴趣和专业特点，内容涉及音乐、美术、体育、传媒、文化、文学等多个领域，展现国内外艺术文化风貌，呈现多元化的态势，让学生了解各个领域不同流派和领军人物，同时注重内容的信息性、时代性和趣味性，从而增强学生跨文化交际意识和提高文化素养。

3. 新颖生动的课后练习：本套教材结合每单元主题，设计形式多样的专项训练，引导学生积极主动参与，进而提高学生学习的主动性。每单元设计了全新的实例模式演练，一方面提高了学生的语言能力，另一方面激发了学生的艺术创作能力和在实际职场中的实践能力及提高团队合作精神。

4. 完整的学习平台：本套教材配有课文音频和电子教案，为教师和学生提供完整便捷的学习平台。

扫下方二维码，可获取配套音频资源。

本套教材内容丰富多彩，建议每单元用 6 学时完成，教师可根据实际情况有所增减。希望本套教材为提升艺术类专业学生的大学英语教学质量，从而推动大学英语改革贡献力量。

由于编者水平有限，诚恳希望广大教师在使用过程中不吝赐教，提出宝贵意见，使这套教材不断得到修订与完善。

编者

2016 年 5 月 15 日

目 录

Unit 1　Visual Arts

Section A　Listening and Speaking
　　　　　Task A　Phonetics—Rhyming Words ················1
　　　　　Task B　Conversations ················2
　　　　　Task C　Passage ················3
　　　　　Task D　Spot Dictation ················4
Section B　Reading
　　　　　Passage A　People Have Been Making Art for a Very Long Time ············4
　　　　　Passage B　Self-Portraits by Vincent van Gogh: Take a Good Look at
　　　　　　　　　　Yourself ················10
　　　　　Passage C　Fast Reading　Genius of European Art ················15
Section C　Grammar
　　　　　主语（一）(Subject Ⅰ) ················17
Section D　Sentence Writing
　　　　　Arts and Crafts: Me-shirt ················20

Unit 2　Music

Section A　Listening and Speaking
　　　　　Task A　General Pronunciation Rules ················23
　　　　　Task B　Conversations ················24
　　　　　Task C　Passage ················25
　　　　　Task D　Spot Dictation ················25
Section B　Reading
　　　　　Passage A　Development of Jazz? ················26
　　　　　Passage B　Celine Marie Claudette Dion ················32
　　　　　Passage C　Fast Reading　Satchmo—A Jazz Superstar ················38
Section C　Grammar
　　　　　主语（二）(Subject Ⅱ) ················40

  Section D Sentence Writing
    Let's Design a Concert Poster! ·· 42

Unit 3 Festivals

  Section A Listening and Speaking
    Task A General Pronunciation Rules ································ 45
    Task B Conversations ·· 45
    Task C Passage ·· 47
    Task D Spot Dictation ··· 47
  Section B Reading
    Passage A A Thanksgiving Story ·· 48
    Passage B Valentine's Day ·· 53
    Passage C Fast Reading Halloween ································ 58
  Section C Grammar
    主谓一致（一）(Subject-Verb Concord Ⅰ) ································ 60
  Section D Sentence Writing
    Celebrate Thanksgiving Day ·· 63

Unit 4 Creative Advertisements

  Section A Listening and Speaking
    Task A General Pronunciation Rules ································ 65
    Task B Conversations ·· 66
    Task C Passage ·· 67
    Task D Spot Dictation ··· 68
  Section B Reading
    Passage A Sweet and Bitter Advertisements ·························· 68
    Passage B The Coca-Cola Hug Machine ······························· 74
    Passage C Fast Reading David Ogilvy: the Man Who Invented
         Modern Advertising ·· 79
  Section C Grammar
    主谓一致（二）(Subject-Verb Concord Ⅱ) ······························ 83
  Section D Sentence Writing
    The Cannes Lions International Festival of Creativity ················· 86

Unit 5 Sports

  Section A Listening and Speaking
    Task A General Pronunciation Rules ································ 89
    Task B Conversations ·· 90
    Task C Passage ·· 91
    Task D Spot Dictation ··· 92

Section B	Reading
	Passage A God of Basketball ··· 92
	Passage B David Beckham ·· 98
	Passage C Fast Reading A Special Extreme Athlete ············· 103
Section C	Grammar
	宾语（一）(Object I) ·· 104
Section D	Sentence Writing
	Color Run ·· 108

Unit 6 Achieving Dreams

Section A	Listening and Speaking
	Task A General Pronunciation Rules ···································· 111
	Task B Conversations ··· 111
	Task C Passage ·· 113
	Task D Spot Dictation ··· 113
Section B	Reading
	Passage A Dream Art ·· 114
	Passage B Teenage Dreams: Nicola Formichetti's Fashion Rebirth ······· 120
	Passage C Fast Reading Pursuing Your Dreams ·················· 125
Section C	Grammar
	宾语（二）(Object II) ··· 127
Section D	Sentence Writing
	What Do You Want to Strive for in Your Lifetime? ···················· 131

Unit 7 Culture

Section A	Listening and Speaking
	Task A General Pronunciation Rules ···································· 133
	Task B Conversations ··· 134
	Task C Passage ·· 135
	Task D Spot Dictation ··· 136
Section B	Reading
	Passage A Teaching People to Think ···································· 136
	Passage B Civil Rights Leader: Martin Luther King, Jr. ············ 142
	Passage C Fast Reading Mayan Civilization ······················· 149
Section C	Grammar
	定语（一）(Attribute I) ··· 150
Section D	Sentence Writing
	Chinese Papercut ·· 154

Unit 8 Psychology

Section A	Listening and Speaking
	Task A General Pronunciation Rules ···································· 155

	Task B Conversations ········· 156
	Task C Passage ········· 157
	Task D Spot Dictation ········· 157
Section B	Reading
	Passage A Pressure ········· 158
	Passage B Three Instant Mood Lifters ········· 162
	Passage C Fast Reading The Meanings of Red, Yellow and Blue ········· 167
Section C	Grammar
	定语（二）(Attribute Ⅱ) ········· 168
Section D	Sentence Writing
	What Is Your Personality Type? ········· 172

Unit 9 Life Beyond the Earth

Section A	Listening and Speaking
	Task A General Pronunciation Rules ········· 173
	Task B Conversations ········· 174
	Task C Passage ········· 175
	Task D Spot Dictation ········· 176
Section B	Reading
	Passage A Are We Alone? ········· 177
	Passage B Close Encounters ········· 182
	Passage C Fast Reading Do Aliens Exist? If So, Will They Kill Us? ········· 189
Section C	Grammar
	状语（一）(Adverbials Ⅰ) ········· 191
Section D	Sentence Writing
	What Happens Once We Find Aliens ········· 195

Unit 10 Architecture

Section A	Listening and Speaking
	Task A General Pronunciation Rules ········· 197
	Task B Conversations ········· 197
	Task C Passage ········· 199
	Task D Spot Dictation ········· 200
Section B	Reading
	Passage A The Art of Building ········· 200
	Passage B Grand Architect ········· 206
	Passage C Fast Reading Wonder of the World: the Taj Mahal ········· 211
Section C	Grammar
	状语（二）(Adverbials Ⅱ) ········· 213
Section D	Sentence Writing
	My House Paint Color! ········· 217

Glossary ········· 219

Unit 1

Visual Arts

Section A Listening and Speaking

Task A Phonetics—Rhyming Words

Tips: Rhyming words are simply defined as a pair of words with identical sound. They do not need to have the same spelling to rhyme.
For example:
cat hat
The words "cat" and "hat" rhyme because they sound the same at the end.
blue shoe
These words rhyme but don't have the same spelling where they rhyme.

Listen to a rhyme and write down the missing words with the appropriate forms of the words given below.

I know all the sounds that the animals _____,
and make them all day from the moment I _____,
I roar like a mouse and I purr like a _____,
I hoot like a duck and I moo like a _____.

I squeak like a cat and I quack like a _____,
I oink like a bear and I honk like a _____,
I croak like a cow and I bark like a _____,
no wonder the animals marvel at _____.

moose   bee   make   me   goose   frog   hog   wake

Task B Conversations

Model Dialogue 1: Meeting for the First Time

1. Listen to the conversation and fill in the blanks with the expressions given below.

David: Hi! My name is David. We haven't met before, have we?

Lucy: No, we haven't! _____.

David: _____, Lucy!

Lucy: _____, David.

David: Are you a new student?

Lucy: Yes, I am. _____?

David: Yeah, me too!

Lucy: What are you studying here?

David: Arts. _____. What about you?

Lucy: _____. But I'm thinking of doing business studies instead.

> 1. Nice to meet you   2. I want to be a painter   3. What about you
> 4. My name is Lucy   5. I'm doing law   6. Same here

2. Role-play a conversation in pairs according to the given situation.

    David and Lucy meet in the library again. They greet each other. David asks Lucy whether she succeeds in changing her major.

Model Dialogue 2: Introduction

1. Listen to the conversation and fill in the blanks with the expressions given below.

Lucy: Ben, this is my friend, David.

Ben: _____.

David: Nice to meet you.

Ben: _____ the school life so far?

David: It's really different from what I expected.

Ben: Don't worry. You'll _____ it in no time.

Lucy: Ben and I are going to the art museum this afternoon. _____?

David: _____, but I have a painting class this afternoon.

Ben: Oh, it's time for class now. _____.

Lucy and Ben: See you!

Unit 1 Visual Arts

1. What do you think about
4. We've got to go
2. get used to
5. Would you like to join us
3. Glad to meet you
6. I'd like to

2. Role-play a conversation in pairs according to the given situation.

Lucy meets her English professor on the way to the museum with Ben. Lucy introduces Ben to her professor.

Task C Passage

Listen to the passage and choose the best answer to each question.

Word Tips:
1. rare [reə(r)] *adj.* 罕见的，不寻常的
2. possession [pə'zeʃn] *n.* 所有物，财产
3. load [ləud] *vt.* 把……装入或装上；*n.* 装载，负荷，工作量

1) What kind of bones did Mr. Grey have?

   A. Common bones.   B. Human bones.

   C. Unusual bones.   D. Useful bones in his work.

2) Why did Mrs. Grey make all the arrangement?

   A. Because she was moving.

   B. Because her husband was busy.

   C. Because her husband collected bones.

   D. Because she cared more for the bones.

3) Why did the man nearly drop the box?

   A. The box was too heavy to carry.

   B. Mrs. Grey told him to treat the box carefully.

   C. His feet were injured.

   D. He thought Mr. Grey was in the box.

Task D Spot Dictation

Listen to the passage three times and fill in the blanks.

> **Word Tips:**
> 1. weapon ['wepən] *n.* 武器，兵器
> 2. sew [səu] *v.* 缝，做针线活
> 3. dweller ['dwelə(r)] *n.* 居民，居住者
> 4. appreciate [ə'pri:ʃieit] *vt.* 欣赏，感激
> 5. weave [wi:v] *v.* 编，织

Cave 1) _____ from the Old Stone Age show us animals and 2) _____. But more importantly, they also show us the **weapons** that were in use in prehistoric times. They show that fire was used, and that people had learned to make **sewing** needles from 3) _____, and that stone tools had been invented for 4) _____ and cutting. Some roughly formed images have been found in the caves, too, showing that cave **dwellers appreciated** the 5) _____ of the human form. In the New Stone Age, people learned to **weave** 6) _____. They didn't have to 7) _____ on animals' skins for clothing.

Section B Reading

Passage A

People Have Been Making Art for a Very Long Time

Pre-reading Questions

1. Where are the earliest drawings likely to be found?
2. What were the most commonly painted animals thousands of years ago?

We all know the French have **refined** tastes for food and drink, but are you surprised that they also made some of the oldest **cave** art? When you're traveling around a **mountainside** in southern France, you are able to **come upon** cave **paintings** of 28 000 to 40 000 years ago! These cave paintings are not only one of the oldest but also the most *elaborated* works of cave art. Can you **imagine** who drew these pictures? How did the **ancient** artists **obtain** their paint colours? What sort of pictures were painted? What was the purpose of these cave paintings?

The earliest cave art was also found in other countries in Europe and the United States. The paintings were mostly about animals. Animals, such as the **buffalo** or horses, were not only used as food but also meant **strength**. **Abstract** art is common, too. **A variety of** dots, lines, signs and **symbols** have been found on the cave walls. All paint colours used in cave paintings were from nature, for example, they used animals blood for painting and their hair for a brush.

As the cave paintings show, people have been making art for a very long time. Long after the cave people, but still thousands of years before you were born, the people in ancient Egypt made beautiful and **amazing works** of art. For the ancient *Egyptians*, art was an important part of their **religion**. There are many wonderful works of the ancient Egyptians, such as the *pyramids*, or the Great Sphinx.

Across cultures different parts of the world and time, the history of painting is a long river of **creativity**, which continues into the 21st century. However, it mainly carried **religious** and **classical** meanings until the early 20th century, only after which time more pure arts have started to **gain favor**.

(301 words)

New Words

refine	[ri'fain]	vt. 精制，改善，使高雅
cave	[keiv]	n. 洞穴
mountainside	['mauntənsaid]	n. 山腰，山坡
painting	['peintiŋ]	n. 绘画，油画
elaborated ★	[i'læbərətid]	adj. 复杂的，精心制作的，精巧的
imagine	[i'mædʒin]	vt. 设想，想象；vi. 想象，猜想，推测
ancient	['einʃənt]	adj. 古代的，古老的；n. 古代人
obtain	[əb'tein]	vt. 获得，得到，达到（目的）；vi. 通行，流行
buffalo	['bʌfələu]	n. 水牛
strength	[streŋθ]	n. 力量，优点
abstract	['æbstrækt]	adj. 抽象的，难解的，抽象派的
symbol	['simbl]	n. 象征，标志，符号
amazing	[ə'meiziŋ]	adj. 令人惊异的

work	[wə:k]	n. （艺术家、作家、作曲家等的）作品，著作
Egyptian ★	[i'dʒipʃn]	n. 埃及人；adj. 埃及的，埃及人的
religion	[ri'lidʒən]	n. 宗教
pyramid ★	['pirəmid]	n. 金字塔
creativity	[ˌkri:ei'tivəti]	n. 创造性，创造力
religious	[ri'lidʒəs]	adj. 宗教的，虔诚的
classical	['klæsikl]	adj. 古典的，经典的
gain	[gein]	vt./vi. 获得，赢得
favor	['feivə]	n. 好感，宠爱，欢心

Useful Expressions

come upon 偶遇，突然发现或遇到
a variety of 多种的，种种

Proper Names

the Great Sphinx [sfiŋks] 狮身人面像

After-reading Activity

Make your own cave drawing (a large cardbox as prop). What would you draw? Why?

Background Information

1. The pyramids（金字塔）

埃及金字塔是古埃及人埋葬国王和王后的陵墓，古埃及人建造金字塔的历史从第三王朝延续到第十三王朝（公元前2686—前2181年），距今已有四千六百多年。埃及的金字塔很多，素有金字塔之国的美称，现存金字塔107座，主要位于首都开罗附近的吉萨（Giza）高原。这一地区有三座较大的金字塔，分别是胡夫金字塔（也叫大金字塔）、卡夫拉金字塔和孟卡拉金字塔，其中最宏伟的是位于吉萨的胡夫金字塔，它已成为埃及国家和文明的象征。

2500年前，古希腊人列出了当时世界七大奇观，如今，七大奇观中只有为首的金字塔经受住了千年岁月的考验留存下来。难怪埃及有句谚语说："人类惧怕时间，而时间惧怕金字塔。"

2. The Great Sphinx（狮身人面像）

大金字塔总共由大约230万块石灰石和花岗岩垒叠而成，中间不用任何黏合材料。而石块与石块之间吻合得天衣无缝，尽管历经4 000多年的风吹雨打，石缝之间都插不进哪怕一把锋利的小刀。每一方石块平均有2.5吨，最重的达到100多吨。以古埃及人当时的劳动力，他们是如何把巨大的石块开采出来，并且运到这里来的？又如何把它们垒砌起来？何以抗拒时间的侵蚀直至今日？而且金字塔的底部四边几乎对着正南、正北、正东、正西，误差小于一度。古埃及人是如何计算得这么精确一直是人们探索而又无法确证的一个谜。

Comprehension

1. Choose the best way to complete each of the following sentences.

1) Animals that meant _____ were often painted on the walls of caves.

   A. beauty   B. strength

   C. mysterious force D. evil

2) After _____ more pure arts began to gain favor.

   A. the late 18th century   B. the late 19th century

   C. the early 20th century   D. the early 21st century

2. Complete the following summary with the words from the passage. The first letter of each missing word is given for your reference.

We all know the French have refined 1) t_____ for food and drink, but are you surprised that they also made some of the oldest 2) c_____ art? When you're 3) t_____ around a mountainside in southern France, you are able to come upon cave 4) p_____ of 28 000 to 40 000 years ago! The earliest art was 5) m_____ about animals. Not only animals that were used as food but also animals that 6) m_____ strength were painted. As the 7) p_____ show, people have been making art for a very long time. The history of painting is a long river of 8) c_____. It mainly carried religious and 9) c_____ meaning until the early 20th century after which time more pure arts gained 10) f_____.

Vocabulary

1. Complete the following sentences with the words given below. Change the form if necessary.

> imagine   ancient   amazing   strength   gain

1) I have _____ favor in my Chinese painting after ten years' efforts.

2) This is really a(n) _____ dance which just brings the house down.

3) We tend to _____ that the Victorians were very prim (循规蹈矩).

4) We should be fully aware of our own _____ and weaknesses.

5) China is recognized as one of the _____ birthplaces of civilization.

2. Complete the following sentences with proper prepositions or adverbs.

1) I came _____ a group of children playing in the street.

2) Two hours _____ a big meal, you are allowed to go swimming.

3) Her skin is white _____ snow.

4) This sort _____ mistakes happen everyday.

Sentence Structure

Combine the following sentences using the structure "not only…but also…".

Sample:

She plays well. She can write music too.

She not only plays well but also can write music.

1) He made a promise. He also kept it.

2) The apartment is inexpensive. It is near my working place, too.

3) Jane can speak Spanish. Tom can speak Spanish, too.

4) Reading books can broaden our horizons. It can also make us wise.

5) Jack is good looking. He is also very rich.

Translation

1. Translate the following English sentences from the text into Chinese.

1) These cave paintings are not only one of the oldest but also the most elaborated works of cave art.

2) Animals, such as the buffalo or horses, were not only used as food but also meant strength.

3) As the cave paintings show, people have been making art for a very long time.

4) For the ancient Egyptians, art was an important part of their religion.

5) The history of painting is a long river of creativity, which continues into the 21st century.

2. Translate the following Chinese sentences into English with the words or phrases given in brackets.

1) 还在很小的时候，他就喜欢绘画了。（have a taste for）

   Even at a young age, he _____.

2) 她在做任何事之前都要得到父母的许可。（obtain）

   She has to _____ before she does anything.

3) 人们基于各种原因去学瑜伽。（a variety of）

   People study yoga _____.

4) 想象一下你坐在那张崭新的大桌子后面。（imagine）

   _____ behind that big new desk.

5) 他赢得了所有导师的青睐。（gain favor）

   He _____ with all the coaches.

Passage B

Self-Portraits by Vincent van Gogh:
Take a Good Look at Yourself

Sometimes an artist paints a **portrait** of himself. This is called a self-portrait. A self-portrait doesn't have to look like a **photograph**. You can paint yourself in many different ways. And each way will say something different about the way you feel about yourself, and the way you want other people to see you.

The **Dutch** painter **Vincent van Gogh** painted many self-portraits during his **lifetime**. He painted himself 37 times between 1886 and 1889. Those self-portraits are **characterized** by **intense** colour **contrasts**. Van Gogh believed that colour expresses something in itself. One cannot do without it; one must **make the most of** it. Vincent was skillful enough to use contrasting colours—green and red, yellow and purple, blue and orange—to **intensify** one another.

One of his self-portraits was created on January 1st, 1889. In this painting, van Gogh looks **calm**, and the gaze of van Gogh is **seldom** directed at the viewer. Many people are surprised by the colours he used. He painted the shadows under his eyes. The green colour contrasted with the red of his hair and beard. Amazingly, van Gogh painted the background in **curved lines** of blue and green. Here the life is shown in tiny waves on the picture—the line of totally **distorted** curve.

Through his self-portraits, we can see a real van Gogh. Van Gogh formed a **unique** style with life experience and **mental** state. He used portrait painting as a method of self-examination, a method to make money and a method of **developing** his skills as an artist. His works and name will never **fade from** people's memory.

You should paint yourselves **as well**. **Whether** you show the whole body **or** only the head and shoulders, your own portrait can **reflect** what you really are.

(295 words)

New Words

portrait	['pɔ:treit]	n. 肖像，肖像画
photograph	['fəutəgra:f]	n. 相片
Dutch	[dʌtʃ]	adj. 荷兰的 n. 荷兰人
lifetime	['laiftaim]	n. 一生，寿命，使用期限
characterize	['kærəktəraiz]	vt. 表示……的典型，赋予……特色
intense	[in'tens]	adj. 紧张的，激烈的，深刻的
contrast	['kɔntra:st]	n. 对比，对照物；v. 对比，成对照
intensify	[in'tensifai]	vt. 强化，加剧
calm	[ka:m]	adj. 平静的，冷静的；v.（使）平静，（使）镇静；n. 镇定，平静
seldom	['seldəm]	adv. 很少，难得；adj. 很少的, 难得的, 稀少的
distorted	[dis'tɔ:tid]	adj. 扭曲的，变形的
unique	[ju:'ni:k]	adj. 独特的，独一无二的
fade	[feid]	vi. 褪去，逐渐消逝；vt. 使褪色；adj. 乏味的，平淡的
mental	['mentl]	adj. 内心的，精神的，思想的
develop	[di'veləp]	v. 发展，开发，冲洗（照片）
reflect	[ri'flekt]	v. 反映，反射，反省

Useful Expressions

make the most of 充分利用

fade from 从……中消逝

as well 也，又

whether…or… 是……还是……

curved lines ★ 曲线

Proper Names

Vincent van Gogh ['vinsənt væn'gəu] 文森特·凡·高（荷兰画家）

Comprehension

1. Mark the following statements *T (true)* or *F (false)* according to the text.

☐ 1) A self-portrait does have to look like a photograph.

☐ 2) Van Gogh believed that one cannot paint without colour.

☐ 3) Many people are surprised by the colours he used to paint his eyes.

☐ 4) The life is shown in curved lines of blue and green on the picture.

☐ 5) Van Gogh believed that we can examine ourselves through portrait painting.

2. Complete the following statements.

1) Sometimes an artist paints a portrait of himself. This is called a _____.

2) Vincent van Gogh painted himself _____ times between 1886 and 1889.

3) Vincent was skillful enough to use contrasting _____ to intensify one another.

4) In one of his self-portraits created in _____ 1st, 1889, van Gogh looks calm, and the gaze of van Gogh is seldom directed at the viewer.

5) Van Gogh used portrait painting as a method of developing his _____ as an artist.

Vocabulary and Structure

1. Put the following words under the corresponding pictures.

portrait   contrast   shadow   curve

1) _____   2) _____   3) _____   4) _____

2. Compare each pair of words and complete the following sentences with the right one. Change the form if necessary.

1) self-portrait, self-portraitist

   I love his _____ in the exhibition.

   Professor Huang is an excellent _____.

2) intense, intensify

   You must _____ your sense of responsibility.

   He was sweating from the _____ heat.

3) skill, skillful

   He is a _____ football player.

   She is interested in the _____ of dancing.

4) create, creation

   God _____ the world.

   Life is the source of literary _____.

3. Complete the following sentences with the words given below. Change the form if necessary.

> contrast   characterize   amazingly   seldom   appearance   unique   develop   reflect

1) We must do our best to _____ the national economy.
2) We should not judge a person by his or her _____.
3) Does this letter _____ how you really think?
4) The boy's room is a complete _____ to the guest room.
5) The book presents a _____ picture of his life experience.
6) The rolling hills _____ this part of England.
7) The girl was _____ courageous.
8) It _____ rains at such a time in winter.

4. Complete the following sentences with the expressions given below. Change the form if necessary.

> make the most of   as well   whether... or...   fade from

1) You decide _____ not to go. It's all up to you.
2) Not only I like this painting, but my mother likes it _____.
3) We shall _____ the opportunity.
4) All memory of her childhood had _____ her mind.

Activity

Planning for a Solo Gallery Show

You've reached the stage in your development as an artist that you've a body of work and have started thinking about a solo gallery show. So, how do you get your paintings into an art gallery?

1. Get familiar with some special English terms about exhibitions.

a solo show 个人秀

gallery 美术馆

exhibition 展览

booth/stand 展位

2. Match the sentences in A with the Chinese equivalents in B.

A

1) Book a location   (   )

2) Choose the right date   (   )

3) Come up with a creative theme   (   )

4) Leave visitors with something they'll remember   (   )

5) Find money-saving ways to promote your show   (   )

6) Last minute details   (   )

B

a) 策划有创意的主题

b) 选择恰当的参展日期

c) 预订展位

d) 最后的细节

e) 采用经济有效的方式宣传你的展览

f) 使你的展览给参观者留下深刻印象

3. Think about what you should pay attention to in order to have a successful solo gallery show.

1) When booking a location for the art show, what should be taken into consideration?

2) How to choose the right date?

3) How to develop your theme?

4) How to decorate your booth to attract the visitors?

5) What are the effective ways to announce your show?

6) After your art work has been completed and ready to hang, what else should you pay attention to?

Passage C Fast Reading

Genius of European Art

A) Once there was a small boy in Florence who loved to watch painters and *sculptors* (雕塑家) at work. He wanted to be an artist, but his father did not like the idea. Little did the man know that his son Michelangelo would become one of the world's most famous artists.

B) Michelangelo began training as an artist at age 13. He was so interested in his art that he often forgot to eat and slept on the floor beside his unfinished artwork. He refused help, even on big projects, so some works took years to complete. Many were never finished.

C) Michelangelo worked in Rome and Florence. In Rome he was **commission**ed (委托制作) to carve a *Pietà* (圣母哀恸). This is a *marble* (大理石) statue showing the Virgin Mary supporting the dead Christ on her knees. The finished work, known as the "Madonna della Pietà", made him famous. And in Florence, Michelangelo spent two years working on a huge block of marble. From it he carved "David", one of the world's finest and best-known sculpture.

D) Between 1508 and 1512, Michelangelo created his most famous work, the paintings on the ceiling of *the Sistine Chapel* (罗马梵蒂冈的西斯廷教堂) in Rome's Vatican. He painted much of the ceiling while lying on his back in a tight *cramp*ed (束缚，限制) position. The *fresco* (壁画) paintings of figures and events from the Bible are huge and splendid. The wall behind the *altar* (祭坛，圣坛) depicts the Last Judgment of humanity by God.

E) Michelangelo was so admired that he became the first European artist whose life story was written during his own lifetime.

Information Match

Please identify the paragraph from which the following information is derived. Each paragraph is marked with a letter.

_____ 1) One of Michelangelo's famous work is the paintings of figures and events on the ceiling of the Sistine Chapel.

_____ 2) Michelangelo's father didn't want him to become an artist.

_____ 3) Michelangelo's biography was written when he was still alive.

_____ 4) Michelangelo was very hard-working, sometimes he forgot to take a rest.

_____ 5) Two of Michelangelo's marble works are Pietà and David.

Background Information

Michelangelo（米开朗基罗）

米开朗基罗（1475年3月6日—1564年2月18日），意大利文艺复兴时期伟大的绘画家、雕塑家、建筑师和诗人，文艺复兴时期雕塑艺术最高峰的代表，与拉斐尔和达·芬奇并称为文艺复兴后三杰。他一生追求艺术的完美，坚持自己的艺术思路，雕刻作品《大卫像》举世闻名，最著名的绘画作品是梵蒂冈西斯廷礼拜堂的《创世记》天顶画和壁画《最后的审判》。他的风格影响了近三个世纪的艺术家。

Section C Grammar

主语（一）(Subject I)

主语表明这句话说的是谁和什么，主语主要由名词、代词或相当于名词的单词、短语或从句充当。

一、名词作主语

The book is the fruit of teamwork.
这本书是团队合作的成果。
A cat has nine lives.
猫有九条命。
Diamond cuts diamond.
强中自有强中手。

二、代词作主语

I have felt a sharp pain.
我感到了剧痛。
That's OK.
这没问题。
Who else did you tell the secret to?
你把秘密还告诉了谁？

三、数词作主语

Two will be enough.
两个就够了。
Two-thirds of the students are international students.
三分之二的学生是留学生。
The fourth is what I like most.
第四个是我最喜欢的。

四、动名词作主语

Skiing is thrilling exercise.
滑雪是很刺激的运动。
A bad beginning makes a bad ending.
不善始者不善终。
It's terrible *not being allowed to smoke at all*.

完全不许吸烟太糟糕了。（为平衡句子结构，用it作形式主语）

五、不定式作主语

To translate this ideal into reality needs hard work.

把理想转变成现实需要辛勤的劳动。

It takes two ***to make a quarrel***.

两个人才吵得起来。（为平衡句子结构，用it作形式主语）

To know everything is to know nothing.

样样皆通，样样稀松。

注意：

1. 不定式作主语时，在很多情况下都可用动名词替代。例如：

To hesitate means failure. = ***Hesitating*** means failure.

犹豫不决就意味着失败。

To know oneself is difficult. = ***Knowing oneself*** is difficult.

有自知之明不容易。

2. 如果作主语的不定式是固定说法，则通常不用动名词替代。例如：

To say is one thing and ***to do*** is another.

说时容易，做时难。

3. 不定式一般表示具体的、特定的行为，通常表示一种目的、愿望或未完成的事情。
   例如：

To finish this task in one day is impossible.

在一天之内完成这项任务是不可能的。

To forgive is to be forgiven.

原谅别人就等于原谅自己。

4. 动名词表示抽象的既成事实或经验。例如：

Working out regularly is good to your health.

经常锻炼身体对健康有好处。

Reading makes a full man.

读书使人完善。

(To be continued)

Exercises

1. Complete the following sentences based on the given Chinese.

1) _____ is most students' pursuit.

取得优异成绩是绝大部分学生的追求。

2) _____ is an insult to him.

将别人称作白痴是对他人的侮辱。

3) _____ is an unforgivable sin here.

在这里，逃课是一种不可原谅的严重错误。

4) _____ will be a great encouragement to him.

这本书的出版对他将是个极大的鼓舞。

5) _____ doesn't really fulfill me.

做妻子和母亲并不能使我感到满足。

6) _____ makes perfect.

熟能生巧。

7) _____ is responsible for the market sales?

你们当中谁负责市场营销？

8) _____ happened to your artist friend?

你那位艺术家朋友究竟怎么了？

2. **Choose the best way to complete each of the following sentences.**

1) _____ is a virtue.

   A. Admit one's mistake　　　　　B. To admit one's mistake

   C. One admits one's mistake　　D. That admitting one's mistake

2) There is no way _____ with John, he is too selfish.

   A. getting along　　B. to get along

   C. get along　　　　D. to getting along.

3) _____ upset all of us.

   A. David suddenly disappeared　　B. David's sudden disappearing

   C. David's suddenly disappear　　D. David suddenly disappearing

4) _____ of a trade never agrees.（同行是冤家）

   A. Two　　　　　B. The two

   C. Being two　　D. Twos

5) _____ to read the book without crying.

   A. This is possible　　B. It seems impossible

   C. That is possible　　D. It is possible that

6) _____ almost seven months to deal with her illness.

   A. It spent her　　B. It took her

   C. She spent　　　D. She took

7) It is no use _____.（覆水难收）

   A. to cry over spilt milk　　B. crying over spilt milk

C. cried over spilt milk   D. in crying over spilt milk

8) — John doesn't seem like the same person.

— _____ so much in the war has made him more thoughtful.

A. Having gone through   B. Had gone through

C. Have gone through   D. To go through

9) Only _____ of all candidates are proved to be qualified.

A. third-four   B. third-fourth

C. three-fourths   D. three-four

10) _____ make light work. （众人拾柴火焰高）

A. A lot of hands   B. Fewer hands

C. A few hands   D. Many hands

Section D   Sentence Writing

Arts and Crafts: Me-shirt

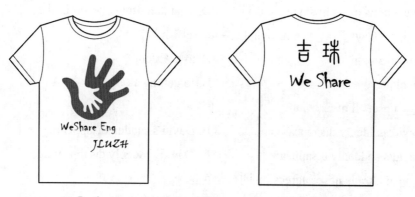

Let's use our artistic skills to create a Me-shirt!

1. What's a Me-shirt?

   Tips: art, writing, personal trait...

   _____

   _____.

2. Why do young people like to wear these kinds of T-shirts?

   Tips: genuine self, pretty, funny...

   _____

   _____.

3. How do you design a Me-shirt?

   Tips: something personal, name, favorite things, family members, pets...

   _____
   _____.

4. Do you plan to have a special Me-shirt party?

   Tips: wear, share, enjoy...

   _____
   _____.

Unit 2

Music

Section A Listening and Speaking

Task A General Pronunciation Rules

A 在重读音节中的发音：

[ei]

1. 在一个辅音字母加上不发音的 e 之前

    例词：m*a*ke, f*a*de, n*a*me, sn*a*ke, t*a*pe, c*a*ke

    特例：h*a*ve [hav], *a*te [et]

2. 在以 -ange 和 -aste 结尾的词中

    例词：ch*a*nge, or*a*nge, str*a*nge, w*a*ste, h*a*ste, t*a*ste

3. 在多数词中位于一个辅音和一个元音之前

    例词：f*a*tal, n*a*sal, r*a*dio, d*a*tum, l*a*bel, p*a*per

[æ]

1. 在闭音节中

    例词：f*a*t, p*a*d, m*a*n, t*a*n, pl*a*n, cr*a*sh

2. 在多数双音节和多音节单词中位于两个或更多辅音字母之前

    例词：p*a*ddle, m*a*mmal, c*a*ndle, *a*mbulance, underst*a*nd, st*a*ndard

[aː]

在 sk, sp, ss, st 之前的多数词中

例词：t*a*sk, b*a*sket, r*a*sp, cl*a*ss, v*a*st, f*a*st

[ɔ]

在闭音节中，位于除了 [k, g, ŋ] 之外的辅音之前，w 和 qu 之后

例词：wh*a*t, w*a*rrior, w*a*sh, qu*a*ntity, qu*a*lify, qu*a*rrel

Task B Conversations

Model Dialogue 1: Talking About Music

1. Listen to the conversation and fill in the blanks with the expressions given below.

Jenny: Hi, Tony, do you like jazz?

Tony: Not really. Actually, _____. And I'm a real fan of Eason Chan, a singer from Hong Kong.

Jenny: _____. Who's it?

Tony: _____? He's one of the most popular Chinese singers. You know, girls go crazy for him. _____.

Jenny: Sorry, you know, I'm not the pop type.

Tony: Never mind!

---
1. I prefer pop music   3. You kidding
2. I've never heard of him   4. I think he's really talented
---

2. Role-play a conversation in pairs according to the given situation.

Tony and Jenny are talking about their favorite musical types. Tony prefers rock music while Jenny loves classical music.

Model Dialogue 2: Talking about a Music Show

1. Listen to the conversation and fill in the blanks with the expressions given below.

David: Hi, Tony, did you watch the show last night, you know, *Sing! China*?

Tony: No, I didn't. The whole family went to my grandparents' house last night. _____.

David: Pity you missed it. It was so exciting. But never mind, you can watch it online.

Tony: Sure. You know, _____, and that's why the program is so attractive, in my opinion.

David: _____! And the coaches are great, and the singers, too.

Tony: You know, actually, I think you're also good enough for the show, why don't you _____?

David: Oh..., Tony, you must be kidding me.

---
1. go and give it a try   3. there're surprises on the stage
2. Definitely   4. It's my grandma's birthday
---

2. Role-play a conversation in pairs according to the given situation.

Jenny and John are talking about a musical show, *I am a Singer*（我是歌手）, which is very popular recently, especially among the youth.

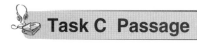

Task C Passage

Listen to the following passage and choose the best answer to each question.

> **Word Tips:**
> save up [seivʌp] *vt.* 储存，积攒
> finance ['fainæns] *n.* 财政，金融，资金
> college ['kɔlidʒ] *n.* 大学，（英国）学院，（尤指私立）中学

1) Who is Laura?
   A. She's a high school student.   B. She's a college student.
   C. She's a teacher.   D. She's a high school graduate.

2) What did Laura do before she went to college?
   A. She went to travel.   B. She went to work.
   C. She just stayed at home.   D. She did volunteer jobs.

3) What troubles did Laura have when she got ready for college?
   A. She didn't have enough money for college.
   B. She just didn't want to go to college.
   C. She's still confused（困惑）about her future.
   D. She wanted to work.

Task D Spot Dictation

Listen to the passage three times and fill in the blanks.

> **Word Tips:**
> literature ['litəritʃə] *n.* 文学，文学作品，著作
> audience ['ɔːdjəns] *n.* 观众，听众

Bruce Lee is the most creative and imaginative person I've even known. He started his 1) _____ when he was 5 years old. At school, he always had many interesting ideas. He loves **literature** as well. He has 2) _____ a book when he was still in high school, and got it published successfully. His families are very 3) _____ him. Now he's working as a 4) _____ for a TV show. He works with a group of brilliant people, and together they have to think of 5) _____ for the program, and most of them are very popular. They have to come up with 6) _____ for the actors or actresses to make the **audience** laugh. It is a job full of 7) _____ . But Bruce loves it and does it well.

Section B Reading

Passage A

Development of Jazz?

Pre-reading Questions

1. How much do you know about jazz music?
2. Is jazz one of your favorite musical styles?

Jazz music is very hard to **define** because it changes all the time. It **has its roots in** America's **folk traditions**, especially in the music of **slaves** taken from Africa. Early jazz **borrowed from** slaves' field work songs and their religious music. The American South, and the city of **New Orleans in particular**, was just right for the birth of jazz to take place. And jazz was the first new style of American music to win an international **audience**.

The first jazz **recording** was made in 1917 by the **Original Dixieland Jazz Band**. Dixieland jazz sprung up in the 1910s in New Orleans and **featured** the loud sound. **Jelly Roll Morton** was one of the most important figures in the early development of jazz. He was a **pianist** and bandleader from New Orleans who published the first jazz **composition** in 1915. **Louis**

Armstrong was another **pioneering** jazz musician from New Orleans. He was well known for solo performances. **In addition to** his musical **contributions**, Armstrong was also an important figure in American history for being one of the first black **entertainers** to **cross over** and be accepted by white audiences.

By the 1930s, a new style of jazz called "**swing**" had **surpassed** Dixieland in popularity. Jazz focused on **rhythm**, **melody**, and a **smoother** sound. **Benny Goodman** was one of the most famous bandleaders of the swing **era**. He helped spread the music to a wider audience of white listeners. Goodman is also famous for leading the first jazz performance at **Carnegie Hall** in 1937.

Jazz has also **been richly influenced by** woman singers. **Billie Holiday**, **Sarah Vaughan**, and **Ella Fitzgerald** are just a few of the **classics**.

Jazz today is more **varied** than ever before and has become more and more popular. Jazz **musicians** from many countries make their own contributions to its development. At festivals, they meet and share their music on every **continent**. In this way jazz continues to grow and change.

(323 words)

New Words

define	[dɪˈfaɪn]	vt. 定义，界定
root	[ruːt]	n. 根，根源
folk	[fəuk]	n. 民族，人们；adj. 民间的，普通平民的
tradition	[trəˈdɪʃn]	n. 传统，惯例
slave	[sleɪv]	n. 奴隶
audience	[ˈɔːdiəns]	n. 观众，读者，听众
recording	[rɪˈkɔːdɪŋ]	n. 记录，录音，唱片
original	[əˈrɪdʒənl]	adj. 原始的，独创的，最初的
feature	[ˈfiːtʃə(r)]	n. 特征，容貌，（期刊的）特辑，故事片；vt. 使有特色；描写……的特征；vi. 起主要作用，作重要角色
pianist	[ˈpiənɪst]	n. 钢琴家，钢琴师
composition	[ˌkɒmpəˈzɪʃn]	n. 作文，作曲，创作
pioneer	[ˌpaɪəˈnɪə(r)]	n. 拓荒者，先驱者；vt. 开拓，做……的先锋
contribution	[ˌkɒntrɪˈbjuːʃn]	n. 贡献，捐赠
entertainer	[ˌentəˈteɪnə(r)]	n. 表演者，艺人
swing	[swɪŋ]	n. 摇摆乐，摇摆舞
surpass	[səˈpɑːs]	vt. 超过，胜过
rhythm	[ˈrɪðəm]	n. [诗]节奏，韵律；[乐]节拍

melody	['melədi]	n. 旋律，曲调
smooth	[smu:ð]	adj. 光滑的，流畅的
era	['iərə]	n. 纪元，年代，时代
classics	['klæsiks]	n. 文学名著，优秀的典范
varied	['veərid]	adj. 各种各样的
musician	[mju'ziʃn]	n. 音乐家
continent	['kɔntinənt]	n. 大陆，陆地

Useful expressions

have its root in 植根于
borrow from 借用
in particular 尤其是，特别
in addition to 除此之外
cross over 横过（河等），穿过
be richly influenced by 受到……很大的影响

Proper Names

New Orleans [nju: 'ɔ:liənz] n. 新奥尔良（美国港口城市）
Diexieland ['diksilænd] 迪克西兰
Original Dixieland Jazz Band 迪克西兰爵士乐队
Jelly Roll Morton ['dʒeli rəu 'mɔ:tən] 杰利·罗尔·莫顿（美国爵士乐作曲家、钢琴家）
Louis Armstrong ['lu(:)is 'a:mstrɔŋ] 路易斯·阿姆斯特朗（爵士乐之父）
Benny Goodman ['beni: 'gudmæn] 本尼·古德曼（美国单簧管演奏家、爵士乐音乐家）
Carnegie Hall [ka:'negi 'hɔ:l] 卡内基音乐厅
Billie Holiday ['bili 'hɔlədei] 比莉·霍利戴（20世纪爵士歌坛三大天后之一）
Sarah Vaughan ['seərə vɔ:n] 莎拉·沃恩（20世纪爵士歌坛三大天后之一）
Ella Fitzgerald ['elə fits'dʒerəld] 埃拉·菲茨杰拉德（20世纪爵士歌坛三大天后之一）

After-reading activity

Jazz, one of the most popular musical styles in the modern world, has been introduced into China for decades. Since then, it has produced great influence on Chinese music. So, what influence do you think jazz brings to Chinese music? And could you please name some of the Chinese jazz singers that you happen to know?

Background Information

1. Louis Armstrong（路易斯·阿姆斯特朗）

提起爵士音乐，人们最先联想到的人，很可能是一位具有小丑般形象的、绰号叫作 Uncle Satchmo（书包嘴大叔）的、活泼可爱的小人物。他是一位声音沙哑的歌手，手中常常拿着一支小号。他以新奥尔良爵士乐风格，在迪克西兰爵士乐配曲下，演奏结构简单、富有戏剧性的作品。这个人就是路易斯·阿姆斯特朗。

阿姆斯特朗首先在爵士乐上成功地使用了拟声唱法，并最终使之成为爵士乐演唱的一大特色。甚至可以说，阿姆斯特朗在某种意义上开创了爵士乐的历史，并因此被称为爵士乐之父。

2. Carnegie Hall（卡内基音乐厅）

该音乐厅是由美国钢铁大王兼慈善家安德鲁·卡内基于1891年在纽约市第57街建立的第一座大型音乐厅。卡内基音乐厅的建筑采用意大利的文艺复兴风格，并有号称世界一流的音响设备。音乐厅建成后的首演式上，由柴可夫斯基担任客座指挥，吸引了全纽约的名门雅士前去观看。多年以来，纽约爱乐乐团一直在此演出，指挥家包括托斯卡尼尼、斯托科夫斯基、布鲁诺·瓦尔特以及伯恩斯坦。能够在这里演出或登台已成为跃登古典与流行音乐乐坛成功的标志。

Comprehension

1. Choose the best way to complete each of the following sentences.

1) Jazz has its roots in American folk tradition, mainly in the music of _____.
   A. native Indians   B. Anglo-Saxons
   C. African slaves   D. traditional style

2) The first jazz recording was made in _____ by the Original Dixieland Jazz Band.
   A. 1910s   B. 1930s   C. 1940s   D. 1950s

2. Complete the following summary with the words from the passage. The first letter of each missing word is given for your reference.

Jazz has its 1) r_____ in the American 2) f_____ traditions. It originated from the music of African slaves. Early jazz borrowed from slaves' field work songs and their religious music. The American South, and the city of New Orleans in 3) p_____ was just right for the birth of jazz to take place. Jelly Roll Morton was one of the most important 4) f_____ in the early development of jazz. He was a 5) p_____ and bandleader from New Orleans who published the first jazz 6) c_____ in 1915. And Louis Armstrong was the most popular singer. Jazz also has been richly influenced by 7) w_____ singers. By the 1930s, jazz focused on rhythm, 8) m_____ and a smoother sound. Jazz today is more 9) v_____ than ever before. Jazz 10) m_____ from many countries make their own contributions to it.

Vocabulary

1. Complete the following sentences with the words given below. Change the form if necessary.

> feature   define   tradition   classics   original

1) _____ the word "love" can be very difficult.
2) She enjoys reading the _____.
3) This is a translation, the _____ copy is in Spanish.
4) He was born in a _____ family.
5) It's a concert _____ music by Mozart.

2. Complete the following sentences with proper prepositions or adverbs.

1) I was _____ my father's home when you called me last night.
2) I have never heard _____ such places.
3) She's _____ to London tomorrow morning.
4) The boys and girls danced _____ the music.

Sentence Structure

Combine the following sentences using the structure "…, especially...".

Sample:

She's good at playing musical instruments. She's good at piano.

She's good at playing musical instruments, especially the piano.

1) The movie is very popular. The movie is popular among the youth.

2) I like all kinds of food. I like the Japanese food.

3) I owe my apology to everybody. I owe my apology to you.

4) I love shopping. I love online shopping.

5) The sky is so blue last week. The sky is so blue on Wednesday.

 **Translation**

1. Translate the following English sentences from the text into Chinese.

1) It has its roots in American's folk traditions, especially in the music of slaves taken from African.

2) Early jazz borrowed from slaves' field work songs and their religious music.

3) Dixieland jazz sprung up in the 1910s in New Orleans and featured the loud sound.

4) By the 1930s, a new style of jazz called "swing" had surpassed Dixieland in popularity.

5) Benny Goodman helped spread the music to a wider audience of white listeners.

2. Translate the following Chinese sentences into English with the words or phrases given in brackets.

1) 在硅滩，每天都会出现很多新创公司。（spring up）

   In Silicon Beach, _____ everyday.

2) 这股潮流很快扩散到全世界。（spread to）

   This fashion _____.

3) 这家公司走娱乐路线。（focus on）

   This company _____.

4) 除了这对双胞胎，杰森和第一任妻子还有一个孩子。（in addition to）

   _____, Jason has another child by his first wife.

5) 他的电影受希区柯克影响很大。（be influenced by）

   _____ by Hitchcock.

Passage B

Celine Marie Claudette Dion

Celine Marie Claudette Dion, a Canadian singer, songwriter, was born on March 30, 1968, in Quebec, Canada. As the youngest of 14 children, she grew up in a **close-knit** musical family. Her parents formed a singing group. They **toured** Canada when Celine was still an **infant**. They later opened a piano bar, where the 5-year-old Celine would perform **to the delight of** customers.

At the age of 12, Celine Dion recorded a **demo** tape of a song she had written with her mother. They sent the tape to the manager and **producer Rene Angelil**. After hearing the tape and inviting Dion to perform for him **in person**, Angelil **signed** her immediately **under the condition** that he would have a complete control over her career. He *mortgaged* his own house to finance her first **album**, *La Voix du bon Dieu* (*The Voice of God*).

By the age of 18, Dion had recorded nine French albums and won **numerous Juno Awards** (the Canadian equivalent of a Grammy Award). In 1988, she won the **Eurovision Song Contest** in **Dublin**, **Ireland**, and her **performance** was **broadcast live** in countries **throughout** Europe, the Middle East, Australia and Japan.

Dion's real **breakthrough** into pop music circle came in 1992, when she recorded the **theme** to Disney's **hit** animated feature *Beauty and the Beast*. The song made it to No. 9 on the **Billboard** Hot 100 and won both a **Grammy** and an **Academy Award**.

Dion's music has been influenced by *genres* ranging from rock and R&B to *gospel* and classical. Her recordings are mainly in French and English, although she also sings in other languages. She has won five Grammy Awards and remains the best-selling Canadian artist in history.

(289 words)

New Words

close-knit	[ˌkləʊsˈnɪt]	adj. 紧密的，组织严密的
tour	[tʊə(r)]	vi. 观光，巡回
infant	[ˈɪnfənt]	n. 婴儿，幼儿
demo	[ˈdeməʊ]	n. 演示，样本唱片
producer	[prəˈdjuːsə(r)]	n. 生产者，制作人
sign	[saɪn]	vt. & vi. 签名；n. 符号，指示牌
mortgage ★	[ˈmɔːgɪdʒ]	n. & vt. 抵押贷款
album	[ˈælbəm]	n. 唱片，相册，集邮簿
numerous	[ˈnjuːmərəs]	adj. 很多的，许多的
performance	[pəˈfɔːməns]	n. 表演，演技，表现
broadcast	[ˈbrɔːdkɑːst]	vt. 广播；n. 电台，电视节目
live	[laɪv]	adj. 活着的，生动的，现场直播的
throughout	[θruːˈaʊt]	prep.（表示时间）自始至终，在……期间；（表示空间）遍及……地域
breakthrough	[ˈbreɪkθruː]	n. 突破
theme	[θiːm]	n.［乐］主题，主旋律
hit	[hɪt]	n. 成功而轰动（或风行）一时的事物（如唱片、电影或戏剧）
billboard	[ˈbɪlbɔːd]	n. 广告牌，告示牌
award	[əˈwɔːd]	n. 奖品；vt. 授予，奖给奖品
genre ★	[ˈʒɒnrə]	n. 种类，体裁，流派
gospel ★	[ˈgɒspl]	n. 福音（书），福音音乐（尤流行于美国南部黑人基督徒中）

Useful expressions

to the delight of sb. 使某人感到开心
in person 亲自，亲身
under the condition 在某种条件下

Proper Names

Celine Marie Claudette Dion [seiˈliːn məˈriː klɔːˈdet ˈdaiən] 席琳·玛丽·克劳德特·迪翁
Rene Angelil [ˈrenei ˈeɪndʒɪlɪl] 雷尼·安杰利（席琳·迪翁的丈夫和经纪人）
Juno Awards [ˈdʒuːnəʊ əˈwɔːd] 朱诺奖（授予加拿大音乐艺术家以及团体的奖项）
Eurovision Song Contest [ˈjʊərəvɪʒn sɒŋ ˈkɒntest] 欧洲电视网歌唱大赛
Ireland [ˈaɪələnd] 爱尔兰（岛）
Dublin [ˈdʌblɪn] 都柏林（爱尔兰首都）

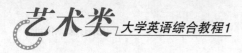

Europe ['jʊərəp] *n.* 欧洲

Grammy Award ['græmi ə'wɔːd] 格莱美奖

Academy Award [ə'kædəmi ə'wɔːd] 学院奖（奥斯卡奖）

Background Information

Eurovision Song Contest（欧洲电视网歌唱大赛）

由欧洲广播联盟（EBU）举办的一年一次的大型歌唱比赛，是欧洲规模最大的歌曲比赛，第一届于1956年在瑞士卢加诺举行，截至2015年已成功举办60届。

Comprehension

1. Mark the following statements *T (true)* or *F (false)* according to the text.

☐ 1) Celine Dion was born in a musical family.

☐ 2) Rene Angelil supported Dion's career financially.

☐ 3) Dion's first album was in English.

☐ 4) Dion's real breakthrough came when she was 18.

☐ 5) The song which won Dion worldwide fame was the theme song she recorded for *Beauty and Beast*.

2. Complete the following statements.

1) At the age of 12, Celine Dion recorded a _____ tape of a song she had written with her mother.

2) Angelil signed her immediately under the condition that he would have a complete _____ over her career.

3) He mortgaged his own house to _____ her first album, *La Voix du bon Dieu* (*The Voice of God*).

4) By the age of 18, Dion had recorded nine _____ albums and won numerous Juno awards.

5) Dion's real breakthrough into _____ music circle came in 1992.

Unit 2 Music

Vocabulary and Structure

1. Put the following words under the corresponding pictures.

> tour   infant   demo   album

1) _____   2) _____   3) _____   4) _____

2. Compare each pair of words and complete the following sentences with the right one. Change the form if necessary.

1) produce, producer

   She has _____ very little work recently.

   He is a well-known _____ .

2) tour, tourist

   We had a _____ of France on this summer vacation.

   Lijiang (丽江) is full of _____ in summer.

3) finance, financial

   _____ for the program comes from the bank.

   Hong Kong is a _____ center.

4) perform, performance

   He is _____ the play written by himself.

   I bought two tickets for the Kong-fu _____ tomorrow night.

3. Complete the following sentences with the words given below. Change the form if necessary.

> award   breakthrough   numerous   broadcast
> live   sign   career   audience

1) Finding another "earth" is a great _____ for human beings.

2) The BBC _____ all over the world.

3) He chose an academic _____ .

4) He won the Grammy _____ for 2010.

5) This show is going out _____ .

6) _____ your name here, please.

7) There are _____ stars in the night sky.

8) The music was performed before an enthusiastic _____ .

4. Complete the following sentences with the expressions given below. Change the form if necessary.

> in person   under the condition   grow up   throughout

1) He _____ in a small town.

2) The winner will be there _____ to collect the prize.

3) _____ his life he had always kept his love for Africa.

4) You can go to the concert _____ that you will keep quiet.

 Activity

Planning for Your Own Concert

You may be a college student majoring in music, or just have talent in music. Actually, you've already earned yourself fame among your friends and schoolmates. Now, you think that you need a bigger stage and decide to have a solo concert on campus. What do you do to best prepare for a solo concert?

1. Get familiar with some special English terms about a concert.

a solo concert 个人演唱会

a concert hall 音乐厅

accompanist 伴奏者

music majors 音乐系学生

menu 曲目单

2. Match the sentences in A with the Chinese equivalents in B.

A

1) Nail down the theme and menu (   )

2) Find accompanists (   )

3) Lease the equipment (   )

4) Choose the date (   )

5) Borrow the hall (   )

6) Publicize the concert (   )

7) Decorate the hall (   )

B

a) 寻找伴奏

b) 敲定主题和歌单

c) 向校方预订演唱大厅

d) 装饰演唱大厅

e) 租赁设备

f) 宣传你的演唱会

g) 确定日期

3. Think about what you should pay attention to in order to have a successful solo concert.

1) What songs would you choose?

2) What theme would you develop?

3) Can you find the equipment?

4) What date would be a better choice?

5) How are you going to publicize the concert?

6) How are you going to decorate the concert hall?

Passage C Fast Reading

Satchmo—A Jazz Superstar

A) A young African American boy sang and danced on a street in New Orleans, Louisiana, in the early 20th century. He hoped to earn some money, as his family was very poor. That boy, Louis Daniel Armstrong, would become one of the world's most famous jazz *trumpet* (小号) players.

B) Armstrong loved music and tried various instruments before finally choosing the *cornet* (短号). The cornet looks like a trumpet but is shaped like a *cone* (锥形). Armstrong became the leader of his school band. Jazz was just beginning to be popular. As a teenager he learned music by listening to pieces played by famous jazz musicians. Later he learned to read music.

C) Armstrong played with jazz bands in Chicago and New York City. He recorded his first solo pieces, "Chimes Blues" and "Tears", in Chicago. In New York he changed from the cornet to the trumpet. He felt the trumpet had a brighter sound and a *flashier* (华丽的) look. By the time Armstrong was 28 years old, he had become very famous. He toured worldwide as a trumpet *soloist* (独奏者) with big bands.

D) Louis Armstrong was *nicknamed* (绰号) "*Satchmo*" (书包嘴) by his fellow musicians. Short for "Satchel Mouth", the name suggested that his mouth was as wide as a large book bag. But the friendly joking was a sign of the great respect jazz musicians showed for Armstrong's talent. His creativity, ability to express emotion, and superior *technical skill* (技巧) were universally admired.

E) Armstrong is also remembered as one of the inventors of what is called "*scat*" (拟声唱法). Sometimes while singing he would sing without lyrics. He would sing a string of sounds instead. His scat singing and *gravelly* (低沉沙哑的) voice became as well known as his face and trumpet.

(344 words)

Information Match

Please identify the paragraph from which the following information is derived. Each paragraph is marked with a letter.

_____ 1) "Satchmo", short for "Satchal mouth", is a nickname, which, however, was a respect to Armstrong's talent.

_____ 2) Jazz was becoming popular when Armstrong was a teenager.

_____ 3) Armstrong is remembered as one of the inventors of what is called "scat".

_____ 4) Armstrong was born in a poor family in New Orleans, Louisiana.

_____ 5) Armstrong started his early career in Chicago and won fame in New York.

Background Information

New York（纽约）

纽约是美国最大的城市。为了与其所在的纽约州相区分，被称为纽约市（官方名称为：The City of New York）。其位于美国东海岸的东北部，是个多族裔聚居的多元化城市，拥有来自97个国家和地区的移民，在此使用的语言达到800种。截至2012年，纽约大约有800万人。纽约（New York）意为"新约克郡"——英荷战争结束后，荷兰战败，被迫将新阿姆斯特丹割让给英国，当时正好是英王查理二世的弟弟约克公爵的生日，于是将新阿姆斯特丹改名为新约克郡，作为送给约克公爵的礼物。另外，由于在20世纪初，纽约对外来移民来说是个崭新的天地，机会到处都是。因此纽约常被昵称为"大苹果"（the Big Apple），便是取"好看、好吃、人人都想咬一口"之意。

Section C Grammar

主语（二）(Subject Ⅱ)

六、名词化的形容词作主语

The disabled are well cared for in our country.

在我们国家，残疾人受到很好的照顾。

The wise know well when to give up.

明智的人懂得什么时候放弃。

The black have the equal rights with the white.

黑人拥有和白人同等的权利。

七、短语作主语

How to do well is an important question.

如何把这件事做好是一个重要问题。

Early to bed and early to rise makes a man healthy.

早睡早起身体好。

Which one to pick is really hard, because there are so many excellent works.

选择哪一个真的太难了，原因在于优秀作品太多了。

八、从句作主语

What has happened proves that our feelings are right.

发生的一切证明我们的感觉是对的。

Whether we'll go or not depends on the weather.

我们是否去要看天气。

That she will succeed is certain.

她会成功是可以肯定的。（陈述句作主语，that 不可省略）

九、it作形式主语和it引导强调句的比较

It 作形式主语代替主语从句（特别是谓语较短时），主语从句的连接词没有变化。例如：

It remains to be seen *if* we are wrong in the matter.

我们是否在这件事上犯了错误还有待于观察。

It is still doubtful *whether* she would play the part.

她是否要扮演这个角色值得怀疑。

It 引导的强调句则是对句子某一部分的强调，必须用连接词 that，其结构是：It is (was) that...

It was in Paris *where* they met for the first time.（误）

It was in Paris *that* they met for the first time.（正确，强调状语，只能用 that）

It was last summer *when* he graduated from the college.（误）

It was last summer *that* he graduated from the college.（正确）

Exercises

1. **Complete the following sentences based on the given Chinese.**

   1) _____ get poorer; _____ get richer.
      穷人越来越穷，富人越来越富。

   2) _____ seem to have gained more favor.
      经典的似乎更受欢迎。

   3) _____ is more experience.
      他需要的是更多的经验。

   4) _____ is still doubtful.
      森林大火是如何引起的仍然让人怀疑。

   5) _____ is unbelievable!
      他们两个一见钟情太不可思议了！

   6) _____ is the parents' headache.
      如何教育这个淘气的孩子是令父母头疼的事。

   7) _____ should be done well.
      值得做的事要做好。

   8) _____ needs the family's discussion.
      是否要把房子卖掉要全家人讨论一下。

2. **Choose the best way to complete each of the following sentences.**

   1) _____ is for him to decide.
      A. When leaving   B. When shall we leave
      C. When we leave   D. When we have left

   2) After a whole day of hard work, all _____ was a nice meal and a good rest.
      A. what he wanted   B. which he wanted
      C. the thing he wanted   D. that he wanted

   3) To a highly imaginative writer, _____ is a pad of paper and a pen.
      A. all are required   B. all required is
      C. all is required   D. all that is required.

   4) _____ is none of your business.
      A. I shall take what measures   B. What measures shall I take
      C. It is what measures I shall take   D. What measures I shall take

5) _____ is power is a famous saying known to all.
   A. What knowledge   B. How knowledge
   C. Where knowledge   D. That knowledge

6) _____ matters little.
   A. He will come or not   B. If or not he comes
   C. Whether he comes or not   D. He comes or not

7) _____ to test the gender of an unborn baby.
   A. This is possible   B. It seems possible
   C. That is possible   D. It is possible that

8) _____ almost seven hours to run through the book.
   A. It spent me   B. It took me
   C. I spent   D. I took

9) _____ art was a relatively late development in the United States.
   A. Not until dance as a performing   B. Dance was a performing
   C. That dance was performed as an   D. Dance as a performing

10) _____ was of no much help to him at that time.
    A. Little could I do   B. What could I do little
    C. The little of which I could do   D. The little that I could do

Section D Sentence Writing

Let's Design a Concert Poster!

Unit 2 Music

1. What is a concert poster?

   Tips: announce/live music performance...

   _____
   _____.

2. How to design a concert poster?

   Tips: name, place, date, time, cost of entry...

   _____
   _____.

3. In what way do you make an eye-catching poster?

   Tips: catchy pictures, colors, interesting elements, less words...

   _____
   _____.

4. Whose concert would you love to attend? Why?

   Tips: special and amazing performance, talented, powerful music, personal experiences, recall teenage years, thrilled...

   _____
   _____.

Unit 3

Festivals

Section A Listening and Speaking

Task A General Pronunciation Rules

A 在非重读音节中的发音：

[æ]

在重读音节前的闭音节中

例词：activity, transport, transform, transfer

[ə]

1. 在重读音节前、后或词尾时

   例词：alone, ability, fantasy, breakfast, umbrella, sofa

2. 在以 -able, -ant, -ance 和 -ancy 结尾的词中

   例词：comfortable, pregnant , annoyance, vacancy, pregnancy

3. 在大多数以 -ate 结尾的名词和形容词之中

   例词：alternate, chocolate, passionate, accurate, private

[ei]

在以 -ate 结尾的动词中

例词：concentrate, translate, navigate, celebrate, facilitate

[i]

在多数以 -age 结尾的词中

例词：heritage, image, passage, sausage, package, baggage

Task B Conversations

Model Dialogue 1: Giving Invitations

1. Listen to the conversation and fill in the blanks with the expressions given below.

David: Hi, Nancy. Winter vacation is coming. _____?

Nancy: I'll go to Yunnan for the holiday. _____, David?

David: I have no idea yet. Maybe I'll just stay at home.

Nancy: _____ to escape from the cold in the North?

David: _____ very attractive.

Nancy: _____ to join me?

David: Well, thanks, Nancy. I'll have to check my schedule first. _____.

> 1. Would you like to
> 2. Would you like
> 3. What's your plan
> 4. How about you?
> 5. Sounds
> 6. I'll call you tonight

2. Role-play a conversation in pairs according to the given situation.

Peter meets Jean in front of the library and asks her about her holiday plan. Jean says she and her roommates will go for Hawaii and asks if Peter would like to join them.

Model Dialogue 2: Accepting or Declining Invitations

1. Listen to the conversation and fill in the blanks with the expressions given below.

Lucy: Ben, Christmas is coming soon. _____ to a party held in Grand Hotel this Friday.

Ben: _____, but my brother will come to see me this Friday. I'll show him around the city then.

Lucy: Well, our party is in the evening, at about 7:00 pm. _____?

Ben: I think I can.

Lucy: Great! Then you can take your brother together to the party. The more people there are, the merrier it will be.

Ben: _____. I will talk with him. I bet he will enjoy it. He is very sociable and crazy about parties.

Lucy: Terrific! Our party will be more enjoyable. _____.

Ben: Oh, no! It's almost time for class. _____. See you.

Lucy: Bye.

> 1. I would like to invite you
> 2. Can you make it
> 3. I can hardly wait
> 4. I'd love to
> 5. That's great
> 6. I have to go now

2. Role-play a conversation in pairs according to the given situation.

Steven invites Jessica to a dinner on Friday evening, but she has no time for it. Then they fix Saturday for it, and Jessica suggests going to a movie after dinner.

Task C Passage

Listen to the passage and choose the best answer to each question.

Word Tips:
1. annual ['ænjuəl] *adj.* 每年的，年年的
2. reunion [ˌriːˈjuːniən] *n.* 团聚
3. official [əˈfiʃl] *adj.* 正式的，官方的
4. lunar ['luːnə(r)] *adj.* 阴历的
5. calendar ['kælində(r)] *n.* 日历
6. take place 发生

1. What festival was mentioned in this conversation?
   A. Valentine's Day.　　　　　B. The Mid-Autumn Festival.
   C. Spring Festival.　　　　　D. Christmas.

2. When is the festival mentioned in the passage?
   A. The fourth Thursday of November.
   B. The ninth day of the ninth Chinese lunar month.
   C. The 15th day of the 8th Chinese lunar month.
   D. The 5th day of the 5th Chinese lunar month.

3. What do people usually have when appreciating the full moon?
   A. Apple pie.　　　　　B. Turkey.
   C. Chocolate.　　　　　D. Moon cakes.

Task D Spot Dictation

Listen to the passage three times and fill in the blanks.

Word Tips:
1. celebrate ['selibreit] *vt.* 庆祝，祝贺
2. bring up 提出（观点等），养育，抚养
3. West Virginia 西弗吉尼亚州

　　Mother's Day is 1) _____ in the USA. It's on the second Sunday in 2) _____. It is a day to thank mothers. On that day mothers usually get flowers and cards.

　　Where does the 3) _____ for the holiday come from? We should thank Miss Anna M. Jarvis. She 4) _____ up the idea of having such a day. She lived in **West Virginia**.

Her mother 5) _____ on May 9, 1905. She loved her mother. She wrote letters to some 6) _____ persons to ask them to 7) _____ a day for their mothers. Then Mother's Day was made on the second Sunday in May by the USA in 1913.

On Mother's Day, children give 8) _____ to their mothers, or the whole family go out and try to do something 9) _____ for their mothers to make them 10) _____.

Section B   Reading

Passage A

A Thanksgiving Story

Pre-reading Questions

1. How much do you know about Thanksgiving Day (such as the date, its origin, traditional food, customs, etc.)?
2. Have you read any moving stories about Thanksgiving Day? Share your answers with your classmates.

My kids and I would be spending the Thanksgiving Day without their father, who had died several months before. The two kids **were sick with** the **flu**. I had only about $2.50 to **last** until the end of the month.

Then I heard the phone ring. It was the **secretary** from the **church**. She said they had something to give us. The secretary met me at the door and **handed** me a **special envelope**. "We think of you and the kids often." she said. I opened the envelope and found two **grocery** *certificates* inside. Each was **worth** $20.

"Thank you very much." I said, and as we **hugged** each other, I cried. Then I went to a **store** and bought some *much-needed* items. As I handed the **cashier** one of the gift certificates, she took it. But she turned her back for what **seemed like** a very long time. I thought something might be wrong.

"This certificate is a real *blessing*," I explained, "Our church gave it to my family." The cashier **turned around** and **replied**, with **giant** tears in her **loving** eyes, "Honey, do you have a **turkey**?" "No." "Anything else for Thanksgiving dinner?" "No, but it's okay," I replied. Handing me the **change**, she said, "I can't tell you exactly why right now, but please go back to the store and buy a turkey, or anything else you need for a Thanksgiving dinner." "Are you sure?" I asked. "Yes! Get whatever you want."

I felt **awkward** as I went back to do some more shopping, but I selected a fresh turkey, a few potatoes, and some juices for the children. Then I went back to the same cashier.

"Now I can tell you," she said, "This morning I **prayed** to help someone today, and then you came!" She **reached** under the **counter for** her **purse**, took out a $20 bill and paid for my groceries. "I'm glad I could help," she said, "Here is my phone number if you ever need anything. God **bless** you, honey."

As I walked to my car, I was deeply **moved** by this stranger's love. I **realized** that God loves my family too, and shows us his love through this stranger's and my church's kind **deeds**.

(373 words)

New Words

flu	[fluː]		*n.* 流行性感冒，流感
last	[lɑːst]		*vi.* 持续；*vt.* 够用，足够维持（某段时间）；*adj.* 最近的，最后的，最不想要的
secretary	['sekrətri]		*n.* 秘书，干事
church	[tʃɜːtʃ]		*n.* [宗] 教堂，教会
hand	[hænd]		*n.* 手，协助，帮助；*vt.* 传递，交给
special	['speʃl]		*adj.* 特殊的，特别的；*n.* 特色菜，特产
envelope	['envələup]		*n.* 信封，封皮
worth	[wɜːθ]		*adj.* 值……钱，值得的；*n.* 财富，财产，价值
hug	[hʌg]		*vt.* 热烈地拥抱，抱紧（某物）；*n.* 拥抱
store	[stɔː(r)]		*n.* 商店
much-needed ★			*adj.* 急需的
item	['aitəm]		*n.* 条款，项目，物品
cashier	[kæ'ʃiə(r)]		*n.* 收银员，出纳员

blessing ★	['blesiŋ]	n. 福气，恩赐
reply	[ri'plai]	n.& vt. 回复，答复
giant	['dʒaiənt]	adj. 巨大的，特大的；n. 巨人，卓越人物
loving	['lʌviŋ]	adj. 充满爱意的，慈爱的，关爱的
turkey	['tə:ki]	n. 火鸡
change	[tʃeindʒ]	n. & vt. 改变，变化；n. 零钱，找头
awkward	['ɔ:kwəd]	adj. 棘手的，使人尴尬的，笨拙的
pray	[prei]	vt. 祈祷，祷求
counter	['kauntə(r)]	n.（商店或酒吧的）柜台；adj. 相反的
purse	[pə:s]	n. 钱包，女用手提包
bless	[bles]	vt. 保佑，为……祈求上帝保佑
move	[mu:v]	vt. & vi. 移动，搬家；vt. 使感动
realize	['ri:əlaiz]	vt. & vi. 认识，领会，实现
deed	[di:d]	n. 行为，行动，事迹

Useful Expressions

be sick with 患……病

grocery certificates ★ 杂货购物券

seem like 看上去像，看起来像

turn around 转身，使调整方向，（使）好转

reach for... 伸手去拿，伸手去够

After-reading Activity

You and your family members are happily preparing a big meal for the coming Spring Festival. Then you happen to know that your neighbor is an old lonely couple, whose daughter and son live in America, unable to come back for the holiday. What will you do to help them?

Background Information

Turkey（火鸡）

Unit 3 Festivals

感恩节是西方国家的传统节日，宴会上有一道必不可少的特色名菜——烤火鸡。为什么要在感恩节吃火鸡呢？这要从感恩节的由来说起。1620年，英国一批清教徒们不堪忍受统治者的迫害，远渡重洋，准备流亡美洲。在大海中漂泊了65天，终于到达了美洲东海岸。当时，此处还是一片荒凉，火鸡和其他野生动物随处可见。时值寒冬，缺衣少食，恶劣的环境正在威胁着他们的生命。在这生死攸关的时刻，当地的印第安人为他们送去了食物、生活用品和生产工具，并帮助他们建立了自己的新家园。为感谢在危难之时帮助过他们的印第安人，同时也感谢上帝对他们的"恩赐"，在11月第四个星期四，将猎获的火鸡制成美味佳肴，盛情款待印第安人，并与他们进行联欢，庆祝活动持续了三天。

此后，每年11月第四个星期四都要举行这样的庆祝活动，招待印第安人食烤火鸡，并在一起举办射箭、跑步、摔跤等体育竞赛，夜晚还围着篝火尽情歌舞，共享欢乐。

Comprehension

1. Choose the best way to complete each of the following sentences.

1) The secretary provided two grocery certificates worth $_____.

   A. 10   B. 20   C. 40   D. 80

2) With the help of the cashier, the author bought _____.

   A. turkey   B. potatoes

   C. some juices   D. All of the above

2. Complete the following summary with the words from the passage. The first letter of each missing word is given for your reference.

My kids and I would be spending the 1) T_____ Day without their 2) f_____ who had died not long before. Unfortunately, the kids were 3) s_____ with flu and I had only $ 2.50 left. Then I received a call from the 4) s_____ from the church. She provided two grocery certificates. I went to a 5) s_____ and bought some much-needed 6) i_____. When I handed the 7) c_____ the gift certificates, it seemed like something was wrong. After knowing that I had nothing for the Thanksgiving, she asked me to go back to the store and get 8) w_____ I want. I did so and 9) s_____ a turkey, some potatoes and some juices. I came to her again and she told me the reason: that morning, she 10) p_____ to help someone. I was just that person. She paid for me by herself as a gift for the holiday.

Vocabulary

1. Complete the following sentences with the words given below. Change the form if necessary.

reply   item   giant   secretary   awkward

1) Fewer than a thousand _____ pandas still live in the wild.

2) This put them in a very _____ position.

3) He _____ that this was absolutely impossible.

4) She wrote down each _____ our teacher had mentioned.

5) The word "_____" comes from the same Latin root as the word "secret".

2. Complete the following sentences with proper prepositions or adverbs.

1) Peter turned the truck _____, and started back for home.

2) The soldier reached _____ his gun.

3) It doesn't seem _____ a good time to tell her such bad news.

4) Recently, she's terribly busy and she's been sick _____ worry.

Sentence Structure

Combine the following sentences using the structure "... , who...".
Sample:
We would be spending the holiday without their father. He had left us several months before.

We would be spending the holiday without their father, who had left us several months before.

1) The old man has a son. He is in the army.

2) Ben is an experienced teacher and he is very popular.

3) Lisa is a new teacher. She loves to chat with students.

4) Our guide was a French Canadian. He was an excellent cook.

5) Jack appears in the reality show. He is more popular than before.

Translation

1. Translate the following English sentences from the text into Chinese.

1) My kids and I would be spending the Thanksgiving Day without their father, who had died several months before.

2) Then I went to a store and bought some much-needed items.

3) Get whatever you want.

4) I felt awkward as I went back to do some more shopping.

5) She reached under the counter for her purse, took out a $20 bill and paid for my groceries.

2. Translate the following Chinese sentences into English with the words given in brackets.

1) 那位老人被确诊患有癌症。(be sick with)

   The old man was diagnosed as _____ cancer.

2) 妈妈伸手把奶瓶拿了过来。(reach for)

   Mama _____ the milk bottle.

3) 她不忍心再转回身去。(turn around)

   She couldn't bear to _____ again.

4) 大部分值得拥有的东西都来之不易。(worth doing)

   Most things _____ never come easy.

5) 格雷斯吓坏了，不能作答。(reply)

   Grace was too scared to _____.

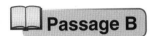

Valentine's Day

Valentine's Day is a festival of romance that **celebrates** love and relationships. Celebrated on February 14th, it is often **marked** by giving **gifts** and spending time with **beloved** ones.

One of the most well-known **symbols** for this festival would be **Cupid** and his **arrows**, and hearts. Cupid became a symbol of Valentine's Day **due to** the fact that he is the Roman God of love. His arrows **cause** his **targets** to **fall in love**.

Valentine's Day started when the *Emperor* Claudius Ⅱ **ruled** Rome. Claudius was so *warlike* and pushed Rome into so many wars. He **had** great **difficulty** finding soldiers for his army. He felt that Roman men just didn't want to leave their family and lovers. To **solve** this problem, he **banned** marriage. But a *priest* called Valentine, who **believed in** love and marriage, continued to **marry** couples **in secret**. When the emperor learned about it, he sent Valentine into **prison**.

While in prison, he **healed** the daughter of his *jailer* and they fell in love with each other. Just before his death, he asked for a pen and paper from his jailer, and **signed** a **farewell** message to her "From Your Valentine", a phrase that lived ever after.

The priest died on February 14th, 270 A.D. Not until a few hundred years later did Valentine's Day was as it is today. At first, this festival **involved** handwritten greetings of love on February 14th. Nowadays, these have almost completely been **replaced** by **commercial** greeting cards. (247 words)

New Words

celebrate	['selibreit]	*vt.* 庆祝，庆贺
mark	[ma:k]	*vt.* 标示，为……做标记；*n.* 成绩，分数，记号

gift	[gift]	n. 礼物，天赋
beloved	[bi'lʌvd]	adj. 心爱的，钟爱的；n. 心爱的人
symbol	['simbl]	n. 象征，标志，符号
arrow	['ærəu]	n. 箭，箭头
cause	[kɔ:z]	vt. 引起，导致；n. 原因，动机，事业
target	['tɑ:git]	n. 目标，对象
emperor ★	['emp(ə)rə]	n. 君主，帝王
rule	[ru:l]	vt. 统治，控制，支配；n. 规则，规定
warlike ★	['wɔ:laik]	adj. 好战的，尚武的
solve	[sɔlv]	vt. 解决（问题）
ban	[bæn]	n. 禁止，取缔；vt. 禁令
priest ★	[pri:st]	n. 牧师，神父
marry	['mæri]	vt. & vi.（使）结婚，娶，嫁；vt. 为……主持婚礼
prison	['prizn]	n. 监狱
heal	[hi:l]	vt. 治愈，愈合
jailer ★	['dʒeilə(r)]	n. 监狱看守
sign	[sain]	vt. & vi. 签名，署名，打手势；n. 符号，手势，指示牌
farewell	[ˌfεə'wel]	n. 告别，欢送；adj. 告别的，送行的
involve	[in'vɔlv]	vt. 涉及，牵涉，参与
replace	[ri'pleis]	vt. 代替，替换，把……放回原处
commercial	[kə'mə:ʃl]	adj. 商业的，贸易的，盈利的

Useful Expressions

due to 因为，由于

fall in love (with sb.) 爱上（某人）

have difficulty (in) doing 做某事有困难

believe in 相信，信奉，信仰

in secret 偷偷地，私下地

Proper Name

Cupid ['kju:pid] 丘比特（罗马神话中的爱神）

Comprehension

1. Mark the following statements *T (true)* or *F (false)* according to the text.

☐ 1) On Valentine's Day, lovers often exchange gifts and spend time together.

☐ 2) Claudius Ⅱ was a peace-loving emperor and was deeply loved by his people.

☐ 3) Priest Valentine was too terrified to marry people since Claudius banned marriage.

☐ 4) While in prison, Valentine fell in love with the jailer's daughter.

☐ 5) Nowadays, most people still prefer handwritten greetings of love on February 14th.

2. Complete the following statements.

1) Valentine's Day is a festival of romance that celebrates _____ and _____.

2) Cupid's arrows cause his targets to _____.

3) Claudius _____ marriage because he felt that Roman men just didn't want to leave their family and lovers.

4) But Priest Valentine, who believed in love and marriage, continued to _____ couples in secret.

5) Just before his death, Valentine signed a farewell message to his love "_____", a phrase that lived ever after.

Vocabulary and Structure

1. Put the following words under the corresponding pictures.

arrow   prison   ban   marry

1) _____ 2) _____ 3) _____ 4) _____

2. Compare each pair of words and complete the following sentences with the right one. Change the form if necessary.

1) involve, involved

The case we are dealing with _____ privacy.

President Clinton was _____ in this scandal (丑闻).

2) solve, solution

Try to find the effective _____ to practical problems.

Step back and you will find a good way to _____ the problem.

3) commerce, commercial

They have made their fortunes from industry and _____.

This _____ bank is willing to lend money to them.

4) celebrate, celebration

More and more young people _____ western festivals.

A wedding is a joyful _____ of love.

3. Complete the following sentences with the words given below. Change the form if necessary.

| mark | heal | symbol | sign |
| cause | target | gift | replace |

1) Her grandmother had the _____ of making people happy.

2) He did well to get such a good _____.

3) Who do you suppose will _____ her on the show?

4) Roses have been widely accepted as the _____ of love.

5) This is the law of _____ and effect or the science of causality (因果关系).

6) I aimed the gun carefully at the _____.

7) Do you love the song "_____ the World" by Michael Jackson?

8) Before an operation, the patient will be asked to _____ a consent form (同意书).

4. Complete the following sentences with the expressions given below. Change the form if necessary.

| due to | have difficulty (in) doing | believe in | in secret |

1) Many students _____ memorizing English words.

2) The two young lovers decided to marry _____, and they did so the very next day.

3) His failure in the exam was _____ his carelessness.

4) I firmly _____ the saying of "No pains, no gains".

Activity

Planning for a Halloween Costume Party

Halloween is coming. As a member of the Students Union, you are required to plan a Halloween Costume Party open to all the students in your university. Then how will you plan it successfully?

1. Get familiar with some special English terms about Halloween.

Halloween 万圣节

costume party 化装舞会，服装派对

dress up 穿上盛装，打扮

Jack-o-lanterns 南瓜灯

mask 面具

scary 恐怖的，可怕的

2. Match the sentences in A with the Chinese equivalents in B.

A

1) Come up with a suitable theme. ( )

2) Make the budget. ( )

3) Make a party check list well in advance. ( )

4) Choose the right date. ( )

5) Put up notices in advance. ( )

6) Prepare food and beverage you can serve. ( )

7) Select the suitable music. ( )

8) Design some interesting games. ( )

B.

a) 提前做好舞会核对清单

b) 确定恰当的日期

c) 策划合适的主题

d) 选择合适的音乐

e) 备好食物和饮料

f) 做出预算

g) 设计一些有趣的游戏

h) 提前张贴海报

3. Think about what you should pay attention to in order to have a successful Halloween Costume Party.

1) What theme would you set for your Halloween Party?

2) When do you think would be suitable to hold the party?

3) How will you decorate to make the party more festive?

4) What game will you prepare to make the party more interesting?

5) What information will the posters include?

Passage C Fast Reading

Halloween

A) On October 31st, dozens of children dress in **costumes** (化妆服), knock on their neighbors' doors and yell "Trick or treat" when the door opens. As they give each child a treat, the neighbors try to guess who is under the **masks** (面具).

B) October 31st was the eve of the **Celtic** (凯尔特人的) new year. The Celts were the **ancestors** (祖先) of the present-day Irish, Welsh and Scottish people. When night fell, people dressed up and tried to look like the dead, hoping that the ghosts would leave peacefully before midnight of the new year.

C) One of the most typical symbols for Halloween is Jack-o-lanterns. According to the legend, Jack, an Irishman, was not allowed into Heaven because he was **stingy** (吝啬的，小气的) with his money. So he was sent to hell. But down there he played tricks on the Devil, **Satan** (撒旦), so he was kicked out of Hell. He was made to walk on the earth forever, carrying a **lantern** (灯笼) to look for a place to stay.

D) Jack-o-lanterns were carved to light nighttime paths and protect people from those evil spirits. Children made Jack-o-lanterns on October 31st from a pumpkin, **hollowed out** (挖空) with the sides having holes and lit by little candles inside. Children would carry them as they went from house to house, begging for food or candies.

E) One of the things that makes this such a wonderful holiday is that you can dress up and pretend to be just about any character you want and still be socially accepted. Be sure to try and order your costumes well in advance to give you plenty of time to make sure that your costume fits properly.

(319 words)

Information Match

Please identify the paragraph from which the following information is derived. Each paragraph is marked with a letter.

_____ 1) Jack could neither stay in Heaven nor in hell but could only carry a lantern to find some place to stay on the earth.

_____ 2) On the night of Halloween, people dressed up to terrify the ghosts to leave peacefully before midnight of the new year.

_____ 3) On Halloween, children would carry Jack-o-lanterns to light paths and protect themselves from these evil spirits when begging for food and candies.

_____ 4) Be sure to order your costume ahead of time in order to make sure that it fits you well.

_____ 5) On October 31st, many children will dress in costumes and wear masks.

Background Information

Trick or treat（不给糖就捣乱）

"不给糖就捣乱"是万圣夜的主要活动。小孩装扮成各种恐怖的样子，逐门逐户按响邻居的门铃，大叫"Trick or treat!"，主人家便会拿出一些糖果、巧克力或是小礼物。

万圣节是儿童们纵情玩乐的好时候。夜幕降临，孩子们便迫不及待地穿上五颜六色的化妆服，戴上千奇百怪的面具，提上一盏"杰克灯"跑到邻居家门前，威吓般地喊着"Trick or treat"。如果大人不用糖果、零钱款待他们，那些调皮的孩子就说到做到：好，你不款待，我就捉弄你。他们有时把人家的门把手涂上肥皂，有时把别人的猫涂上颜色。这些小恶作剧常令大人啼笑皆非。当然，大多数人家都非常乐于款待这些天真烂漫的小客人。所以万圣节前夜的孩子们总是肚子塞得饱饱的，口袋装得满满的。

Section C Grammar

主谓一致（一）（Subject-Verb Concord I）

主谓一致是指语法形式上要一致，即用作主语的名词中心词和谓语动词在单、复数形式上一致。一般情况下，主谓之间的一致关系由以下三个原则的支配：语法一致原则、意义一致原则和就近原则。

一、语法一致

语法一致是指主语和谓语从语法形式上取得一致：主语是单数形式，谓语也采取单数形式；主语是复数形式，谓语也采取复数形式。

He often *goes* out with his friends in the town.
他经常和镇上的朋友一起出去。

These young drink a lot, and laugh and sing and *there are* often fights.
这些年轻人喝很多酒，又笑又唱，还经常打架。

1. 不定式、动名词以及从句作主语时应看作单数，谓语动词用单数。例如：

    Going too far is as bad as not going far enough.
    过犹不及。

    Sometimes *to lose love is* to hold it too tightly.
    有时失去爱是因为抓得太紧。

2. 不定代词 one, every, each, everybody, everyone, one of, no one, nothing, nobody, someone, somebody, either, neither, many a 等作主语或是修饰主语时应看作单数，谓语动词用单数。例如：

    Many a student *takes* a walk on campus after dinner.
    许多学生晚饭后在校园里散步。

    Every boy and girl in our college *shows* great interest in extra-curriculum activities.
    我们学院的每个男生和女生对课外活动都表现出很大的兴趣。

3. 表示国家、机构、事件、作品等名称的专有名词作主语时应看作单数，谓语动词用单数。例如：

    The Netherlands has been known for producing flowers, especially tulips.
    荷兰以盛产花卉而闻名，特别是郁金香。

    Aesop's Fables is a book about animal stories that were told in Greece almost 2 500 years ago.
    《伊索寓言》是一本讲述动物的故事书，这些故事早在 2 500 多年前的希腊就传诵了。

The World Health Organization (***WHO***) ***continues*** to be deeply concerned with the people affected with Ebola in Africa.

世界卫生组织（世卫组织）继续对非洲感染埃博拉病毒的人民表示深切关怀。

4. 当 a portion, a series of, a kind of, the number of 等与名词构成名词短语作主语时应看作单数，谓语动词用单数。例如：

A series of Korean dramas ***is*** usually shot at the shortest time because of the high expenses.

由于成本高昂，因此一部韩剧通常都在最短时间内拍摄出来。

The number of fans to Korea dramas ***is*** amazing in the world due to the spread of Korean Wave.

由于韩流的传播，韩剧在全世界粉丝的数量惊人。

A kind of rose in the garden ***smells*** very pleasant.

这座花园里有一种玫瑰香气怡人。

5. 由 some, several, both, few, many, a number of 等词修饰主语，或是由它们自身作主语时应看作复数，谓语动词用复数。另外，由 and 连接两个主语时，谓语一般用复数。例如：

Hiking and camping are popular outdoor activities.

远足和露营是受欢迎的户外活动。

Both of us ***are*** fond of watching American movies.

我们俩都喜欢看美国电影。

A number of graduates ***are*** planning to study abroad.

许多毕业生打算去国外留学。

6. 由 a lot of, most of, any of, half of, two fifths of, sixty percent of, some of, none of, the rest of, all of 等词修饰主语，如果后接不可数名词，或是单数形式的名词作主语时应看作单数，谓语动词用单数；但如果后接可数名词的复数形式作主语时应看作复数，谓语动词用复数。例如：

A lot of water has to be stored if the electricity is cut off tomorrow.

如果明天断电，要多存些水。

A lot of books about children education ***have been*** published recently.

最近出版了许多关于儿童教育的书籍。

All that ***is*** now just water under the bridge.

一切都付之东流。

Exercises

1. Complete the following sentences based on the given Chinese.

   1) A little boy and a girl _____ at the party.

   一个小男孩和一个小姑娘在晚会上跳舞。

2) A needle and thread _____ under the bed.

在床下面找到了针线（穿了线的针）。

3) Each of the students _____ a musical instrument.

每个学生都带了一件乐器。

4) This kind of flowers _____.

这种花是有毒的。

5) One million pounds _____.

一百万英镑是一大笔钱。

6) Seventy percent of the surface of the earth _____ by sea.

地球表面的70%覆盖着水。

7) Neither of them _____.

他俩谁都不知道答案。

8) Jogging _____ your heart.

慢跑对心脏有好处。

2. Choose the best way to complete each of the following sentences.

1) Somebody _____ to see you.

 A. wants   B. want   C. is wanting   D. is to want

2) Some of the most famous dramas _____ been broadcast via networks.

 A. has   B. are   C. have   D. is

3) In many African tales, the monkey and several other animals _____ clever, and the human beings _____ shown to be usually foolish.

 A. are...are   B. are...is   C. is...is   D. is...are

4) Some parts of Japan _____ many feet of snow every winter.

 A. is getting   B. are getting   C. gets   D. get

5) Most of the buildings in the city center _____ made of bricks.

 A. have   B. are   C. has   D. get

6) Among all his works, none _____ as popular as this one.

 A. is   B. are   C. has   D. have

7) Three-fourths of the people _____ against the plan.

 A. is   B. are   C. has   D. have

8) Many a passenger _____ killed in the accident.

 A. are   B. have   C. has   D. is

9) Niagara Falls, one of the most amazing natural wonders in North America, _____ more than 25 000 years old.

 A. has   B. have   C. are   D. is

10) That he has grown up in a rich family _____ him to choose his way of life.

    A. allow   B. allows   C. is allowed   D. are allowed

Section D   Sentence Writing

Celebrate Thanksgiving Day

1) When is Thanksgiving Day celebrated in the US?

    Tips: celebrate, fourth Thursday of November...

    _____

    _____.

2) Why do Americans celebrate Thanksgiving Day?

    Tips: settlers, America, starvation, harvest, Indians ...

    _____

    _____.

3) How do westerners celebrate Thanksgiving Day?

    Tips: family dinner, turkey, apple pie, football match...

    _____

    _____.

4) Do Chinese celebrate Thanksgiving Day in China? Why or why not?

    Tips: give thanks, have reunion dinner /non-traditional holiday

    _____

    _____.

Unit 4

Creative Advertisements

Section A Listening and Speaking

Task A General Pronunciation Rules

字母组合

1. ae

   [eə] 例词：*ae*roplane, *ae*rophotography, *ae*rate

   [i(:)] 例词：formul*ae*, *ae*sthete, *ae*sthetics

2. ai/ay

   [ei] 例词：p*ai*n, m*ai*l, w*ai*t, tr*ai*t, l*ay*, tr*ay*, pl*ay*

   特例：s*ai*d [sed], s*ay*s [sez], *ai*sle [ail], pl*ai*t [plæt] pl*ai*d [plæd]

   [i] 在 ai 非重读时

   例词：mount*ai*n, barg*ai*n, fount*ai*n, portr*ai*t

   [-] 在有些单词词尾的 -tain 中, ai 不发音

   例词：Brit*ai*n, cert*ai*n, curt*ai*n

3. air

   [eə] 例词：h*air*, p*air*, f*air*, rep*air*, ch*air*

4. al

   [ɔ:] 在 k 之前

   例词：t*al*k, w*al*k, ch*al*k, st*al*k, b*al*k, c*al*k

   [a:] 在 m, f, ve 之前

   例词：c*al*m, p*al*m, h*al*f, c*al*f, h*al*ve, c*al*ves

   [ɔ:l] 在除 k, m, f, ve 之外的辅音字母之前

   例词：*al*ter, s*al*t, *al*so, b*al*d, *al*ways

5. all

   [ɔ:l] 例词：b*all*, t*all*, f*all*, sm*all*, w*all*, c*all*

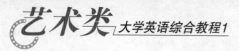

Task B Conversations

Model Dialogue 1: Making a Complaint

1. Listen to the conversation and fill in the blanks with the expressions given below.

> **Word Tips:**
> 1. refund ['ri:fʌnd] *n.* 退款；偿还数额
> 2. replacement [ri'pleismənt] *n.* 更换
> 3. inconvenience [ˌinkən'vi:niəns] *vt.*（使）……不便
> 4. in no time 立刻

Judy: What can I do for you, sir?

Tim: It's about this phone.

Judy: What seems to be the problem?

Tim: Sometimes _____.

Judy: Did you accidentally drop it on the floor, sir?

Tim: No and I only bought it three days ago. _____, I'm very disappointed.

Judy: I'm so sorry _____. Would you like a refund or a replacement?

Tim: _____, please.

Judy: Well, we'll _____ for you in no time.

> 1. there's no signal on this phone
> 2. you've been inconvenienced
> 3. I'd like a replacement
> 4. I have to say
> 5. get this phone changed

2. Role-play a conversation in pairs according to the given situation.

　　May is making a complaint to the salesclerk about her skirt she bought last week. May is asking for a refund, but the salesclerk says that clothes at a discount are not refundable. At last, May agreed to have her skirt fixed up.

Model Dialogue 2: Asking for Action

1. Listen to the conversation and fill in the blanks with the expressions given below.

> **Word Tips:**
> 1. the front view one 朝街房
> 2. rear room 背街房
> 3. upgrade [ʌp'greid] *vt./vi.* 升级，使升级
> 4. It's too much for me 让我难以忍受

Unit 4 Creative Advertisements

Assistant Manager: How can I help you?

Customer: I'm sorry _____, but can you help me with this? I want to change a room, it's too noisy.

Assistant Manager: Oh, I see. Your room is the front view one. I'll check if _____.

Customer: My wife was woken up several times by the noise of the traffic outside. She said _____.

Assistant Manager: I'm awfully sorry, sir. But _____ today.

Customer: Can we _____?

Assistant Manager: Yes, we'll manage it right away.

1. it was too much for her	4. there is any rear room left
2. to bother you	5. upgrade to a sea view room
3. we don't have any spare room	

2. Role-play a conversation in pairs according to the given situation.

Agatha is complaining to the assistant manager about the heat in the room. The assistant manager checked the air-conditioner and found it broke down. The assistant manager offers to change another room for Kevin.

Task C Passage

Listen to the passage and choose the best answer to each question.

Word Tips:
1. necktie ['nektai] *n.* 领带
2. request [ri'kwest] *n.* 要求，需要
3. purchase ['pə:tʃəs] *n.* 购买，购买行为，购置物
4. solution [sə'lu:ʃn] *n.* 解决，溶解

1) Why did Mr. Hall want to return the necktie?

   A. He didn't like its style.

   B. His family thought it's too expensive.

   C. His family didn't think the color fit him.

   D. There was quality problem with the tie.

2) Why did Mr. Hall get angry?

   A. The sales clerk refused to refund it.

   B. The sales clerk refused to exchange it.

C. The sales manager refused to see him.

D. The sales manager was rude to him.

3) According to the passage, what's the purchase-return rule?

A. All the goods are not refundable.

B. Even if there's quality problem, they could only exchange it, but couldn't make the refund.

C. All the goods could be refunded.

D. Only the goods with quality problem could be refunded.

Task D Spot Dictation

Listen to the passage three times and fill in the blanks.

Word Tips:
1. target ['tɑːgit] *n.* 目标
2. appeal [ə'piːl] *vi.* 有吸引力，提请注意
3. grab [græb] *v.* 抓住，夺取

When 1) _____ an advertisement, keep the **target** customers in mind. Even the cleverest ad won't work if it doesn't attract the target 2) _____ . Are you looking for a certain age group? Or are you looking for people with a 3) _____ ? Whatever it is, try to get a clear picture of who your dream consumer is and why he or she would be interested in what you're advertising.

Remember: it needs to 4) _____ your audience as much as possible and avoid 5) _____ to them. You need to 6) _____ children's attention by colors, sounds and pictures. Young people 7) _____ humor and tend to follow the fashion. Adults will be more interested in quality and value.

Section B Reading

Passage A

Sweet and Bitter Advertisements

Pre-reading Questions

1. What is advertising according to the passage?

2. What negative impact do **advertisements** have on the children?

*"If you do your job correctly, social media will tell you that, yes, you are the most **talked-about** thing in the world today."* —***Tom Bernardin***, *CEO of **Leo Burnett Company**, which is one of the most **successful advertising** agencies in the world.*

Advertising is **providing** information, calling attention to something that you want to sell or **promote**. It is important for companies to **advertise** in order to build a brand, to sell your products or services, and to make money. If an advertisement for a product attracts the **consumers**, they **tend to** buy it often or **at least** give it a try.

Advertisement reaches people through different kinds of advertising. For instance, some ***ad-filmmakers*** are **designing** new ways of attracting the kids to buy their products. They use simple, strong natural **image**s and the power of creativity to talk to children.

Some advertisements **focus on** healthy food products and can help **improve** the **diet** of a child, if they are **attractive** enough.

Certain advertisements, with strong messages **encourage** the kids to **pursue** their dreams such as becoming a doctor, scientist or an **engineer**.

However, the ad-filmmakers should remember that the commercials can also **have negative impact on** children. They tend to **persuade** their parents to buy the products shown in the commercials, whether useful or not.

Junk foods, such as pizzas, burgers and soft drinks, are heavily promoted during children's programs. This develops a favor for fatty, **sugary** and fast foods in kids. These unhealthy eating habits would probably make many children become **overweight**.

For the **overall** development of the kids, parents should give proper guide to the children and limit the time in watching the commercials. Kids should be encouraged to spend more time in **socializing**, playing, reading and exercise.

(298 words)

New Words

advertisement	[əd'vɜːtismənt]	n. 广告，宣传
successful	[sək'sesfl]	adj. 成功的，有成就的
advertising	['ædvətaiziŋ]	adj. 广告的，广告业的；n. 广告，做广告
provide	[prə'vaid]	vt. & vi. 提供，供给，供应
promote	[prə'məut]	vt. 促进，提升，促销
advertise	['ædvətaiz]	vt. & vi. 做广告，做宣传
consumer	[kən'sjuːmə]	n. 消费者
design	[di'zain]	vt. 设计，绘制
image	['imidʒ]	n. 形象，影像

improve	[im'pru:v]	vt. & vi. 提高，改善，改良
diet	['daiət]	n. 日常饮食，规定饮食；vt. & vi.（使）节制饮食
attractive	[ə'træktiv]	adj. 引人注目的，有吸引力的
encourage	[in'kʌridʒ]	vt. 鼓励，鼓舞
pursue	[pə'sju:]	vt. 继续，追求
engineer	[ˌendʒi'niə(r)]	n. 工程师
negative	['negətiv]	adj. 负面的，消极的，否认的
impact	['impækt]	n. 影响，冲击，碰撞
persuade	[pə'sweid]	vt. 说服，使信服
sugary	['ʃugəri]	adj. 含糖的，甜的
overweight	[ˌəuvə'weit]	adj. 超重的，过重的
overall	[ˌəuvər'ɔ:l]	adj. 全面的，综合的
socialize	['səuʃəlaiz]	vi. 参与社交，联谊
talked-about ★	[tɔ:kət'əbaut]	adj. 谈论的
ad-filmmaker ★	[æd' film' meikə]	n. 广告片制作人

Useful Expressions

tend to 倾向，易于

at least 至少

focus on 集中于

have an impact on 对……有影响

Proper Names

Tom Bernardin [tɒm bə'na:djən] 汤姆·贝尔纳丁（人名）（美国李奥·贝纳全球主席及行政总裁）

After-reading Activity

If you are creative director of an advertising agency, what product would you like to advertise for young children? Why?

Background Information

Leo Burnett Company（李奥·贝纳广告公司）

李奥·贝纳广告公司是一家美国广告公司，1935年由李奥·贝纳创立，现在是全球最大的跨国广告公司之一。在全球80多个国家设有将近100个办事处，拥有一万多名员工，年营业额在20亿美元上下，在全美大型广告公司之中名列前茅。李奥·贝纳（Leo Burnett, 1891—1971）是该广告公司的创始人。

李奥·贝纳的客户包括全球 25 个最有价值品牌当中的 7 个,如麦当劳、可口可乐、迪士尼、万宝路等。

李奥·贝纳(亚太)集团公司被评为"2001 年度亚太地区最佳广告公司"。李奥·贝纳于 1979 年进入中国市场,业务网络包括香港、广州、上海和北京。李奥·贝纳在中国的客户包括麦当劳、菲亚特、惠氏、箭牌、美标和中国电信等。

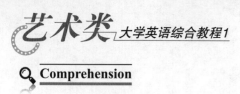

Comprehension

1. Choose the best way to complete each of the following sentences.

1) Leo Burnett Worldwide is one of the largest and most successful _____ agencies in the world.

   A. travel   B. ticket
   C. trade   D. advertising

2) The unhealthy eating habit for fatty, sugary food would make children _____.

   A. slim   B. thin
   C. overweight   D. slender

2. Complete the following summary with the words from the passage. The first letter of each missing word is given for your reference.

Advertising is to 1) p_____ information and call attention to the products that you want to sell or 2) p_____ in order to make money. Advertisement 3) r_____ people through different kinds of advertising. For instance, some ad-filmmakers are 4) d_____ new ways of attracting the kids to buy their products. They use very 5) s_____, natural 6) i_____ to talk to children. However, some commercials have 7) n_____ impact on people, especially on the children. Therefore, for the 8) o_____ development of the kids, parents should give proper guide to the children and 9) e_____ them to spend more time in 10) s_____, playing, reading and exercise.

Vocabulary

1. Complete the following sentences with the words given below. Change the form if necessary.

| provide | attractive | pursue | encourage | impact |

1) Ice cream and candies are _____ to children.

2) The company didn't _____ further details about its business decision.

3) This book has a great _____ on its readers.

4) Children should be _____ to be independent thinkers.

5) Everyone has the right to _____ his/her dreams.

2. Complete the following sentences with proper prepositions or adverbs.

1) I tend _____ think that he is right.

2) As students, we should focus our mind _____ studies.

3) His brave deeds have had a great impact _____ our spirit.

4) Having a favor _____ low-fat food will keep us fit.

Sentence Structure

Rewrite these sentences using the structure "It is+adj+(for sb.) to do…"

Sample:

To translate this sentence into English is hard for you.

It is hard for you to translate this sentence into English.

1) To get to the bus stop in such a short time is impossible for you.

2) To study hard in college is important for students.

3) To learn from others is necessary for us.

4) To cross the busy street is dangerous for little kids.

5) To finish the work in less than one hour is difficult for us.

Translation

1. Translate the following English sentences from the text into Chinese.

1) Advertising is providing information, calling attention to something that you want to sell or promote.

2) If an advertisement for a product attracts the consumers, they tend to buy it often or at least give it a try.

3) They use simple, strong natural images and the power of creativity in his advertisements to talk to children.

4) However, the ad-filmmakers should remember that the commercials can also have negative impact on the children.

5) Kids should be encouraged to spend more time in socializing, playing, reading and exercise.

2. Translate the following Chinese sentences into English with the words given in brackets.

1) 至少有 5 000 名运动员参加上海国际马拉松长跑。（at least）

   There are _____ Shanghai International Marathon.

2) 今年我们会议的议题将会关注消费者权益。（focus on）

   This year our meeting _____ the consumers' rights.

3) 匆忙时往往会犯错。（tend to）

   We _____ when in a hurry.

4) 他的演说对听众产生了深远的影响。（have an impact on）

   His speech _____.

5) 超市不得不降价促销。（promote）

   The supermarket had to _____.

Passage B

The Coca-Cola Hug Machine

A Coke **vending** machine was **installed** overnight at the **National University of Singapore**. People were pleasantly surprised to see a regular-looking Coca-Cola vending machine, with the words "hug me" in large letters on the logo front. Instead of money, this machine **responds** only to the **currency** of hugs. **Specifically**, you have to squeeze the sides of the soda **dispenser** in a specific way to make a free Coke come out. Those **bold** enough to hug the machine **were rewarded with** cans of ice-cold Coca-Cola and left with huge smiles on their faces.

The **innovative** idea is part of the "Open Happiness" **marketing strategy** created by advertising firm **Ogilvy & Mather**. This strategy is to deliver happiness in an **unexpected**, innovative way to **engage** not only the people present, but the audience **at large**.

Positioning this *stunt* at a university is a smart move in Singapore, where public signs of **affection** have long been **discouraged**, but are **on the rise** among the young. Coke is positioning itself as a non-**threatening** friend to **demonstrating** youth. You hug the machine, and it returns the **favour** with a Coke. Because vending machines have feelings too.

The **campaign** has been such a success that there are plans to **roll** them **out** across Asia. The **influence** was amazing. There were more and more people waiting to give hugs.

This is one of the most famous advertisement that Ogilvy has helped to build for Coca-Cola. Ogilvy is trying its best to **instill** the **belief** that its job is to make advertising that sells, and the advertising that sells best is advertising that builds brands.

(271 words)

New Words

hug   [hʌg]   *n. & vt.* 拥抱，紧抱

vending	['vendiŋ]	n.（尤指在公共场所）贩卖
install	[in'stɔːl]	vt. 安装，安顿，任命
respond	[ri'spɔnd]	vt. & vi. 回答，响应 vi. 作出反应，回报或回复
currency	['kʌrənsi]	n. 货币，通用，流通
specifically	[spə'sifikli]	adv. 特有地，明确地
dispenser	[di'spensə(r)]	n. 自动售卖机，配药师，自动取款机（或饮水机等）
specific	[spə'sifik]	adj. 明确的，特种的，具体的；n. 特性，细节
bold	[bəuld]	adj. 醒目的，勇敢的，无畏的；n. 粗体字，黑体字
innovative	['inəveitiv]	adj. 革新的，创新的
unexpected	[ˌʌnik'spektid]	adj. 想不到的，意外的
engage	[in'geidʒ]	vt. 吸引住，聘用；vi. 与……建立密切关系，从事
position	[pə'ziʃn]	n. 位置，地位，职位；vt. 安置，把……放在适当位置
stunt ★	[stʌnt]	n. 惊险动作，特技，噱头
affection	[ə'fekʃn]	n. 喜爱，慈爱，情感或感情
discourage	[dis'kʌridʒ]	vt. 使气馁，使沮丧
threatening	['θretniŋ]	adj. 胁迫的，险恶的
demonstrate	['demənstreit]	vt. 证明，展示，演示；vi. 示威游行
favour	['feivə]	n. 好感，宠爱，关切；vt. 支持，赞成
campaign	[kæm'pein]	n. 运动，活动
influence	['influəns]	n. 影响力，影响；vt. 影响，感染
instill	[in'stil]	vt. 逐步灌输
belief	[bi'liːf]	n. 信念，信条

Useful Expressions

respond to 对……作出回应
be rewarded with 拿……作为奖励
on the rise 在增加，在上涨
at large 总体地，（囚犯）在逃，逍遥法外
roll out 推出，铺开

Proper Names

Coca-Cola [ˌkəukə 'kəulə] 可口可乐

National University of Singapore ['næʃnəl,juːniˈvɜːsəti əv,siŋgəˈpɔː] 新加坡国立大学

Singapore [,siŋgəˈpɔː] *n.* 新加坡（东南亚国家）

Ogilvy & Mather [,ɔːdʒilˈviː ˈmæðə(r)] 奥美广告公司

Comprehension

1. Mark the following statements *T* (*true*) or *F* (*false*) according to the text.

☐ 1) Pepsi got an idea of "hugging the vending machine in order to get a free drink".

☐ 2) The Open Happiness campaign took place in Singapore.

☐ 3) This campaign was a great success and had influenced many countries in Europe.

☐ 4) This "hugging machine for free coke" part was designed by Ogilvy & Mather.

☐ 5) Ogilvy believes that the advertising that sells best is advertising that builds brands.

2. Complete the following statements.

1. There stands a vending machine which gives out free cans of Coke in return for _____.

2. Instead of paying money, people have to squeeze the sides of the _____ to get a free can of Coke.

3. Public signs of affection have long been _____, but are on the rise among the young.

4. You hug the machine, and it returns the _____ with a Coke.

5. The campaign has been such a _____ that there are plans to roll them out across Asia.

Vocabulary and Structure

1. Put the following words under the corresponding pictures.

hug   currency   a vending machine   logo

1) _____   2) _____   3) _____   4) _____

2. Compare each pair of words and complete the following sentences with the right one. Change the form if necessary.

1) hug, hugger

Mary is a tree _____ .（环保分子）

She gave her mother a big _____.

2) discourage, discouragement

She was _____ in her marriage.

Despite all these _____, she refused to give up.

3) unexpected, expected

His _____ arrival threw our plan into confusion.

The overpayment equals the _____ loss of the loan (贷款).

4) belief, believe

He comes to me in the _____ that I can help him.

I _____ that he will make the right decision.

3. Complete the following sentences with the words given below. Change the form if necessary.

| innovative | campaign | place | discourage |
| rise | influence | specific | instill |

1) Higher living costs have swallowed up (抵消) our pay _____.

2) He was one of the most creative and _____ engineers of his generation.

3) I asked him to be more _____ on this issue.

4) The _____ lasted from May to July.

5) Please _____ the book on the shelf after you finish reading it.

6) We must _____ a sense of duty in our children.

7) Her _____ in the company remained undiminished (不减的).

8) The loss of the match didn't _____ them.

4. Complete the following sentences with the expressions given below. Change the form if necessary.

| respond to | be rewarded with | on the rise | at large |

1) The people _____ are hoping for great change.

2) The number of homeless is still _____.

3) He didn't _____ her hug.

4) Make the extra effort to impress the buyer and you will _____ a quicker sale.

Activity

Designing Your Business Cards

 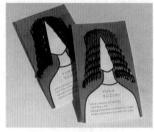 

Suppose someday in the future, you start your own business. When you meet face-to-face with clients, or when you happen to run into someone you might want to do business with, having business cards is surely a great way to promote your images. So, how do you design your own business cards?

1. Get familiar with some special English terms about business cards.

logo 标识，标志

contact information 联系信息

title 头衔

typeface 字体，字样

2. Match the sentences in A with the Chinese equivalents in B.

A

1) Use your logo as the basis. Make it the largest element on the card. (　　)

2) Keep it simple. Do not cram too much information on the card. (　　)

3) Do include the essentials—your name, title, company name, contact information (address, phone and fax numbers, email and Wechat username). (　　)

4) Make sure the typeface is easily readable. (　　)

5) Try to be creative and make it an appeal. (　　)

B

a) 尽量有创意，使之具有吸引力。

b) 确保字体清晰可辨。

c) 以标识为基准，使之成为名片上最重要的元素。

d) 囊括基本信息，包括你的姓名、头衔、公司名称及联系方式（地址、电话和传真、电子邮箱及微信号等）。

e) 简洁，不要堆砌太多信息。

3. **Think about what you should pay attention to in order to design a creative card.**

1) What size, shape would you like to choose to make your business card stand out?

2) What kind of print appeals to people?

3) What is crucial for a creative card?

4) For efficient connections, what would you include on your business card?

Passage C Fast Reading

David Ogilvy: the Man Who Invented Modern Advertising

A) David Mackenzie Ogilvy, the founder of Ogilvy & Mather Worldwide, was born in England on June 23, 1911. He used to be a cook in Paris and a salesman in England. After World War Ⅱ, Ogilvy bought a farm in Pennsylvania and became a farmer. But several years later, he admitted his limitations as a farmer and moved to New York.

B) In 1948, he built one of the world's largest and most respected advertising agency (which eventually became Ogilvy & Mather Worldwide) with the financial help of London agency Mather & Crowther. He changed the rules of the game and created a number of very famous advertisements.

C) The 1950's was the golden age for Oglivy's advertising company. He handled accounts such as Dove (多芬), Hathaway Shirts (哈撒韦衬衫), Schweppes (怡泉苏打水) and Rolls Royce (罗尔斯·罗伊斯). The agency was so successful by 1957 that Ogilvy turned away 50 clients that year.

D) In the 1960's, Oglivy handled accounts such as Sears (西尔斯百货公司), General Foods (通用食品公司), Shell (壳牌), American Express (美国运通公司) etc.

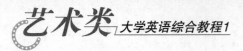

E) Ogilvy was perhaps best known for being the "apostle of brand image" (品牌形象的倡导者). He believed that every ad is part of a long-term investment in the personality of the brand. He also believed that advertising is based on the ability to sell, not entertain, and that it should be based on research about what consumers want. Ogilvy once said that the consumer was just like a wife and the man should not insult her intelligence.

F) Just as Roman says it, that Ogilvy invented modern advertising. Upon his death in 1999 at age 88, advertising executive Jerry Della Femina said, "He (Oglivy) will be the last advertising man whose death will be marked on the front of the New York Times." (369 words)

Information Match

Please identify the paragraph from which the following information is derived. Each paragraph is marked with a letter.

_____ 1) Ogilvy believed that advertising should be based on research about what consumers want.

_____ 2) Ogilvy handled accounts for Shell.

_____ 3) Ogilvy invented modern advertising.

_____ 4) Ogilvy used to be a farmer.

_____ 5) In 1948, Ogilvy built one of the world's largest and most respected advertising agency.

Background Information

1. Dove（多芬）

多芬，1957 年在美国诞生，是全球著名的从事美容行业的女性品牌。多芬推崇的美是自然的，是由女性自己积极创造的，可以带来自信，并且是由内而外散发出来的美。多芬的美是自我定义的，是有思想的美，它的美不仅仅是外在的，也是内在的。60 多年来，多芬一直用真人来做广告。就像多芬的英文名字 Dove 一样，这是一个象征着希望、快乐、和平以及所有积极事物的名字。

2. Hathaway（哈撒韦衬衫）

哈撒韦衬衫是缅因州小城沃特威的一个小公司里虔诚的手艺人缝制的，他们老老少少在那里工作了整整 110 多年。1951 年，奥美广告公司创意总监大卫·奥格威为哈撒韦衬衫设计了广告，就是让模特儿乔治·蓝吉尔戴上一只眼罩。这一绝妙设计使得品牌的销售额从 500 万美元上升到 1 300 万美元。而戴眼罩的男人这一创意广告连续使用了 30 年。

哈撒韦衬衫使用世界各地最有名的布料来缝制，衣领裁剪精致，能使人看起来更年轻、更高贵。

3. Schweppes（怡泉）

源自 1792 年的英国，苏打水十大品牌之一，可口可乐公司旗下饮料品牌，在世界各地拥有许多忠实的消费者，拥有维多利亚一世女王及英国皇室供应苏打水的特许权。

4. Rolls Royce（罗尔斯·罗伊斯）

英国罗尔斯·罗伊斯公司，简称"罗罗"，成立于1906年，创始人是Charles Stewart。以燃气轮机技术为核心，活跃在民用航空、国防、船舶和能源四个环球市场上。罗尔斯·罗伊斯产品中最著名的是军用和民用发动机，目前它是全球第二大军用发动机和第二大民用发动机制造商。"劳斯莱斯"和"罗尔斯·罗伊斯"均由英文Rolls Royce翻译而来，二者的不同在于：生产汽车的叫劳斯莱斯，生产发动机的叫"罗尔斯·罗伊斯"。

5. Sears（西尔斯百货公司）

美国西尔斯百货公司，创立于1886年，是世界十大购物网站之一。以向农民邮购起家，成为世界最大的私人零售企业之一。1900年，当货到付款的销售方式刚刚兴起时，西尔斯公司马上实行"先货后款"的方式。这一变化使西尔斯公司在这一年超过了其竞争对手沃德公司，成为美国零售业销售额排行榜的第一名。西尔斯公司于2005年被美国凯马特（Kmart）并购，组成美国第三大零售业集团。

6. Shell（壳牌）

荷兰皇家石油于1890年创立，并获得荷兰女王特别授权，因此被命名为荷兰皇家石油公司。壳牌集团今天已发展成为世界最大的国际石油公司：创下了油气深水开发的世界纪录；国际液化天然气技术先驱；全球最大的汽车燃油和润滑油的零售商；世界最大的化工产品经营者之一。

7. American Express（美国运通公司）

公司创立于 1850 年，总部设在美国纽约。美国运通公司是全球最大的独立信用卡公司。在美国运通公司提供的众多金融、旅游产品及服务中，美国运通卡为知名度最高的产品。美国运通公司也是全球最大的旅游服务公司，在全世界 120 多个国家拥有近 2 300 个美国运通旅游办事处。美国运通公司是在反映美国经济的道琼斯工业指数 30 家公司中唯一的服务性公司。

Section C Grammar

主谓一致（二）(Subject-Verb Concord Ⅱ)

二、意义一致

意义一致是指从意义角度来解决主谓一致问题。有时主语形式上为单数，但意义上却是复数，那么谓语根据其意义也用复数形式；而有时主语形式上为复数，但意义上却是单数，那么谓语根据其意义也用单数形式。

1. 当主语后面接由 as well as, as much as, accompanied by, including, in addition to, more than, no less than, rather than, together with 等引导的词组时，其谓语动词的形式要根据主语自身的单、复数而定。即这些词所引导的词组不影响主语自身的单、复数形式，而且它们与主语之间有"，"隔开。例如：

Energy, along with heat and light, *is* provided by the sun.
太阳提供给我们的有能量，还有光和热。

The house, with all its furniture, *was* sold to the young man.
这座房子，连同里面的家具全部卖给了那个年轻人。

2. 表示金钱、时间、价格或度量衡的复合名词作主语时，通常把这些名词看作一个整体，谓语一般用单数。

Twenty years stands for a long period in one's life.

二十年在人的一生里意味着一段很长的时期。

A hundred dollars is enough for a student to spend on food for one month.

一百块钱足够一个学生一个月的伙食了。

3. 形容词前加定冠词即"the+ 形容词"作主语时，其意义若是指个人或是抽象概念应看作单数，谓语动词用单数；但如果其意义是指一类人则应该看作是复数，那么谓语动词也应该用复数。例如：

I have bought two necklaces; ***the red is*** for myself and ***the blue is*** for my mother.

我买了两条项链，红色的留给自己，蓝色的是送妈妈的。

The young usually ***consider*** the old conservative, that's why the generation gap exists.

青年人常认为老年人保守，那就是代沟存在的原因。

4. 当 and 连接两个并列主语在意义上指同一人、同一物、同一事或者同一概念时，应看作单数，谓语动词用单数。

Bread and butter is delicious.

涂了黄油的面包很美味。

The iron and steel industry is very important to our life.

钢铁工业对我们的生活很重要。

5. 集体名词作主语时，谓语动词的数取决于主语的意义：主语表示整体时视为单数，谓语动词用单数；主语表示集体中的个体成员时视为复数，谓语动词用复数。常见的集体名词有：army, audience, cattle, class, club, committee, crowd, family, government, group, majority, minority, people, police, public, staff, team 等，其中 cattle, people, police 一般看成复数形式。例如：

The family is one of nature's masterpieces.

家庭是大自然创造的杰作之一。

His family were all around him when he died.

他临终时全家人都守在他身旁。

There ***are*** many herds of ***cattle*** in the meadow.

牧场上有许多牛群。

三、就近原则

就近原则是指谓语动词的人称和数常常与最邻近的主语保持一致。常出现在这类句子中的连词有：or, either…or…, neither…nor…, not only…but also… 等。例如：

Either I or ***they are*** responsible for the result of the matter.

不是我，就是他们要对那件事的后果负责任。

Neither I nor ***he is*** able to judge them here.

这里，我不能对他们做出评判，他也不能。

Unit 4 Creative Advertisements

Exercises

1. Complete the following sentences based on the given Chinese.

1) _____ receive benefit, while the conceited reap failure.
   谦受益，满招损。

2) Ancient and modern arts history _____.
   古代艺术史和现代艺术史是我们的必修课程。

3) Not only he but also all his family _____ concerts.
   不仅他自己，他全家人都对音乐会感兴趣。

4) Tom, along with his friends, _____ every Saturday.
   汤姆及其朋友们每到周六都去滑雪。

5) Neither of us _____ fairly.
   我们两个都没受到公平对待。

6) _____ that ends well.
   结果好一切都好。

7) _____ made of genuine leather.
   这双鞋是真皮制成的。

8) Between the two buildings _____.
   在两栋楼之间矗立着一座雕像。

2. Choose the best way to complete each of the following sentences.

1) The club secretary and monitor _____ asked to make a speech at the meeting yesterday.
   A. is   B. was   C. are   D. were

2) Five hundred miles _____ a long distance.
   A. is   B. was   C. are   D. were

3) Every boy and girl _____ invited to the art show.
   A. have been   B. has been   C. are   D. were

4) The son, rather than his parents, _____ responsible for the disaster.
   A. have been   B. has been   C. are   D. is

5) Not only Mary but also her parents _____ pleased to spend the leisure time together.
   A. have   B. has   C. feel   D. feels

6) The bookstore had not ordered _____ texts for all the children of different ages.
   A. plenty of   B. enough   C. as many   D. enough of

7) —What did you see? —We saw _____ police there.
   A. many   B. much   C. little   D. the

8) Birds of a feather _____ together.

| A. are flying | B. flies | C. flock | D. flocks |

9) —Do you want to wait? —Three years _____ too long for me to wait.

| A. are | B. is | C. was | D. Were |

10) Time and tide _____ no man.

| A. waits for | B. wait | C. waits | D. wait for |

Section D   Sentence Writing

The Cannes Lions International Festival of Creativity
戛纳国际创意节

1. What is the Cannes Lions International Festival of Creativity?

   Tips: celebration of creativity, international advertising awards, in the form of...

   _____

   _____.

2. Is the Cannes Lions somehow related to the Cannes Film Festival?

   Tips: advertising professional, establish, similar recognition to...

   _____

   _____.

3. What message can you get from the 1st print advertisement on this page?

   Tips: stay awake, responsibility, shoulder, safety, depend on...

   _____

   _____.

Unit 4 Creative Advertisements

4. What message can you get from the 2nd print advertisement on this page?

   Tips: species, die out, killing, take actions, protect, benefit, humankind...

   _____

   _____

   _____.

Unit 5

Sports

Section A Listening and Speaking

  Task A General Pronunciation Rules

字母组合

1. ar

   在重读音节中的发音：

   [ɑː] 在词尾或在辅音之前

   例词：c*ar*, b*ar*, st*ar*, f*ar*, h*ar*d, p*ar*t, al*ar*m, f*ar*m

   [æ] 在 r 之前

   例词：c*ar*rot, c*ar*ry, m*ar*riage, n*ar*row, b*ar*rier

   [eər] 在元音之前

   例词：v*ar*y, st*ar*e, gl*ar*e, w*ar*y, p*ar*ent

   [ɔː] 在词尾且在 w 之后或在一个辅音之前

   例词：w*ar*, w*ar*m, w*ar*n, aw*ar*d, rew*ar*d

   在非重读音节中的发音：

   [ə] 例词：forw*ar*d, popul*ar*, doll*ar*, stand*ar*d

2. au

   [ɔː] 在单词的开头或中间

   例词：*au*to, *au*tumn, *au*dio, *au*thor, c*au*se, p*au*se, f*au*lt

3. augh

   [ɔː] 例词：t*augh*t, c*augh*t, d*augh*ter, n*augh*ty

   特例：laugh [lɑːf]

4. aw

   [ɔː] 位于词尾或在 n/l 之前

   例词：s*aw*, l*aw*, dr*aw*, d*aw*n, l*aw*n, crawl

Task B Conversations

Model Dialogue 1: Talking about English Learning

1. Listen to the conversation and fill in the blanks with the expressions given below.

> **Word Tips:**
> 1. earphone ['iəfəun] *n.* 耳机，听筒
> 2. wonder ['wʌndə] *v.* 想知道，怀疑
> 3. repeat [ri'pi:t] *vt.* 重复，复制
> 4. VOA (Voice of America) 美国之音

Lisa: Excuse me. Are you also here _____?

Joy: (Earphones off) Oh…hello. Sorry?

Lisa: I was wondering if you are also waiting for the lecture to start.

Joy: Yes. _____ about English learning at college.

Lisa: Hah… me too. By the way, what were you listening to just now?

Joy: Special English on VOA. You know that helps me a lot _____.

Lisa: Really? How?

Joy: Well, it is so slowly that _____.

> 1. I am very interested in the topic
> 2. I can hear clearly and repeat at the same time
> 3. waiting for the lecture
> 4. in my English pronunciation and listening

2. Role-play a conversation in pairs according to the given situation.

Two freshmen are waiting for the English lecture to start. They talk about how to improve English pronunciation and listening.

Model Dialogue 2: Learning English in the Library

1. Listen to the conversation and fill in the blanks with the expressions given below.

> **Word Tips:**
> 1. dictation [dik'teiʃən] *n.* 听写，命令
> 2. distract [dis'trækt] *vt.* 转移，分心
> 3. bother ['bɔðə] *vt.* 烦扰，打扰
> 4. give it a shot 试一试

Lisa: (Whispering) Hey, Janet, can you just _____?

Janet: What? I can't hear you.

Lisa: Stop reading with your earphones in.

Janet: Oh...OK, but _____?

Lisa: I just can't focus on my dictation. _____.

Janet: Sorry, Lisa. I've never felt that. I just can't help reading it out while listening to Special English.

Lisa: _____ you are listening to, like me.

Janet: Thanks. Good idea. I'll give it a shot.

1. Your reading is too distracting
2. You can write down the sentences
3. stop reading while listening
4. is that bothering you

2. Role-play a conversation in pairs according to the given situation.

Lisa and Janet are on their way back to the dorm after morning reading. Lisa tells Janet a new method of learning English.

Task C Passage

Listen to the passage and choose the best answer to each question.

Word Tips:
1. rusty ['rʌsti] *adj.* 迟钝的，生锈的
2. rhythm ['riðəm] *n.* 节奏，韵律
3. quarterfinal [kwɔːtə'fainəl] *n.* 四分之一决赛
4. tournament ['tuənəmənt] *n.* 锦标赛，联赛

1) What was the result of the match Federer took part in?
   A. 6-4, 6-4. B. 4-6, 4-6.
   C. 7-5, 6-2. D. 5-7, 2-6.

2) Where did Federer work out this time?
   A. Switzerland. B. In Rogers Cup.
   C. In Montreal. D. In US Open.

3) What happened to John Isner in Cincinnati this year?
   A. He won the match.
   B. He lost the match.

C. He didn't play the match.

D. He didn't finish the match because of an injury.

Task D Spot Dictation

Listen to the passage three times and fill in the blanks.

> **Word Tips:**
> 1. indoors ['indɔːz] *adv.* 在室内
> 2. immediately [i'miːdiətli] *adv.* 立即，立刻
> 3. throughout [θruːˈaut] *prep.* 贯穿，遍及
> 4. professional [prəˈfeʃənəl] *adj.* 专业的，职业的

James Naismith, a 1) _____ education teacher in America, wanted to create a team sport that could be played indoors during the winter. Therefore, he 2) _____ the game of basketball in 1891.

People immediately enjoyed basketball's 3) _____ and fast action. In just a few years, both men and women were playing basketball at schools and sports 4) _____ throughout North America. It became so popular that people started 5) _____ money to watch basketball games. American soldiers took the game to Europe during World War One.

In 1936, basketball became part of the 6) _____ at the Olympic Games. About the same time, college basketball was becoming a 7) _____ national sport in the United States. The best college players went on to play for professional teams.

Section B   Reading

Passage A

God of Basketball

Pre-reading Questions

1. How much do you know about Michael Jordan?

2. Who do you think would win in a one-on-one basketball game between Michael Jordan and LeBron James?

Michael Jordan has said he believes he could beat **LeBron James** if they two are in a **one-on-one** basketball game when both are in their **prime**. The former star, now 50, said there's a long list of players he would've liked to have played one-on-one, James included.

Years ago, I was too, asked a **weird** "if" question: Who would win if **late Bruce Lee** and **Mike Tyson** were in a street fight? **To be frank**, I hate both "if" questions, **much less** about Jordan. What a waste of time! He is God of Basketball, isn't he?

Beyond doubt, Michael Jordan is the greatest basketball player of all time. His amazing **leaping** ability earned him the nickname "Air Jordan". His success in basketball includes **Rookie** of the Year, Five-time **NBA MVP**, Six-time NBA **champion**, Six-time NBA Finals MVP, **Defensive** Player of the Year, Ten scoring titles, etc. As an **outstanding athlete** with excellent physical **soundness**, great **artistry** and strong **competitive** desire, Jordan **single-handedly redefined** the NBA superstar.

In fact, the game has **undergone radical** changes since the days of Jordan. And when we **circle back** to the *contrived* **comparison**, we may find there is no way to reach an answer or to **turn back the clock** and get one.

Still, there remain people like Jordan—and many fans as well—who love these **unending** comparisons. As for me, I don't care who Jordan could beat one-on-one and I just love him like many do.

Oh, and Lee would beat Tyson in a street fight. And both would beat Jordan.   (258 words)

New Words

weird	[wiəd]	*adj.*	怪诞的，超自然的，奇异的
prime	[praim]	*n.*	精华，全盛
late	[leit]	*adj.*	已故的，迟到的
leap	[li:p]	*vi.*	跳，冲动的行动 *vt.* 跳过，使跳跃
rookie	['ruki]	*n.*	新手，新人（俗称"菜鸟"）
champion	['tʃæmpiən]	*n.*	冠军
defensive	[di'fensiv]	*adj.*	防御的，防守的，辩护的，自卫的

outstanding	[aut'stændiŋ]	adj. 杰出的，显著的
athlete	['æθli:t]	n. 运动员，体育家
soundness	['saundnis]	n. 健康，稳固
artistry	['ɑ:tistri]	n. 艺术性，工艺
competitive	[kəm'petətiv]	adj. 竞争的，比赛的，有竞争力的
single-handedly	['siŋgl-'hændidli]	adv. 单手的，单枪匹马的
redefine	[ˌri:di'fain]	v. 重新定义，再定义
comparison	[kəm'pærisn]	n. 比较，对照
contrived ★	[kən'traivd]	adj. 人为的，做作的
undergo	[ʌndə'gəu]	v. 经历
radical	['rædikəl]	adj. 激进的，根本的
circle	['sə:kl]	n. 圆，圈子；vt. 圈出，包围，绕……运转；vi. 环绕，盘旋
unending	[ʌn'endiŋ]	adj. 不断的，无止境的

Useful Expressions

one-on-one 一对一的

to be frank 坦白地说

much less 更不用说，不及

beyond doubt 毫无疑问

turn back the clock 时光逆转

Proper Names

Michael Jordan ['maikəl 'dʒɔ:dən] n. 迈克尔·乔丹（人名）

LeBron James [lə 'brɔn 'dʒæmz] n. 勒布朗·詹姆斯（人名）

Bruce Lee [bru:s 'li:] n. 李小龙（人名）

Mike Tyson [maik taisən] n. 迈克·泰森（人名）

NBA (National Basketball Association) 美国职业篮球协会

MVP (Most Valuable Player) 最有价值球员

After-reading Activity

What information about basketball is important to you, NBA, MVP or Yao Ming?

Background Information

1. NBA（美国职业篮球协会）

美国国家篮球协会（National Basketball Association），简称NBA，为北美的职业篮球组织，由三个职业体育联盟组成：美国职业篮球联盟（NBA）、美国女子职业篮球联盟（WNBA）以及NBA发展联盟（NBA Development League）。其中NBA是世界上水平最高的篮球联赛，也是美国四大职业体育联赛之一。NBA拥有30支球队，分属两个分区（Conference）：东部联盟和西部联盟；30支球队当中有29支位于美国，另外一支来自加拿大的多伦多。

2. MVP（最有价值球员）

"MVP"是"最有价值球员"的意思。是由美国国家篮球协会所授予的奖项，是联盟所有奖项中含金量最高的一个个人奖项，必须由联盟总裁亲自颁发。MVP有四种：常规赛MVP、总决赛MVP、全明星赛MVP、新秀挑战赛MVP。当选MVP有两个重要条件：一要有超强的个人能力；二要率球队取得好成绩。其中，MVP霸者是在一年内同时获得三大MVP的人，历史上有3人做到：威里斯·里德（1970），迈克尔·乔丹（1996, 1998），沙奎尔·奥尼尔（2000）。

Comprehension

1. Choose the best way to complete each of the following sentences.

1) Michael Jordan has won _____ MVPs in total.

    A. 5   B. 6   C. 11   D. 12

2) Who will win in a one-on-one game between Jordan and James?

    A. Jordan.   B. James.

    C. Not mentioned.   D. No way to give an answer.

2. Complete the following summary with the words from the passage. The first letter of each missing word is given for your reference.

    Michael once said he could 1) b_____ James in a one-on-one basketball game when both were in their 2) p_____. Beyond 3) d_____, Jordan is regarded as the best basketball player ever, no only because of his amazing 4) l_____ ability which earned him the nickname "Air Jordan", but also of his excellent physical 5) s_____, great artistry and strong competitive 6) d_____.

    Actually, the game has changed a lot since Jordan's time. In response to the 7) c_____ between Jordan and James, it is impossible to get a definite answer and 8) t_____ back the clock.

    There are people like Jordan all the time. So are people who like to make 9) u_____ comparison. Anyway, there is no point comparing Jordan with others. He is 10) g_____ of basketball.

Vocabulary

1. Complete the following sentences with the words given below. Change the form if necessary.

prime	outstanding	late	undergo	remain

1) The _____ president, Nelson Mandela was one of the greatest in modern world.

2) This is an _____ example of strict economy.

3) We've had a series of athletes like Jordan, trying to come back well past their _____.

4) He _____ three months of treatment in Chicago before returning to Boston.

5) She felt like _____ here, side by side with her family and friends and all the victims of the earthquake.

2. Complete the following sentences with proper prepositions or adverbs.

1) Nadal (纳达尔) was regarded as the King of Clay (红土之王) when _____ his prime.

2) It is a waste _____ time discussing this with them.

3) I suggest that you finish the first draft and then circle _____ to the beginning.

4) She said she would never ever marry someone _____ him.

Sentence Structure

Combine the following sentences using the structure "much less".

Sample:

You have no time to finish the task. You can't do anything else right now.

You have no time to finish the task, much less do anything else right now.

1) He has never been outside of the town. He hasn't been abroad, either.

2) The cat can't jump over the low shrub. It can't jump over the tall tree, either.

3) He couldn't speak Italian. He couldn't write in Italian.

4) They wouldn't take a drink. They wouldn't stay for a dinner, either.

5) So many young people can't afford a bath room in big cities. Nor can they afford a big house.

Translation

1. Translate the following English sentences from the text into Chinese.

1) The former star, now 50, said there's a long list of players he would've liked to have played one-on-one, James included.

2) To be frank, I hate both "if" questions, much less about Jordan.

3) As an outstanding athlete with excellent physical soundness, great artistry and strong competitive desire, Jordan single-handedly redefined the NBA superstar.

4) Still, there remain people like Jordan—and many fans as well—who love these unending comparison.

5) And when we circle back to the contrived comparison, we may find there is no way to reach an answer or to turn back the clock and get one.

2. Translate the following Chinese sentences into English with the words given in brackets.

1) 坦白来讲，我对这类电影不太感兴趣。（frank）

   _____ I am not so interested in film of this type.

2) 蜘蛛侠单枪匹马就制服了这个抢劫犯。（single-handed）

   The Spider Man _____.

3) 我没有办法在嘈杂的环境下专心看书。（no way）

   _____ in noisy surroundings.

4) 稍后我会回转去书店帮你找到这本杂志。（circle back）

   _____ to find the book for you.

5) 毫无疑问，刘翔是中国最出色的运动员之一。（doubt）

   _____, Liu Xiang _____ in China.

David Beckham

As David Beckham **announces** his **retirement** after a win at **PSG**, he can **reflect with** pride **on** a career that has truly attracted wide public attention.

Beckham's **CV** is **a roll of** honours of Europe's greatest clubs. **Cynics** may point to his **limitations** but he was special and **diligent** enough to be well-known. He has played for **Manchester United**, **Real Madrid**, **AC Milan**, **Paris St-Germain**, and **LA Galaxy**. These names **counter** any argument and provide a powerful answer to anybody daring to doubt him.

Beckham won six **league** titles at Manchester United as well as two **FA Cups**, the highest of many highs coming in the **Nou Camp** in May 1999. He is the first British player to win titles in four countries—**obvious** evidence of a professional life played out on the widest stage.

It was hard to imagine Beckham was at a time, **regarded as** the nation's bad guy when he was **sent off** for kicking out at **Argentina's Diego Simeone** in the 1998 World Cup in France. His team lost the game. It took him time to **win back** the nation's affections yet it was **accomplished** at last.

Fortunately, Beckham was **elevated** to the status of England's football *saviour* when his last-minute **free-kick** earned a **draw** against Greece at **Old Trafford** and **secured** their place at the 2002 World Cup in Japan and South Korea.

And this is where we **have regret about** perhaps the great disappointment of Beckham's career—he never truly played in World Cup **in the manner** he would have wished. **Imperfection** is, in a sense, perfection, isn't it?

(267 words)

New Words

announce	[ə'nauns]	vt.	宣布，播报
retirement	[ri'taiəmənt]	n.	退休，退役
reflect	[ri'flekt]	vt. & vi.	反射（光、热、声或影像），反映，考虑，反省
cynic ★	['sinik]	n.	愤世嫉俗者，犬儒学派的人
limitation	[ˌlimi'teiʃn]	n.	限制，限度
diligent	['dilidʒənt]	adj.	勤奋的，勤勉的，用功的
latterly	['lætəli]	adv.	近来，最近，后来
counter	['kauntə]	vt.	反击，还击
league	[liːg]	n.	联盟；社团
obvious	['ɔbviəs]	adj.	明显的，显著的
accomplish	[ə'kʌmpliʃ]	vt.	完成，达到（目的）
elevate	['eliveit]	vt.	提升，举起
saviour ★	['seivjə]	n.	救世主，救星
draw	[drɔː]	n.	平局，抽签
secure	[si'kjuə]	vt.	保护，争取到
imperfection	[ˌimpə'fekʃn]	n.	不完美，瑕疵

Useful Expressions

reflect (with pride) on（自豪地）回想……

CV (Curriculum Vitae) 简历

a roll of 一卷

be regarded as 被当作是……，被认为是……

send off 寄出，罚出场

have regret about 为……感到遗憾

win back 重获，赢回

free kick （足球）任意球

in the manner 以某种方式

Proper Names

David Beckham [deivid 'bekhæm] 大卫·贝克汉姆（人名）

PSG 巴黎圣日耳曼（Paris Saint Garment 的简称）

Manchester United ['mæntʃistə juː'naitid] 曼彻斯特联队（简称"曼联"）

Nou Camp [njuː kæmp] 诺坎普球场（西班牙巴塞罗那队主场馆）

FA Cups [fa: kʌps] 英格兰足总杯（The Football Association Challenge Cup 的简称）

Real Madrid [ri:l mə'drid] 皇家马德里队（简称"皇马"）

AC Milan ['ei 'si: mi'læn] AC 米兰

Paris St-Germain ['pæris seint dʒə'mein] 巴黎圣日耳曼（简称为"PSG"）

LA Galaxy [ˌel'ei 'gæləksi] 洛杉矶银河队

Argentina [ˌa:dʒən'ti:nə] 阿根廷

Diego Simeone [di'eigəu 'simiən] 迭戈·西蒙尼（人名）

Old Trafford [əuld 'træfəd] 老特拉福德球场（位于英格兰）

Comprehension

1. Mark the following statements *T* (*true*) or *F* (*false*) according to the text.

☐ 1) Beckham has played for 6 clubs worldwide.

☐ 2) He isn't the first British player to win titles in four countries.

☐ 3) British people never spoke ill of him.

☐ 4) He succeeded in winning back the love from British people.

☐ 5) He made great contribution for his team in 2002 World Cup.

2. Complete the following statements.

1) David Beckham announces his _____ after a win at PSG.

2) He had some _____ according to some cynics.

3) The tittles he won are clear _____ of a professional life played out on the widest stage.

4) 1998 World Cup was held in _____.

5) He was elevated to the status of England's football _____ when his last-minute free-kick helped his team secure their place at the 2002 World Cup.

Vocabulary and Structure

1. Put the following words about football under the corresponding pictures.

corner kick   penalty kick   shooting   goal keeping

1) _____   2) _____   3) _____   4) _____

Unit 5 Sports

2. Compare each pair of words and complete the following sentences with the right one. Change the form if necessary.

1) announce, announcement

   Beckham _____ his engagement to Victoria in 2003.

   She made her _____ after talks with the chairman.

2) retire, retirement

   The proportion of the population who are over _____ age has been growing in the past few years.

   Though _____, Beckham is still working on some projects related to football.

3) cynic, cynical

   A _____ is a man who knows the price of everything and the value of nothing.

   He was so _____ that he looked down upon everything that made life valuable.

4) affect, affection

   More than one million people have been _____ by the virus.

   She thought of her ex-boyfriend with _____ on Chinese Valentine's Day.

3. Complete the following sentences with the words given below. Change the form if necessary.

limitation	elevate	security	affection
imperfection	draw	imagination	counter

1) As you travel westward, does the _____ get higher?

2) The doctor cured his disease, using the techniques I once thought _____.

3) The dog has a strong _____ for its owner.

4) The game has _____ huge crowds.

5) The director's _____ seems to have dried up.

6) The fear was that the enemy has launched its own _____ attack in the battle.

7) _____ food and water must be supplied after the earthquake.

8) Your resources are _____. So invest them only on things that give you the most return.

4. Complete the following sentences with the expressions given below. Change the form if necessary.

reflect on	have no regret about	win back	in a careful manner

1) The only thing you can do is to carry out the plan _____.

2) Your decision _____ well _____ your judgment.

3) And if she never comes, you will _____ it.

4) Booksellers are trying their best to raise their profit online and _____ the customers.

 Activity

Planning for a TV Interview

You are planning a live TV interview with a famous football team from your city. What questions would you like to ask them?

1. Get familiar with some special English terms about interviews.

live interview 直播采访

interviewee 被采访者

unexpected situation 突发状况

ascertain the time 确认时间

2. Match the sentences in A with the Chinese equivalents in B.

A

1) Confirm interview theme (　　)

2) Get a whole picture of the interviewees (　　)

3) Design major questions for the interview (　　)

4) Be ready for unexpected situation (　　)

5) Ascertain interview time with interviewees (　　)

6) Last minute details. (　　)

B

a) 最后要关注的细节

b) 对采访对象进行全面了解

c) 为突发情况做准备

d) 列出采访提纲, 提出采访的主干问题

e) 与被采访对象确定采访时间

f) 确定采访的主题

3. Think about what you should pay attention to in order to have a successful TV interview.

1) How do you choose the right date?

2) How do you develop your theme?

3) What are the effective ways to advertise the interview?

4) After your interview has been completed, what else should you pay attention to?

Passage C Fast Reading

A Special Extreme Athlete

A) The legend of Arthur begins months ago, deep in the Amazon *jungles* (丛林) of *Ecuador* (厄瓜多尔), where a team of *Swedish* (瑞典的) athletes was preparing for another difficult 430-mile race through mountain and jungle. Dirty and hungry, the extreme athletes in a worldwide competition had just a *cracked* (破开的) can of meat—and that's when they saw him, Arthur.

B) They offered the poor animal, dirty and bleeding, a Swedish meatball. The dog ate it up. And from that moment on, the dog wouldn't leave the team's side. They thought he would disappear back into the jungle. But he didn't.

C) Arthur completed the remaining miles of the Adventure Racing World Series—an extreme event that calls on the athlete to endure difficulties while hiking, *trekking* (艰苦跋涉), biking and *kayaking* (划独木舟) over hundreds of miles—and has since become more and more famous.

D) When the Swedes fell into mud, so did Arthur. When they slept on the ground, so did Arthur. When they *paddled* (划桨) their kayaks, Arthur swam beside, "They started with four team members—but finished with five," the members of Peak Performance Adventure Racing Team wrote. One added on Facebook: "I came to Ecuador to win the World Championship. Instead, I got a new friend."

E) "I almost cried in front of my computer, when receiving the decision!" the team posted on their Facebook page. "The team is *thrilled* (十分兴奋的) and happy knowing that Swedish *authorities* (当局) approved Michael's application to bring Arthur back to Sweden. A big important piece in the work to get Arthur on the plane is done." And when they got off the plane in Sweden, there he was again, Arthur.

(320 words)

Information Match

Please identify the paragraph from which the following information is derived. Each paragraph is marked with a letter.

_____ 1) Arthur was poor and hungry when offered some food by the athletes.

_____ 2) Arthur endured many difficulties and finished the race.

_____ 3) Arthur was regarded as the fifth member of the team.

_____ 4) The team got approval from the Sweden authorities to bring Arthur back to Sweden.

_____ 5) The race was actually a competition with a team of extreme athletes involved.

Background Information

1. Story Background（故事背景）

2014年，一个由迈克尔·林诺德等四个瑞典人组成的越野小组报名参加了极限越野世界锦标赛，在约40天的时间内，他们要完成430多英里的路程。当行进到厄瓜多尔雨林时，他们遇到一只筋疲力尽、浑身是泥的流浪狗亚瑟，迈克尔喂了它一个肉丸子，却没想到流浪狗却始终不愿意离开他们，不论赛事多么艰难、多么危险，它依然坚定地跟着队伍，不离不弃地完成了400多英里的长途跋涉。尽管在行进的过程中，组织方出于安全问题，一度拒绝了亚瑟跟队伍继续前行，但四人小组说服了组织方，让亚瑟留在队伍中并继续比赛，他们最终成为队友。在比赛结束后，迈克尔将亚瑟带回了瑞典，同自己一起愉快地生活。

2. Extreme Off-road Race（极限穿越比赛）

极限穿越比赛是一种有组织的户外极限运动，是指在一定时间和区域内，主要依靠徒步完成由起点到终点的过程。在此过程中，选手们将经历山川、河流、高山、丛林等不同赛段，因此它对参赛选手的野外综合技能要求较高，集登山、攀岩、漂流、溯溪、野外生存于一体，一般要求穿越人员必须具备强健的体能、稳定的心理素质、坚持不懈的毅力以及乐于助人的团队精神。

Section C Grammar

宾语（一）(Object I)

宾语是动作的对象或承受者，一般跟在及物动词或介词的后面，可分为动词宾语，介词宾语。宾语主要由名词、代词或相当于名词的单词、短语或从句充当。

一、名词作宾语

Some paintings have a religious *theme*.

有些画以宗教为主题。

In the spring of 1953, Kahlo had the only *exhibition* of her work in Mexico.

1953年春，卡洛在墨西哥举办了她唯一的一次画展。

二、代词作宾语

At school, Dickens' teacher beat *him* with a cane for laughing too loudly.

在学校，狄更斯的老师用棍子打他，理由是他笑声太大了。

Which is the closest planet to the sun?

哪个是离太阳最近的行星？

三、动名词作宾语

Isn't it a *blessing* in disguise?

难道不是因祸得福吗？

People have imagined *living in outer space*.

人们一直想象在外太空居住。

四、不定式作宾语

I want *to put a bug in your ear*.

我要提醒你一点事。

She knows what she wants of life and refuses *to sacrifice an inch*.

她知道自己想要什么样的生活，拒绝牺牲其中的任何一点。

注意：动名词和不定式都可以作宾语，但有些动词只能接动名词作宾语，有些动词只能接不定式作宾语；还有些动词既可以接动名词，又可以接不定式作宾语。

1. 只能接动名词作宾语的动词有：

admit, advise, allow, appreciate（感激）, avoid（避免）, can't help, consider, delay（耽搁、延期）, enjoy, excuse, fancy（想象、设想）, finish, imagine, keep, mind, miss, permit, practice, suggest, give up, insist on（坚持）, object to（反对）, put off（推迟）, look forward to…（期望）。例如：

She *can't help shedding tears.*

她忍不住流下了眼泪。

Do you *object to my speaking to him* about it?

我去和他谈谈这事，你有意见吗？

2. 只能接不定式作宾语的动词有：

agree, ask, care, choose, dare, decide, demand, expect, hope, learn, long（渴望）, manage, offer, plan, pretend, promise, refuse, wait, want, wish…。例如：

He *agreed to pay* me for the drawings.

他答应向我支付这些画的钱。

Peter *offered to teach* them water-skiing.

彼得主动提出教他们滑水。

3. 有些动词既能加不定式作宾语，又能加动名词作宾语。两者意思基本相同。如 begin, start, like, hate, continue 等。但有些动词两种形式在意思上有很大的差别，例如：

① remember to do sth. 记住（别忘记）要做某事

    remember doing sth. 记得（回忆起）过去曾经做过某事

    ⎧ Please *remember to* post the letter for me.
    ⎨ 请记得给我寄信。
    ⎪ I *remember posting* (or having posted) the letter.
    ⎩ 我记得已经寄了信。

② forget to do sth. 忘记要做某事

    forget doing sth. 忘记了曾做过某事

    ⎧ He *forgot to lock* the door.
    ⎨ 他忘了锁门。
    ⎪ He *forgot ever having locked* the door.
    ⎩ 他忘记已经锁了门。

③ regret to do sth. 对现在要发生的事表示"抱歉、遗憾"

    regret doing sth. 对已经发生的事表示后悔

    ⎧ I *regret to inform* you that you are laid off.
    ⎨ 我很遗憾地通知你被裁员了。
    ⎪ She *regretted giving up* her home five years ago.
    ⎩ 她很遗憾五年前放弃了自己的家。

④ stop to do sth. 停下来去做某事

    stop doing sth. 停止做某事

    ⎧ They *stopped to work*.
    ⎨ 他们停下来开始工作。
    ⎪ They *stopped working*.
    ⎩ 他们停止了工作。

⑤ try to do sth. 设法……，试图……

    try doing sth. 试一试，试试看

    ⎧ I *try to remember* all the good times I've had here.
    ⎨ 我尽力记住我在这里曾经度过的美好时光。
    ⎪ I *have tried painting* my self-portrait.
    ⎩ 我试着画一幅自画像。

⑥ mean to do sth. 打算……，有……的意图

   mean doing sth. 意味着，就是

> I don't **mean to hurt** your feelings.
> 我不是有意伤害你的感情的。
>
> Managing well **means communicating** well.
> 良好的管理需要有效的沟通。

Exercises

1. Complete the following sentences based on the given Chinese.

1) Fanny Elssler's style of ballet borrowed from _____.
   芬妮·爱思勒的芭蕾舞风格取自于民间舞蹈。

2) They stopped _____.
   他们停下来开始讨论这个问题。

3) I regret _____ before he left.
   我后悔在他离开之前没跟他说再见。

4) Do you fancy _____?
   你有空想不想去看场电影？

5) I don't know why he refused _____.
   我不知道他为什么拒绝接受我们的邀请。

6) How can you expect me _____?
   你怎能指望我相信你的承诺？

7) They are considering _____.
   他们正在考虑自己创业。

8) He was born with _____.
   他是嘴巴含着银汤匙出生的。

2. Choose the best way to complete each of the following sentences.

1) I feel like _____ a long walk. Would you like _____ with me?
   A. taking ... going   B. to take ... going
   C. taking ... to go   D. to take ... to go

2) You should keep on _____ English every day in order to improve it.
   A. to practice to speak   B. to practice speaking
   C. practicing to speak   D. practicing speaking

3) Do you still remember _____ to your birth place eight years ago?
   A. taken   B. to take   C. to be taken   D. being taken

4) I should say sorry to him. I regret _____ to help him that day.

   A. refusing   B. to refuse   C. refused   D. refuse

5) I look forward to _____ you in the near future.

   A. hear from   B. hearing from   C. hear to   D. hearing to

6) I enjoyed _____ rugby.

   A. playing   B. playing the   C. to play   D. to play the

7) The son has promised _____ for a long visit.

   A. coming   B. come   C. to come   D. to coming

8) They demanded _____ US troops.

   A. removing   B. remove   C. to removing   D. to remove

9) I am _____ with envy. (我羡慕极了)

   A. blue   B. green   C. pink   D. red

10) She longed _____ him again.

   A. to see   B. to seeing   C. having seen   D. see

Section D   Sentence Writing

Color Run

1. What is Color Run?

   Tips: throw at, participant, 5K course, dress in white, rainbow...

   _____

   _____.

2. How do you prepare your hair for color run?

   Tips: wet, apply...to , olive oil, barrier, dye (染料), wash, shampoo...

_____
_____.

3. What is the colored powder made from?

   Tips: corn starch, food grade (食品级), dye, bright colors...

   _____
   _____.

4. Would you like to take part in the Color Run if it is being held in your city? Why/why not?

   Tips: fun, interesting, happiest 5km on the planet, rainbow, dangerous, hurt, eye, protection...

   _____
   _____.

Unit 6

Achieving Dreams

 ## Section A   Listening and Speaking

 ### Task A General Pronunciation Rules

E 在重读音节中的发音:

[iː]

1. 在单音节单词词尾

   例词: me, he, she, we, be

2. 在一个辅音字母加上不发音的 e 之前

   例词: these, delete, complete, eve, theme

3. 在多数词中位于一个辅音字母加一个元音字母之前

   例词: even, evening, legal, thesis, media

[e]

1. 在闭音节中

   例词: bet, send, forget, less, neck, west

2. 在双音节单词或多音节单词中位于两个或两个以上辅音字母之前

   例词: secretary, segment, fellow, plenty, splendid

3. 在倒数第三个重读开音节中

   例词: celebrate, regular, specify, melody, penetrate

 ### Task B Conversations

Model Dialogue 1: If I were a millionaire...

1. Listen to the conversation and fill in the blanks with the expressions given below.

Dave: Wow, I read from the newspaper that so many people won the lottery and became millionaires...

Lisa: It seems that _____.

Dave: Yes, I hope I could be the lucky one.

Lisa: Well, if you had a million dollars suddenly, what would you do?

Dave: I would _____. Maybe a big house and a luxury car...

Lisa: Do you really think money can buy happiness?

Dave: Sort of... Money can make me feel happy. Money helps us _____— family, education, health care and so on.

Lisa: But _____ is the real happiness. In the long run, more money won't necessarily give you more joy, day-to-day. It won't help you feel closer to your friends and family.

Dave: _____.

---
1. support the things we care about most 4. There's something in what you said
2. emotional well-being 5. buy anything I like
3. you are green with envy

---

2. Role-play a conversation in pairs according to the given situation.

Dave believes money can buy happiness and his family will have no money concerns if he has a lot of money. Lisa disagrees. They argue with each other about how to balance between making money and time spent with family.

Model Dialogue 2: Introduction

1. Listen to the conversation and fill in the blanks with the expressions given below.

Susan: What can I do for you?

Bob: Yes. I'd like to change some US dollars. Could you tell me what _____ for US dollars is?

Susan: It's _____ per hundred US dollars.

Bob: I want to change some US dollars.

Susan: _____?

Bob: 2 000 US dollars total.

Susan: Please fill out _____.

Bob: Okay.

Susan: Please _____. I will do it for you as soon as possible.

---
1. 621 RMB 4. How much would you like to change
2. the exchange form 5. wait a minute
3. today's exchange rate

2. Role-play a conversation in pairs according to the given situation.

Ann is in the bank and wants to change some US dollars into Chinese yuan.

Task C Passage

Listen to the passage and choose the best answer to each question.

Word Tips:
1. wealthy ['welθi]] *adj.* 富有的
2. definitely ['definətli] *adv.* 明确地；一定地；肯定地
3. damage ['dæmidʒ] *vt./vi.* 损害，毁坏
4. seek [si:k] *vt.* 寻找；追求

1) When the speaker's grandfather is ill, what does he come to realize?
   A. It's important to make more money.
   B. Money means nothing if you have no health.
   C. Working overtime is necessary.
   D. If they were rich, the grandfather wouldn't suffer a lot.

2) What is the speaker's attitude towards working overtime?
   A. It will not damage our health when we are young.
   B. It will damage our health slowly even if we don't feel it.
   C. It is necessary to work overtime because we want to be rich.
   D. It is the best way to make progress in our career.

3) What's our main concern when we are ill?
   A. Money and health.   B. Health and love.
   C. Money and love.   D. Health and work.

Task D Spot Dictation

Listen to the passage three times and fill in the blanks.

Word Tips:
1. turn out 结果，发生
2. bring up 提出，提起
3. engage [in'geidʒ] *vi.* 从事，使从事
4. connect [kə'nekt] *vi.* 连接，结合

When was the last time you dreamed? I'm talking about dreaming and 1) _____ something that you really want in your life. I bet when you were younger, you dreamed all the time, but something happened and it didn't 2) _____ . That's 3) _____ when you slowly 4) _____ on dreaming. Or maybe you have achieved your dreams and didn't want to create new ones. Don't worry. That's common. Often people get busy in their 5) _____ and forget to dream. Or they're afraid to dream because it 6) _____ lots of disappointments. It's comfortable to live without burdens, but that's not where the fun is in life. Having dreams 7) _____ you in your life, makes it more exciting, and **connects** you to yourself and what's important to you.

Section B   Reading

Passage A

Dream Art

Pre-reading Questions

1. Where does inspiration come from? Is dream a source of inspiration?
2. Have you ever tried to record your dreams? What was the most memorable dream you ever had?

Dream art is any form of art directly **based on** material from dreams, or which employs dream-like **imagery**. **Historical** records of dreams in art are as old as **literature** itself. For instance, there are descriptions of major **characters'** dreams in *Bible*. However, dreams as art **appear** to be a later development.

In European literature, the Romantic Movement emphasized the value of emotion and *irrational* inspiration. **"Visions"**, whether from dreams or enchantment, **served** as raw material and **were taken to represent** the artist's highest creative potential. In the late 19th and early 20th centuries, *symbolism* and *expressionism* introduced dream imagery into visual art. The famous **playwright August Strindberg coined** the term "dream play" for a style of **narrative** that did not **distinguish** between **fantasy** and reality.

The invention of film and **animation** brought new possibilities for vivid **depiction** of nonrealistic events. But films **consisting** entirely **of** dream imagery have **remained** a **rarity.** Comic books and **comic strips** have explored dreams somewhat more often. Starting with **Winsor McCay**'s popular newspaper strips, the trend toward **confessional** works saw an increasing number of artists drawing their own dreams. A Harvard psychologist **identifies** modern dream-inspired art such as paintings including **Jasper John**'s *Flag,* much of the work of **Jim Dine**, novels **ranging from** *Sophie's Choice* to works by **Anne Rice** and **Stephen King** and films including **Robert Altman**'s *Three Women.* He also describes how **Paul McCartney**'s *Yesterday* was heard by him in a dream and most of **Billy Joel**'s music has **originated in** dreams.

Dream material continues to be used by a wide range of **contemporary** artists for various purposes. This practice is considered to be of a **psychological** value for the artist-independent of the artistic value of the results.

(294 words)

New Words

imagery	['imidʒəri]	n. 形象，意象
historical	[his'tɔrikl]	adj. 历史的，史学的
literature	['litrətʃə]	n. 文学，文艺，著作
character	['kærəktə(r)]	n. 角色，性格
appear	[ə'piə(r)]	vi. 出现，显得，似乎
irrational ★	[i'ræʃənl]	adj. 非理性的
inspiration	[ˌinspə'reiʃn]	n. 灵感，鼓舞
vision	['viʒn]	n. 幻想，远见，视力
represent	[ˌrepri'zent]	vt. 代表，表现
symbolism ★	['simbəlizəm]	n. 象征主义
expressionism ★	[ik'spreʃənizəm]	n. 表现主义
playwright	['pleirait]	n. 剧作家
coin	[kɔin]	vi. 杜撰，创造
narrative	['nærətiv]	adj. 叙事的，叙事体的
distinguish	[di'stiŋgwiʃ]	vi. 区别，区分
fantasy	['fæntəsi]	n. 幻想
animation	[ˌæni'meiʃn]	n. 动画片

depiction	[dɪˈpɪkʃn]	n. 描写，描绘
remain	[rɪˈmeɪn]	vi. 保持，依然
rarity	[ˈreərəti]	n. 罕见，珍贵
confessional ★	[kənˈfeʃənl]	adj. 忏悔的，自白的
identify	[aɪˈdentɪfaɪ]	vt. 辨别出，识别
originate	[əˈrɪdʒɪneɪt]	vi. 发源，起源
contemporary	[kənˈtemprəri]	adj. 当代的，同时代的
psychological	[ˌsaɪkəˈlɒdʒɪkl]	adj. 心理的，心理学的

Useful Expressions

base on 基于，建立在……基础上
serve as 充当，起……作用
consist of 由……组成，由……构成
comic strips 连环漫画
range from 从……到……范围

Proper Names

August Strindberg [ˈɔːgʌst ˈstrɪndbɜːrg] 奥古斯特·斯特林堡（瑞典剧作家）
Winsor McCay [ˈwɪnzə maɪˈkeɪ] 温瑟·麦凯（美国著名漫画家和动画导演）
Jasper John [ˈdʒæspə dʒɒn] 贾斯珀·约翰（美国战后著名艺术家）
Jim Dine [dʒɪm daɪn] 吉姆·迪恩（美国波普艺术家）
Anne Rice [æn raɪs] 安妮·赖斯（美国当代著名小说家）
Stephen King [ˈstiːvən kɪŋ] 史蒂芬·金（美国畅销书作家）
Robert Altman [ˈrɒbət ˈɔːltmən] 罗伯特·阿特曼（美国著名电影导演）
John Sayles [dʒɒn ˈseɪlz] 约翰·赛尔斯（美国独立导演、编剧、作家）
Paul McCartney [pɔːl məkˈkʌtni] 保罗·麦卡特尼（英国音乐家、创作歌手及作曲家）
Billy Joel [ˈbɪli ˈdʒəʊəl] 比利·乔尔（美国天才歌手、钢琴家、作曲家、作词家）

After-reading Activity

Unit 6 Achieving Dreams

Everybody has normal dreams every single night. These dreams offer insight from mind. And these insights are based on your thoughts, experiences from the day before, sometimes memories from long ago. Can you draw a picture of your most unforgettable dream? Then ask your classmates to interpret the meaning of your dream according to your picture.

Background Information

1. Symbolism（象征主义）

象征主义，名词源于希腊文 Symbolon，它在希腊文中的原意是指 "一块木板（或一种陶器）分成两半，主客双方各执其一，再次见面时拼成一块，以示友爱" 的信物。几经演变，其义变成了 "用一种形式作为一种概念的习惯代表"，即引申为任何观念或事物的代表，凡能表达某种观念及事物的符号或物品就叫作 "象征"。它与通常人们用的比喻不同，它涉及事物的实质，含义远较比喻深广。是 19 世纪末在英国及西方几个国家出现的一种艺术思潮。

2. Expressionism（表现主义）

表现主义是艺术家通过作品着重表现内心的情感，而忽视对描写对象形式的摹写，往往表现为对现实扭曲和抽象化的做法，尤其用来表达恐惧的情感，因此，主题欢快的表现主义作品很少见。从这个定义上来说，马蒂斯·格吕内瓦尔德与格雷考的作品也可以说是表现主义的，但是一般来说表现主义仅限于 20 世纪的作品。

Comprehension

1. Choose the best way to complete each of the following sentences.

1) Dream art is any form of art based on material from _____.
   A. imagination   B. inspiration
   C. dreams   D. fantasy

2) _____ continued to be used by many contemporary artists for various purposes.
   A. Fantasy story   B. Fable
   C. Dream material   D. Fiction

2. Complete the following summary with the words from the passage. The first letter of each missing word is given for your reference.

Dream art is any form of art based on 1) m_____ from dreams. Historical records of dream art are as old as 2) l_____ itself. However, dreams as art 3) a_____ to be a later development. In European literature, the Romantic Movement emphasized the value of emotion and irrational 4) i_____ . In the late 19th and early 20th 5) c_____ , symbolism and expressionism introduced dreams imagery into visual art. The 6) i_____ of film and animation makes vivid 7) d_____ of nonrealistic events become possible. Comic books and comic strips have 8) e_____ dreams to a great extent. Dream art even arouses experts' attention. A Harvard psychologist 9) i_____ modern dream-inspired art ranging from painting to music by famous artists. Besides, dream material is considered to be used by a wide range of 10) c_____ artists for various purposes.

Vocabulary

1. Complete the following sentences with the words given below. Change the form if necessary.

> originate   distinguish   character   represent   imagery

1) The main _____ in the fiction is a girl who lost her parents in the war.
2) Where did the style of painting _____?
3) This painting tells a vivid _____ of dreams.
4) Could you _____ the two voices (嗓音)?
5) The comment does not _____ our views.

2. Complete the following sentences with proper prepositions or adverbs.

1) The film is based _____ a true story.
2) She introduced me _____ the author of *Harry Potter*.

3) The house consists _____ five rooms.

4) The celebration started _____ a huge firework display.

Sentence Structure

Combine the following sentences using the structure "as… as ...".

Sample:

My coffee is good. Your coffee is the same good as my coffee.

You coffee is as good as mine.

1) I am tall. He is the same tall as me.

2) Basketball is popular here. Football is the same popular here.

3) The old lady's hair is white. The old lady's hair is the same white as snow.

4) My brother works hard. I work the same hard as my brother.

5) He knows little about music. I know the same little about painting as he knows about music.

Translation

1. Translate the following English sentences from the text into Chinese.

1) Dream art is any form of art directly based on material from dreams, or which employs dream-like imagery.

2) "Visions", whether from dreams or enchantment, served as raw material and were taken to represent the artist's highest creative potential.

3) In the late 19th and early 20th centuries, symbolism and expressionism introduced dream imagery into visual art.

4) The famous playwright August Strindberg coined the term "dream play" for a style of narrative that did not distinguish between fantasy and reality.

5) Dream material continues to be used by a wide range of contemporary artists for various purposes.

2. Translate the following Chinese sentences into English with the words given in brackets.

1) 他们强调健康饮食的重要性。（emphasize）

   They _____ healthy eating.

2) 老师的这番话被认为是对他的夸奖。（be taken into）

   What the teacher said _____ a compliment to him.

3) 这个观念起源于古希腊。（originate in）

   The idea _____ ancient Greece.

4) 这个班级的学生年龄从 15 岁至 50 岁不等。(range from)

   The ages of the students _____.

5) 他继续工作直到深夜。(continue to)

   He _____ late into the night.

Passage B

Teenage Dreams:
Nicola Formichetti's Fashion Rebirth

Nicola Formichetti, a creative whiz kid in fashion, was born in Japan and grew up in Rome and Tokyo. As a child he **trained as** a classical pianist. But moving to London and **getting involved in** fashion industry became his greatest **desire**. He used the excuse of attending an architecture school to get to London pursuing his dream. In London he began working at a **boutique** called "*The Pineal Eye*". While working at "*The Pineal Eye*", Formichetti was spotted by fashion editor **Katy England** and she offered him a monthly page at *Dazed & Confused* called "Eye Spy". In 2005, he was named the **magazine**'s fashion director. Eventually, he was **promoted** to become the magazine's creative director in 2008.

Now he enjoys the global **reputation** as the artistic director of the Italian fashion **label Diesel** and for being a frequent **collaborator** with singer-songwriter and performance artist Lady Gaga. Rather than **sticking to** design alone, he keeps his eyes on everything from design and **graphics** to selling and marketing. Nicola, **along with** his brother, creates the Nicopanda line based on the panda cartoon that looks like Nicola. In May 2012, Nicola opened Nicopanda **pop up stores** at **Lane Crawford** in Beijing and Hong Kong.

His influence is varied. Although he is **rank**ed the most **influential stylist** in the world, his influence on culture is greatest. Previously the role and influence of stylists were more limited. While other stylists become designers, he is the first to **take control of** a major fashion house. And he is **interpreted as** the most **prominent** example of a stylist becoming a power **broker** within the industry. However he hates to be called an **elitist** in fashion. As he tells in an interview, he is a simple person and really works hard to live his teenage dreams.

What is your teenage dream? Are you working hard to pursue your dream? Never say that your dream will forever be a dream. Go ahead, plan on making that dream a reality and watch how great you can achieve your goals.

(338 words)

New Words

desire	[di'zaiə(r)]	n. 渴望，欲望
boutique	[bu'ti:k]	n. 精品店，专卖流行衣服的小商店
magazine	[ˌmægə'zi:n]	n. 杂志
promote	[prə'məut]	vt. 提升，促进
reputation	[ˌrepju'teiʃn]	n. 名誉，声望
label	['leibl]	n. 标签，商标
collaborator ★	[kə'læbəreitə(r)]	n. 合作者
graphics ★	['græfiks]	n. 图像，图形
rank	[ræŋk]	vt. 评定等级，名列，位居
influential	[ˌinflu'enʃl]	adj. 有影响力的
stylist	['stailist]	n. 设计师，造型师
prominent	['prɔminənt]	adj. 杰出的，显著的
broker	['brəukə(r)]	n. 经纪人，代理人
elitist	[i'li:tist]	n. 优秀人才，杰出人物

Useful Expressions

train as 受过……训练
get involved in 涉及，参加……活动
stick to 坚持做某事
along with 和……一起
take control of 控制
interpret as 把……看作，把……理解为
pop up stores（短期经营）时尚潮店

Proper Names

Nicola Formichetti [ni'kɔː lʌ fɔrmi'keti] 尼克拉·弗米切提（著名造型师、设计师、时尚编辑）
Diesel [dizl] 迪赛（意大利著名时尚品牌）
Katy England ['keti 'iŋglənd] 凯蒂·英格兰（英国著名造型师、时尚编辑）
Lane Crawford ['lein 'krɔfəd] 连卡佛（亚洲最具影响力的时装及生活专门店）

Comprehension

1. Mark the following statements *T* (*true*) or *F* (*false*) according to the text.

☐ 1) As a child, Nicola was trained as a designer.

☐ 2) Nicola is an artistic director of the Italian fashion label Diesel.

☐ 3) Nicola only pays attention to fashion design.

☐ 4) Nicola has become an example of a stylist and a power broker within the industry.

☐ 5) Nicola enjoys being called an elitist in fashion.

2. Complete the following statements.

1) Nicola Formichetti was born in J_____ and grew up in R_____ and T_____.

2) While working at "*The Pineal Eye*", Formichetti was spotted by fashion e_____ Katy England.

3) Now Nicola Formichetti enjoys the global reputation as the a_____ director of the Italian fashion label Diesel.

4) Nicola Formichetti hates to be called an e_____ in fashion.

5) Nicola Formichetti really works hard to live his t_____ dreams.

Vocabulary and Structure

1. Put the following words under the corresponding pictures.

teenage   magazine   boutique   label

1) _____ 2) _____ 3) _____ 4) _____

Unit 6 Achieving Dreams

2. **Compare each pair of words and complete the following sentences with the right one. Change the form if necessary.**

1) creative, create

   He _____ a bad impression at the interview.

   She is a good designer. She is so _____.

2) fashion, fashionable

   What is the latest _____ in cloth?

   Decoration of this style is highly _____.

3) perform, performance

   It is an excellent _____.

   She is _____ at the National Theatre.

4) style, stylist

   The writer's _____ is very clear and simple.

   He is the best fashion _____ in Europe.

3. **Complete the following sentences with the words given below. Change the form if necessary.**

| reputation | spot | influential | prominent |
| elitist | rank | promote | desire |

1) She is _____ as one of the world's top players.

2) The stature was in a _____ position outside the railway station.

3) Most of these fossils(化石) are too small to be easily _____ .

4) She has a burning _____ for knowledge.

5) She has built up a high _____ as a pianist.

6) He is an _____ in computer field.

7) This was a highly _____ work.

8) He has been _____ from assistant manager to manager.

4. **Complete the following sentences with the expressions given below. Change the form if necessary.**

| train as | get to | stick to | interpret as |

1) It's right to _____ the principles, but not to stand on.

2) Your silence could be _____ refusal.

3) She _____ an engineer in college.

4) What time does the train _____ London?

123

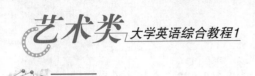

Activity

Planning for a Dream Fund

As a member of the Innovation and Venture Base of your college, starting your own business on campus has always been your dream. But you have to raise a sum of venture capital fund as a start. So, how do you turn your visionary career into actual practice?

1. Get familiar with some special English terms about exhibitions.

venture capital 创业基金

design proposal 设计方案

brainstorming 头脑风暴

fund management 基金管理

seed money 本钱

finance 资助

sponsor 资助人

2. Match the sentences in A with the Chinese equivalents in B.

A

1) Choose creative minds to form your team   (   )

2) Search for responsible sponsors   (   )

3) Select potential and profitable business direction   (   )

4) Do researches on how much seed money you need   (   )

5) Study management guidance   (   )

6) Last minute details   (   )

B

a) 寻找可靠的资助人

b) 学习管理指南

c) 最后的细节

d) 挑选有利可图的商业发展方向

e) 选择有创新头脑的队友

f) 研究需要多少本金

3. Think about what you should pay attention to in order to have a full preparation.

1) When choosing creative minds as your team members, what should you put into consideration?

2) How to search for responsible sponsors?

3) How to select to find potential and profitable business direction?

4) How to figure out how much money you need as a start and how to make a budget?

5) How to build mutual trust (相互信任) between you and your sponsor?

6) After your fund has been completed and your dream ready to carry out, what else should you pay attention to?

Passage C Fast Reading

Pursuing Your Dreams

A) Following your dreams is usually *easier said than done* (说起来容易做起来难). When watching a movie about someone following his or her dreams, and the fixed **formula** (公式) leads you to believe that, after one or two **hiccups** (中断) and a couple of hours, you'll eventually get exactly what you wanted. However, in the real world, for most of us, the road to our dreams is long, challenging and unexpected.

B) Of course, it doesn't mean that the pursuit isn't worthwhile—in fact, the experience of pursuing your dreams is often rewarding and enlightening. In trying to put the pursuit of dreams into *perspective* (看法), you should keep the following quotes in mind.

C) 1) "You have to dream before your dreams can come true." —A. P. J. Abdul Kalam.

Some people kill their potential by refusing to think "what if?" and ignoring what's truly important to them in life. You have to start dreaming before you can achieve anything.

D) 2) "Don't give up on your dreams, or your dreams will give up on you." — John Wooden.

The moment you believe you can't do it, everything else comes to nothing. Never stop believing.

E) 3) "I have lots of things to prove to myself. One is that I can live my life fearlessly."

— Oprah Winfrey.

Fear is a limiting factor, and it's present in all of us, but moving past that fear is essential for success.

F) 4) "Love what you do and do what you love. Don't listen to anyone else who tells you not to do it. You do what you want, what you love. Imagination should be the center of your life."

— Ray Bradbury.

Ignore everybody who tries to tell you what to do or think. Follow your own instincts and goals.

G) Be sure to think about this list the next time you feel frustrated in the pursuit of your dreams. By adopting the perspectives of people who have already achieved their dreams, you can be inspired and remain determined in achieving your goals.   (356 words)

Information Match

Please identify the paragraph from which the following information is derived. Each paragraph is marked with a letter.

_____ 1) In the pursuit of your dreams, you should follow your own instincts and goals.

_____ 2) You have to start dreaming before your dreams can come true.

_____ 3) Although fear is present in all of us, but overcoming that fear is essential for success.

_____ 4) The road to our dreams is long and challenging.

_____ 5) You should always believe in yourself.

Background Information

1. Abdul Kalam（阿卜杜勒·卡拉姆）

印度前总统阿卜杜勒·卡拉姆（Abdul Kalam）于1931年10月15日出生。在获得航空技术博士学位后，卡拉姆开始在印度斯坦航空公司工作。卡拉姆为印度的导弹研制做出了杰出贡献，被誉为"印度导弹之父"。2002年7月，卡拉姆当选为印度第12届总统，2007年卸任，是第一位当选印度总统的职业科学家。

他喜欢文学和印度古典音乐，是一位诗人。他还是个素食主义者，不饮酒，信奉伊斯兰教。他的信条是："只有强大才能得到尊重。"

2. John Wooden（约翰·伍登）

约翰·伍登（John Wooden）是美国篮球史上以运动员和教练员双重身份入选奈史密斯篮球荣誉纪念馆的唯一一人。他曾在执教加州大学洛杉矶分校棕熊队的27年中拿到了10个NCAA冠军，包括空前绝后的7连冠（1967—1973），同时他所执教的球队还曾获得88场连胜的纪录。伍登曾六次赢得大学最佳教练员称号。他所获得的荣誉数不胜数。他培养出的巨星弟子包括阿卜杜尔·贾巴尔以及比尔·沃顿等。

3. Oprah Winfrey（奥普拉·温弗瑞）

奥普拉·温弗瑞（Oprah Winfrey），1954年1月29日出生于密西西比州，美国演员，制片，主持人。她是当今世界上最具影响力的女性之一，她的成就是多方面的：主持电视谈话节目"奥普拉脱口秀"，30岁出头成为无可争议的"脱口秀女皇"；2002年，被普林斯顿大学授予荣誉博士学位；获"鲍勃·霍普人道主义奖"；2003年获"马里恩·安德森奖"；美国第一位黑人亿万富翁。

4. Ray Bradbury（雷·布拉德伯雷）

雷·布拉德伯雷（Ray Bradbury，1920— ）是美国科幻、奇幻、恐怖小说作家。1946年获得了"最佳美国短篇小说奖"。其中较著名的有：《火星纪事》、《太阳的金苹果》、《R代表火箭》、《明天午夜》等。

布拉德伯雷是世界闻名的科幻小说家，受爱伦·坡影响很大，作品常常通过噩梦似的情景影射残酷的现实，但正当你对生活感到绝望时，又往往会突然发生新的转机，这反映了作者的一种哲学思想：他认为人生无常，命途多舛，既可能乐极生悲，也可能绝处逢生。

Section C Grammar

宾语（二）(Object II)

五、宾语从句

置于动词、介词等词性后面起宾语作用的从句叫宾语从句。宾语从句的语序必须是陈述语序。宾语从句的引导词有：

连词：that (that 常可省略), whether, if

代词：who, whose, what, which

副词：when, where, how, why 等。

（一）that 引导的宾语从句（在非正式场合 that 可以省略）

My child often complains *that his teacher is too strict.*

我的孩子经常抱怨说他的老师太严厉。

I have realized *that it is getting dark*.

我意识到天渐渐黑了。

注意：当主句谓语动词是 think, believe, suppose, expect 等词，而宾语从句的意思是否定时，常把否定转移至主句表示。例如：

I *don't* think it is right for him to spend his spare time that way.

我觉得他那样消磨时间是不对的。

Most people *didn't* believe that Mozart, a little boy of five years old, could write such beautiful music.

大多数人认为，年仅五岁的莫扎特写不出那么优美的音乐。

（二）由 whether, if 引导的宾语从句

由 whether, if 引导的宾语从句，实际上是一般疑问句演变而来的，意思是"是否"。宾语从句要用陈述句语序。一般说来，在宾语从句中 whether 与 if 可以互换使用，但在特殊情况下 if 与 whether 是不能互换的。例如：

I wonder *whether (if)* I might have a word with Mr Abbot?

请问我能否和阿博特先生说几句话？

只能用 whether，不能用 if 引导的宾语从句：

1. 在带 to 的不定式前。

   We are discussing *whether to explore the cave.*

   我们在讨论要不要勘探这个岩洞。

2. 在介词的后面。

   I'm *thinking of whether* we should visit the Great Lakes.

   我在想我们要不要参观五大湖。

3. 直接与 or not 连用时。

   I don't know *whether* comets would bring bad luck *or not*.

   我不知道彗星是否会带来厄运。

只能用 if 不能用 whether 引导的宾语从句：

1. if 引导条件状语从句，意为"如果"。

   The students will have sports meet *if it is sunny.*

   如果天气晴朗，学生就会开运动会。

2. if 引导否定概念的宾语从句时。

He asked *if I didn't come to class yesterday.*

他问我是不是昨天没来上课。

3. 引导状语从句 even if（即使）和 as if（好像）时。

He talks *as if he has known all about it.*

他谈话的口气好像他知晓了一切。

（三）连接代词和连接副词引导的宾语从句

这样的宾语从句实际上是由特殊疑问句变化而来的，宾语从句要用陈述句语序。英语中的连接代词有：who, whom, whose, which, what 在句中担任主语、宾语、定语或者表语。

I can't remember *which teachers I had*.

我记不清哪些老师教过我。

Instead of complaining about what's wrong, be grateful for *what's right*.

别抱怨不好的事，要对好的事心存感恩。

英语中的连接副词有：when, where, why, how 句中担任状语的成分。

He knew *where Henry Carter had gone*.

他知道亨利·卡特去了哪里。

I can't understand *why they don't want us*.

我不明白为什么他们不想要我们。

Exercises

1. Complete the following sentences based on the given Chinese.

1) Let's suppose (that) _____.

让我们假设，有一天这事发生在你身上。

2) Our teacher told us _____ in the solar system.

老师告诉我们地球是太阳系中的一颗行星。

3) Did you ever wonder _____?

你想过那些超级名模是如何做到惊艳的吗？

4) Some artists paint _____.

有些画家把想象中所见到的东西画下来。

5) It would be more accurate to say _____.

更为准确地说，儒勒·凡尔纳（Jules Verne）创造了科幻小说。

6) Many people ask _____.

许多人问上帝是否存在。

7) Many students think it important _____.

许多学生认为充分利用业余时间很重要。

8) Do you know _____ in Korea ?

你知道在韩国，哪个数字是厄运数字吗？

2. Choose the best way to complete each of the following sentences.

1) I am not sure _____ there is afterlife.

   A. whether   B. that   C. weather   D. why

2) Do you know _____ ?

   A. what good he can get from this   B. what good can he get from this

   C. what good does he get from this   D. he can get what good

3) — Could you tell me _____ she has a crush on? — Her friend's brother, David.

   A. that   B. whose   C. whom   D. which

4) — What are you reading? — A book about _____.

   A. how was Israel founded   B. how Israel was founded

   C. how Israel was found   D. how was Israel found

5) — Do you know _____ the president's address is?

   — He may live at No.234 or No. 235 of Maple Street. I'm not sure of _____.

   A. where ... which   B. where ... what

   C. what ... that   D. what ... where

6) There is not much difference between the two. I really don't know _____.

   A. what should I choose   B. which I should choose

   C. which should I choose   D. what I should choose

7) What you said to him about finance is just to teach a fish _____. (班门弄斧)

   A. to swim   B. swim

   C. how to swim   D. swimming

8) I wonder _____ such an important question.

   A. why did they leave aside   B. how did they leave aside

   C. how they left aside   D. why they left aside

9) There is a child inside all of us, _____ we realize it or not. And sometimes we return to that child like state.

   A. if   B. whether

   C. as   D. which

10) My wife asked me _____ last night.

   A. where I stayed over   B. where did I stay over

   C. where I have stayed over   D. where had I stayed over

Section D Sentence Writing

What do You Want to Strive for in Your Lifetime?

1) Why do you come to college?

   Tips: opportunity, transform from…to…, take time, passionate about…

   _____
   _____.

2) What are you seeking in life?

   Tips: spirituality, career, self-development, keep in sight…

   _____
   _____.

3) Take time to ponder what really matters to you? Before you answer the question, think about what gives you happiness and fulfillment?

   Tips: come in one's mind, bring one's joy, give somebody a sense of…

   _____
   _____.

4) What do you really want to achieve and how to achieve your goal?

   Tips: direction, make the most of, focus on, strive for…

   _____
   _____.

Unit 7

Culture

Section A Listening and Speaking

Task A General Pronunciation Rules

E 在非重读音节中的发音：

[i]

1. 在重读音节前或后的音节中且位于辅音字母之前

   例词：b*e*gin, *e*motion, *e*xcuse, d*e*liberate, t*e*lephone, *e*lephant

2. 在名词复数形式的结尾 -es 和单数第三人称的动词词尾 -es 中且位于 [s, z, ʃ, tʃ, dʒ] 之后

   例词：hous*es*, ros*es*, dish*es*, branch*es*, wag*es* , ris*es*, pass*es*, wash*es*, watch*es*, chang*es*

3. 在动词词尾 -ed 中且位于 [t, d] 之后

   例词：start*ed*, faint*ed*, wait*ed*, decid*ed*, expand*ed*, pretend*ed*

4. 在词尾 -et 中

   例词：pock*et*, wall*et*, mark*et*, tick*et*, jack*et*

5. 在双音节单词词尾 -est 中，包括形容词的最高级形式

   例词：harv*est*, bigg*est*, old*est*, long*est*, short*est*, small*est*

[ə]

1. 在词尾 -ent, -ment, 和 -ence (ency) 中

   例词：equival*ent*, argum*ent*, governm*ent*, intellig*ence*, ag*ency*

2. 在后缀 -let, -less, -ess, -ness 中

   例词：book*let*, tab*let*, voice*less*, wire*less*, host*ess*, waitr*ess*, sad*ness*, kind*ness*

[-]

1. 在词尾不发音

   例词：appl*e*, mic*e*, ton*e*, fin*e*, blous*e*, hors*e*, pal*e*

2. 单数第三人称的动词词尾 -es 中且位于除了 [s, z, ʃ, tʃ, dʒ] 之外的辅音之后时不发音

   例词：hik*es*, vot*es*, tak*es*, suppli*es*, decid*es*, multipli*es*

Task B Conversations

Model Dialogue 1: Are You All Right?

1. Listen to the conversation and fill in the blanks with the expressions below.

Bob: You look so pale. _____?

Amy: Not really. I have a cold and I hate the cold weather.

Bob: _____. Did you see the doctor?

Amy: Not yet, but I've taken some medicine.

Bob: You should have some rest. Maybe you should ask for a sick leave.

Amy: But then I will miss some classes. You know the exam is coming.

Bob: _____. I can help you with it later.

Amy: Oh. _____. Maybe I should listen to you.

Bob: Drinking more water will be helpful, too. _____.

Amy: I hope so. _____.

```
1. Don't worry about the schoolwork        4. I am sorry to hear that
2. Are you all right                       5. Thanks for your concern
3. I really hope you can be better soon    6. You are so sweet
```

2. Role-play a conversation in pairs according to the given situation.

Bob and Amy meet in the library. Bob asks Amy whether she has recovered.

Model Dialogue 2: You Poor Thing!

1. Listen to the conversation and fill in the blanks with the expressions given below.

Lucy: Ben, what's the problem? You look sad.

Ben: Well. I broke up with Amy.

Lucy: Oh, I'm sorry. _____?

Ben: She said I don't love her.

Lucy: We all know that's not true. _____?

Ben: She wanted me to buy her a purse when we were shopping together, but I couldn't afford that purse. _____.

Lucy: You can explain to her. Oh. _____.

Ben: More than that, I am disappointed.

Lucy: Oh, you poor thing. You know _____.

Ben: But it is hard to forget her. I thought we love each other.

Lucy: I know. _____. Try to cheer up.

Ben: Thank you.

---
1. It's too expensive for me
2. But everything will be OK
3. There are plenty of fish in the sea
4. What happened
5. You must be heartbroken
6. Why did she think so

---

2. Role-play a conversation in pairs according to the given situation.

Amy meets Ben in the canteen. Ben broke up with his girlfriend. Amy comforts him.

Task C Passage

Listen to the passage and choose the best answer to each question.

Word Tips:
1. culture shock 文化冲击
2. vacation [və'keiʃən] *n.* 假期，休假
3. expose [ik'spəuz] *vt.* 揭露，使暴露，使曝光
4. adjust to 适应
5. host country 东道主国家
6. custom ['kʌstəm] *n.* 习惯，风俗

1) What causes culture shock? _____.

   A. Fear   B. Cultural differences

   C. Anxiety   D. Foreign language

2) In order to adjust to the new environment in the shortest time, you'd better _____.

   A. learn a foreign language in a short time

   B. learn about the culture of the host country

   C. stay with the people of the host country all the time

   D. forget your own culture

3) Which one is *not* the right way to overcoming culture shock?

   A. You'd better plan it and expect it.

   B. You should take the courage to face it.

   C. You'd better learn more about the custom and religion of the host country.

   D. You'd better return to your motherland when you miss home.

Task D Spot Dictation

Listen to the passage three times and fill in the blanks.

> **Word Tips:**
> 1. Asian ['eiʃən] *adj.* 亚洲的，亚洲人的
> 2. value ['vælju:] *v.* 重视；*n.* 价值
> 3. tend to 往往，倾向于
> 4. virtue ['və:tju] *n.* 美德，优点
> 5. informal [in'fɔ:m(ə)l] *adj.* 非正式的
> 6. request [ri'kwest] *v.* 请求；*n.* 要求

  In **Asian** cultures, group membership and "face" (面子) are highly 1) _____ . How one is seen by others 2) _____ be more 3) _____ to an individual here. Politeness is a 4) _____ **virtue**, and communication is often indirect to 5) _____ offending (得罪) one another. Direct words are often considered 6) _____ by those who cherish (珍惜) 7) _____. Many young people, however, and those who know more about 8) _____ cultures, have developed more direct, 9) _____ styles. With globalization (全球化), the more open and direct communications will be 10) _____.

Section B   Reading

Passage A

Teaching People to Think

Pre-reading Questions

1. How much do you know about the ancient **Greece**?
2. Do you know **Socrates**? What do you know about him? Have you read about Socrates and **Plato**?

  "*By all means, marry. If you get a good wife, you'll become happy; if you get a bad one, you'll become a* **philosopher**.*"*

                  — *Socrates*

  Socrates lived in **Athens**, Greece, almost 2,500 years ago. He is considered one of the greatest philosophers and teachers of all time. He actually wrote none of his teachings down, but many of the things he said were recorded by others.

Socrates was a person full of **curiosity**. From the time he was a young man, Socrates searched for **wisdom** and truth. He gained wisdom by asking questions. Socrates didn't give lectures or tell people what to think. Instead, he asked questions. It is to improve the student and his understanding. It forces the students to open their minds to all possibilities. It can lead a student to think in a different way that will **boost** his confidence and bring about more knowledge and understanding.

Socrates felt that throughout your life, it's important to know yourself, to **figure out** who you are and what you really want to do. Socrates helped people realize "True knowledge exists in knowing that you know nothing."

Socrates **challenged false** ideas people had about things like love and **courage**. He would break down the ideas people held. Then he built new ideas. Socrates felt that this was what **philosophy** was all about. Since then, many great philosophers have used this method to find truth.

Some people said that Socrates thought too much. Sometimes Socrates would stand in one **spot** and think for many hours without moving or saying a word. Socrates often **angered** people because he made them feel **embarrassed** when they could not answer his questions.

Eventually, the leaders of Athens put Socrates in **prison** because they thought that he made young people **misbehave** and that he did not believe in the gods of Athens. As a **punishment**, they made Socrates drink a **deadly poison**. Socrates could have run away, but he chose to stay and accept his punishment. He believed he had a duty to **obey** the law. One of Socrates' students, Plato, became a famous teacher himself. He wrote down many of Socrates' conversations so that his ideas would be **preserved** for many future **generations**. (393 words)

New Words

philosopher	[fə'lɔsəfə(r)]	*n.* 哲学家，哲人
curiosity	[kjuəri'ɔsiti]	*n.* 好奇心，好奇
wisdom	['wizdəm]	*n.* 智慧，才智
boost	[buːst]	*vt.* 促进，提高；*vi.* 宣扬；*n.* 提高，增加，吹捧
lecture	['lektʃə]	*n. & vt.* 演讲，教训
challenge	['tʃæləndʒ]	*vt.* 向……挑战；*n.* 挑战，怀疑
false	[fɔːls]	*adj.* 错误的，伪造的
courage	['kʌridʒ]	*n.* 勇气，胆量

philosophy	[fə'lɔsəfi]	n. 哲学，哲理，人生观
spot	[spɔt]	n. 地点，斑点，污点；vt. 认出，发现
anger	['æŋgə(r)]	vt. 触怒，激怒；n. 愤怒
embarrassed	[im'bærəst]	adj. 尴尬的，窘迫的
eventually	[i'ventʃuəli]	adv. 最终，终于
leader	['li:də(r)]	n. 领导者，领袖
prison	['prizn]	n. 监狱
misbehave	[ˌmisbi'heiv]	vi. & vt. 行为不礼貌，使行为不端
deadly	['dedli]	adj. 极端的，非常的，致命的
punishment	['pʌniʃmənt]	n. 惩罚，处罚，刑罚
poison	['pɔizn]	n. 毒药，毒；vi. & vt. 下毒，使中毒
obey	[ə'bei]	vt. 遵守，服从
preserve	[pri'zə:v]	vt. 保存，保留，保护
generation	[ˌdʒenə'reiʃn]	n. 一代（约30年），一代人

Useful Expressions

figure out 计算出，弄明白，解决，想出
search for 寻找，搜寻
break down 毁掉，分解，发生故障
pay for 为……而付钱，赔偿
put sb. in prison 把某人关进监狱，关押

Proper Names

Greece [gri:s] 希腊
Socrates ['sɔkrəti:z] 苏格拉底（公元前469?—前399 古希腊哲学家）
Plato ['pleitəu] 柏拉图（约公元前427—约前347 古希腊哲学家）
Athens ['æθinz] 雅典（希腊首都）

After-reading Activity

Do you really know yourself? Sometimes it is important to know who you really are and what you really want to do. Think about these questions.

Background Information

1. Socrates（苏格拉底）

苏格拉底（约公元前469—前399年）是古希腊雅典人，著名的思想家、哲学家、教育家、公民陪审员，他和他的学生柏拉图，以及柏拉图的学生亚里士多德被并称为"古希腊三贤"，更被后人广泛地认为是西方哲学的奠基者。苏格拉底原为雕刻匠，后来倾心于教育研究，并以培养青年的完善道德为己任。他主张有知识的人才具有美德，才能治理国家，强调"美德就是知识"，知识的对象是"善"，知识是可教的，但并不是从外面灌输的，而是先天就有的。把人先天就有的、潜在的知识、美德诱发出来，这就是教育。他还首先发明和使用了以师生共同谈话、共商问题、获得知识为特征的问答式教学法。

2. Plato（柏拉图）

柏拉图（约公元前427—前347年），古希腊伟大的哲学家，也是西方哲学乃至整

个西方文化最伟大的哲学家和思想家之一，其创造或发展的概念包括：柏拉图思想、柏拉图主义、柏拉图式爱情等。柏拉图的主要作品为《理想国》，与柏拉图大多数著作一样，以苏格拉底为主角用对话体写成，这部"哲学大全"不仅是柏拉图对自己此前哲学思想的概括和总结，而且是当时各门学科的综合，它探讨了哲学、政治、伦理道德、教育、文艺等各方面的问题，以理念论为基础，建立了一个系统的理想国家方案。

3. Ancient Greece（古希腊）

古希腊是西方历史的开源，持续了约650年（公元前800年—前146年）。位于欧洲南部，地中海的东北部，包括今巴尔干半岛南部、小亚细亚半岛西岸和爱琴海中的许多小岛。公元前五六世纪，特别是希波战争以后，经济生活高度繁荣，产生了光辉灿烂的希腊文化，对后世有深远的影响。古希腊人在哲学思想、历史、建筑、科学、文学、戏剧、雕塑等诸多方面有很深的造诣。这一文明在古希腊灭亡后，被古罗马人破坏性地延续下去，从而成为整个西方文明的精神源泉。

Comprehension

1. Choose the best answer for the following sentences according to the passage.

1) Socrates is the _____ of Plato.

   A. teacher   B. student

   C. friend   D. relative（亲戚）

2) How did Socrates die?

   A. He was murdered（谋杀）.   B. He was hung（绞杀）.

   C. He drank deadly poison.   D. He had an accident.

2. Complete the following summary with the words from the passage. The first letter of each missing word is given for your reference.

　　Socrates lived in ancient 1) G_____ around 2 500 years ago. He was very 2) c_____ and liked asking questions. By asking questions, he helped people

3) r_____ "True knowledge exists in knowing that you know nothing." Sometimes Socrates would stand in one 4) s_____ thinking for hours. But he often made people feel 5) e_____ when they could not answer his questions. 6) E_____ the leaders of Athens put Socrates in 7) p_____ because they thought that he made young people misbehave. As a 8) p_____, they made Socrates drink a deadly 9) p_____. Socrates could have run away, but he chose to stay and accept his punishment. He believed he had a duty to 10) o_____ the law.

Vocabulary

1. Complete the following sentences with the words given below. Change the form if necessary.

| future | obey | realize | embarrassed | accept |

1) Eventually, he _____ his dream of becoming a policeman.
2) She is really _____ by her son's bad table manners.
3) They talked about their _____ plans.
4) I really hope that you can _____ my invitation.
5) Drivers must _____ the traffic rules.

2. Complete the following sentences with proper prepositions or adverbs.

1) On our way to the village, our car broke _____.
2) He was put _____ prison because he poisoned his roommate.
3) He was quite willing to pay _____ my lost bike.
4) I am sure that I can realize my dream _____ future.

Sentence Structure

Combine the following sentences using the structure "with…" or "without…".

Sample:

I can think for hours. I don't move or speak.

I can think for hours without moving or speaking.

1) He went into the bedroom. He held a cup of milk in his hand.
2) She saw me. Her mouth was wide open.
3) The little girl left the gift shop. Her eyes were full of tears.
4) They left the meeting room. They didn't say anything.
5) Jack was walking on the street. There was a book under his arm.

1. Translate the following English sentences from the text into Chinese.

1) From the time he was a young man, Socrates searched for wisdom and truth.

2) Socrates challenged false ideas people had about things like love and courage.

3) It forces the students to open their minds to all possibilities.

4) Socrates often angered people because he made them feel embarrassed when they could not answer his questions.

5) Socrates could have run away, but he chose to stay and accept his punishment.

2. Translate the following Chinese sentences into English with the words given in brackets.

1) 为了满足好奇心,我们去了巴尔的摩。(curiosity)

　　_____ we traveled to Baltimore.

2) 我听不懂老师在讲什么。(figure out)

　　I can't _____.

3) 公司面临着三月之内要盖完那座大楼的挑战。(challenge)

　　The company _____ of completing the building in three months.

4) 我们需要大胜一场来增强信心。(boost)

　　We need a big win to _____.

5) 我们必须守法。(obey)

　　We must _____.

Civil Rights Leader: Martin Luther King, Jr.

　　Martin Luther King, Jr., was born on 15 January 1929 in Atlanta, Georgia. He was the second son in his family. He was a very bright student and a talented speaker. King received his **Ph.D.** in **Systematic Theology** from **Boston University** in 1955.

　　King was a **minister** and a student of the Indian leader **Mahatma Gandhi**. He believed that **nonviolence** was the most **powerful** way for people to make their points. This meant **demanding** one's rights through **peaceful** means, such as **strikes** and protests, not by fighting.

　　On December 1, 1955, a black woman named Rosa Parks refused to give up her seat on a bus to a white man. As a result, she was **arrested** for breaking the city's law. At that time the law said that black people had to sit only in **certain** seats of trains and buses and use different bathrooms. Rosa Parks' action **sparked protests** by black **residents**. And Martin Luther King, Jr. was **chosen** as their leader.

However, black people still didn't receive the same **civil rights** as white people. In 1963, King **organized** a historic march to Washington to show the importance of solving the nation's racial problems. There, King **delivered** a powerful speech to about 250 000 people: "I have a dream that my four children will one day live in a nation where they will not be judged by the colour of their skin, but by the **content** of their character". In his dream, he hoped that someday all people would be **equal**, like brothers. This speech came to be regarded as one of the greatest speeches in the world. It helped put civil rights at the top of the list of **reforms** in the United States.

At the age of thirty-five, Martin Luther King, Jr. was **awarded** the **Nobel Prize for Peace** in 1964. He became the youngest man to have received the Prize. Unfortunately, after one strike in April 1968, King was **shot** dead by a white man. To honor him, in 1986, the US government established Martin Luther King, Jr. Day (the third Monday of every January, which is King's birthday) as a national holiday.

(357 words)

New Words

civil	['sivl]	*adj.* 公民的，国内的
arrest	[ə'rest]	*vt.* 逮捕，拘捕
certain	['sə:tn]	*adj.* 某些，某一，确信的
spark	[spa:k]	*vt.* 引发，发出火花；*n.* 火花
protest	['prəutest]	*n.* 抗议；*vt. & vi.* 反对，抗议
resident	['rezidənt]	*n.* 居民
choose	[tʃu:z]	*vt./ vi.* 选择，挑选，选出
minister	['ministə(r)]	*n.* 牧师，部长
nonviolence	['nɔn'vaiələns]	*n.* 非暴力，非暴力政策
powerful	['pauəfl]	*adj.* 强大的，强有力的
demanding	[di'ma:ndiŋ]	*adj.* 强人所难的，强求的
peaceful	['pi:sfl]	*adj.* 和平的，爱好和平的，安静的
strike	[straik]	*n.* 罢工；*vt.* 打击，撞击
organize	['ɔ:gənaiz]	*vt.* 组织，安排，使有条理
march	[ma:tʃ]	*n.* 游行示威，行军；*vi.* 前进，行军
deliver	[di'livə(r)]	*vt.* 发表，递送
content	['kɔntent]	*n.* 内容，（书等的）目录，满足
equal	['i:kwəl]	*adj.* 平等的，相同的

reform	[ri'fɔːm]	n. 改革，改良，改造；vt. & vi. 改善
award	[ə'wɔːd]	vt. 授予，赠予；n. 奖
unfortunately	[ʌn'fɔːtʃənətli]	adv. 不幸的是，遗憾的是
shoot	[ʃuːt]	vi. 射击，射杀
establish	[i'stæbliʃ]	vt. 建立，创立

Useful Expressions

Systematic Theology ★ [ˌsistə'mætik θi'ɔlədʒi] 系统神学
give up 放弃，交出
the same as 与……相同
such as 比如，诸如
because of 因为，由于
be regarded as 被认为是

Proper Names

Ph.D. 文学博士，哲学博士（Doctor of Philosophy 的缩写）
Boston University ['bɔʃtən ˌjuːni'vəːsəti] 波士顿大学
Rosa Parks ['rəuzə 'paːks] 罗莎·帕克斯
Martin Luther King, Jr. ['maːtin 'luθəkiŋ 'dʒuːniə(r)] 马丁·路德·金
Mahatma Gandhi [mə'hætmə 'gændiː] 圣雄甘地
Washington, D.C. ['wɔʃiŋtən 'diː'siː] 华盛顿特区（DC 是 District of Columbia 的缩写）

Background Information

1. Martin Luther King, Jr.（马丁·路德·金）

　　马丁·路德·金（1929 年 1 月 15 日—1968 年 4 月 4 日），著名的美国民权运动领袖。1948 年大学毕业。1948 年至 1951 年期间，在美国东海岸的费城继续深造。1963

年，马丁·路德·金觐见了肯尼迪总统，要求通过新的民权法，给黑人以平等的权利。1963年8月28日，在林肯纪念堂前发表了《我有一个梦想》的演说。1964年年度诺贝尔和平奖的获得者。1968年4月，马丁·路德·金前往孟菲斯市，领导工人罢工后，被人刺杀，年仅39岁。从1986年起，美国政府将每年1月的第3个星期一定为马丁·路德·金全国纪念日。

2. Mahatma Gandhi（圣雄甘地）

莫罕达斯·卡拉姆昌德·甘地(1869年10月2日—1948年1月30日)，尊称圣雄甘地，是印度民族解放运动的领导人和印度国家大会党领袖。他是现代印度的国父，也是提倡非暴力抵抗的现代政治学说——甘地主义的创始人。他的精神思想带领国家迈向独立，脱离英国的殖民统治。他的"非暴力"哲学思想影响了全世界的民族主义者和争取能以和平变革的国际运动。

3. Civil Rights Movement（美国民权运动 1955—1968年）

美国民权运动指的是第二次世界大战后美国黑人反对种族隔离与歧视，争取民主权利的群众运动。

4. Nobel Prize（诺贝尔奖）

诺贝尔奖是以瑞典著名的化学家、硝化甘油炸药的发明人阿尔弗雷德·贝恩哈德·诺贝尔的部分遗产（3 100万瑞典克朗）作为基金创立的。诺贝尔奖分设物理、化学、生理

或医学、文学、和平五个奖项，以基金每年的利息或投资收益授予前一年世界上在这些领域对人类作出重大贡献的人，1901年首次颁发。诺贝尔奖包括金质奖章、证书和奖金。1968年，瑞典国家银行在成立300周年之际，捐出大额资金给诺贝尔基金，增设"瑞典国家银行纪念诺贝尔经济科学奖"，1969年首次颁发，人们习惯上称这个额外的奖项为诺贝尔经济学奖。

Comprehension

1. Mark the following statements *T* (*true*) or *F* (*false*) according to the text.

☐ 1) Martin Luther King, Jr's action sparked protests by black residents.

☐ 2) Mahatma Gandhi believed that nonviolence was the most powerful way for people to protest.

☐ 3) In 1963, black people received the same rights as white people.

☐ 4) King was awarded the Nobel Prize for Literature in 1964.

☐ 5) Martin Luther King, Jr. Day is a U.S. national holiday.

2. Complete the following statements.

1) Martin Luther King, Jr. was chosen to lead the protests of the black _____.

2) Mahatma Gandhi was the _____ of Martin Luther King, Jr..

3) King _____ a powerful speech on the topic "I have a dream."

4) King's dream was that someday all people would be _____.

5) In April 1968, King was _____ dead.

Vocabulary and Structure

1. Put the following words under the corresponding pictures.

　　　　shoot　　　　spark　　　　award　　　　minister

1) _____　　2) _____　　3) _____　　4) _____

2. Compare each pair of words and complete the following sentences with the right one. Change the form if necessary.

1) lead, leader

As the _____ of the company, she can give us orders.

Too much work and too little rest often _____ to illness.

2) choose, choice

You must _____ your friends carefully.

We have no _____ but to go to school.

3) peace, peaceful

The _____ talks between the two counties are useless.

We should deal with the problem with _____ means.

4) sit, seat

This room can _____ 100 people.

He asked me to _____ near him.

3. **Complete the following sentences with the words given below. Change the form if necessary.**

| arrest | speech | equal | organize | protest |

1) All people are created _____.

2) He was _____ because of drunk driving.

3) These people are _____ against the new rules.

4) The headmaster gave us a _____ at the beginning of this term.

5) As the team leader, how would you _____ your team?

4. **Complete the following sentences with the expressions given below. Change the form if necessary.**

| give up | be regarded as | because of | such as |

1) I like eating a lot of fruits, _____ apples, pears, bananas and so on.

2) After he got married, he _____ smoking.

3) She _____ the best teacher in the school.

4) The flight was delayed _____ the heavy snow.

Activity

Preparing for a Speech

As an art student, you may be dreaming to have your solo show or win a special award one day. At the beginning of your show or after you win the prize, you will need to give a speech.

Think about how to present an engaging speech.

1. **Translate the following sentences and get familiar with them, as they can be useful in your speech.**

1) Good morning, ladies and gentlemen.

2) I am glad to have the opportunity to deliver a speech.

3) Right, let's get started.

4) Thanks for your attention.

2. **Match the sentences in A with the Chinese equivalents in B.**

A

1) Good preparation.   (   )

2) Speak from your heart.   (   )

3) Use humor.   (   )

4) Use body language.   (   )

5) Vary your pitch.   (   )

6) Keep it simple.   (   )

B

a) 运用好形体语言

b) 准备一定要充分

c) 保持内容简单易懂

d) 语调要抑扬顿挫

e) 加一点小幽默

f) 演讲要真诚

3. Think about what you should pay attention to in order to have a successful speech.

1) How to choose a good topic to attract people's attention?

2) How to develop the topic ?

3) How to conquer your fear when speaking in front of a large audience?

4) How could you prepare yourself including clothes, makeup...?

5) Besides the questions mentioned above, what else should you pay attention to?

Passage C Fast Reading

Mayan Civilization

A) Mayan Civilization is as mysterious as its disappearance. The Maya Empire grew up in a *region* (地区) of Mexico and Central America. Between about A.D. 200 and 900, the Maya built many religious centers and cities in this area. It reached the peak of its power and influence around the sixth century A.D.

B) The Mayans were remembered for many reasons. They had 365-day solar *calendars* (历法), invented number system and developed a writing system. They were the only Central Americans of their time to develop writing.

C) The Mayans left behind a surprising amount of impressive architecture and artwork. Most of the great stone cities of the Maya were abandoned by A.D. 900. Their huge *temples* (寺庙) were really great wonders. Every temple consisted of four sides, each side had 91 steps and at the top there was an extra step. This is special due to the fact that the total number of the steps is also the number of days in a year.

D) One of the things that is most memorable is their *religion* (宗教). The Maya *worshiped* (敬奉) several gods and even offered human *sacrifices* (祭品). Many of their buildings are decorated with the face of *Chac* (恰克), the rain god. He was an important god in their farming society. It is said that the Mayans would draw blood and offer it to the Gods. The Mayans believed that their King had a link to the Gods and could communicate with them.

E) Why Mayan culture disappeared is sill unknown to this day. The cities were entirely empty by the time the Spanish arrived in the 16th century. Some people have studied it and found that it fell apart because it was too over populated and there was not enough food for everyone. The *decline* (衰落) may have been because of weather changes, disease, or war—or a combination of these things.

(318 words)

Information Match

Please identify the paragraph from which the following information is derived. Each paragraph is marked with a letter.

_____ 1) The Mayan developed a 365-day solar calendar.

_____ 2) The Mayans were excellent at architecture, for example, building stone cities and tall temples.

_____ 3) The Mayan cities were entirely empty in the 16th century.

_____ 4) The golden period of the Mayan Civilization is between about A.D. 200 and 900.

_____ 5) Chac was an important god in the Mayan farming society.

Background Information

玛雅文明，是古代分布于现今墨西哥东南部、危地马拉、洪都拉斯、萨尔瓦多和伯利兹5个国家的丛林文明。虽然处于新石器时代，却在天文学、数学、农业、艺术及文字等方面都有极高的成就。与印加帝国及阿兹特克帝国并列为美洲三大文明（阿兹特克帝国与玛雅文明位于中美洲；印加帝国位于南美洲安第斯山一带）。

Section C Grammar

定语（一）(Attribute I)

定语是用来修饰、限定、说明名词或代词的品质与特征的，主要由形容词担任。此外，名词、代词、数词、副词、介词短语以及动词不定式（短语）、分词和定语从句等都可用作定语。

一、形容词作定语

Different countries and cultures also produce ***different*** styles of architecture.

不同的国家和文化也诞生不同的建筑风格。

Even though he died in 1828, Francisco Goya is considered by some to be a "*modern*" painter.

虽然弗朗西斯科·戈雅卒于 1828 年,他仍然被认为是"现代派"画家。

Mozart often blended *popular* and *classical* music to create *new* styles of music。

莫扎特经常把通俗音乐和古典音乐融合,创作出全新风格的音乐。

二、数词作定语

Nine times out of ten, he will succeed in the examination.

十之八九他会考及格的。

Two heads are better than one.

集思广益。

I have the *fir*st prize in my back pocket.

头等奖已是我囊中之物。

三、物主代词作定语

Patience is *his* strong suit.

忍耐是他的长处。

His parents tried in every way to satisfy *his* needs.

他的父母尽力在各方面满足他的需求。

A quarter of all children are unhappy about *their* looks.

所有孩子当中有四分之一对自己的长相不满意。

四、介词短语作定语

Portugal is famous for its many varieties of wine, *including Port and Madeira.*

葡萄牙以盛产各种葡萄酒而闻名,包括波尔图和马德拉。

He is a wolf *in sheep's clothing.*

他是一只披着羊皮的狼。

Asia is home *to many kinds of animals*.

亚洲是很多动物的家园。

五、名词或名词所有格作定语

Isabel Allende was a journalist in Chile, as well as a *short-story* writer.

伊莎贝尔·阿连德是智利的记者,也是一个短篇小说家。

Four hundred years later, people still enjoy reading *Shakespeare's* plays.

四百年之后,人们仍然喜欢阅读莎士比亚的戏剧。

There are five *woman* doctors in the hospital.

这家医院有五位女医生。

六、副词作定语

On my way *home*, I continued telling him my exciting traveling experiences.

在回家的路上，我继续跟他讲我那些激动人心的旅行经历。

I'm so lucky to be chosen for a trip *abroad*.

我真幸运，被选中出国旅行。

Most of the people *here* enjoy Chinese food.

这里大多数人喜欢中国菜。

七、不定式作定语

Perhaps in years *to come* we shall meet again.

或许在未来岁月中我们还会相见。

I'm not going with you, I have other fish *to fry*.

我不和你一起去，我还有别的事。

八、分词作定语

He is a hard *boiled* egg.

他是一个面冷心热的人。

The girl *combing her hair* by the window is Martha.

在窗边梳头的女孩叫玛莎。

In the United States, some jazz and blues have their roots in folk songs *brought over hundreds of years ago by African slaves*.

在美国，某些爵士乐和蓝调都扎根于民俗音乐，是几百年前由非洲的奴隶带过来的。

Exercises

1. Complete the following sentences based on the given Chinese.

1) _____ in this movie sounds wonderful.

   这个电影里的背景音乐非常美妙。

2) He turned the radio down so that he shouldn't disturb _____.

   为了不打扰楼下的老太太，他把收音机音量调低了。

3) The missing girl was last seen _____.

   那个失踪的女孩最后被看到是在沙盒里玩。

4) Being in an _____ day after day, many people are city-pale.

   每天待在空调房里，许多人面色苍白。

5) We live in _____.

   我们住在一间面朝大海的房间。

6) We're greatly amused by _____.

   看到正在升起的太阳，我们都非常快乐。

7) I thought she had _____ shot at the job.

   我认为她得不到这个工作。

8) My eagerness _____ kept lifting me out of my seat.

   我想到外面世界的渴望总是让我跃跃欲试。

2. Choose the best way to complete each of the following sentences.

1) China is a _____ country, while Japan is a _____ country.
   A. developing ... developed   B. developed ... developing
   C. developing ... developing   D. developed ... developed

2) The lady _____ to you by me yesterday is our president's daughter.
   A. introducing   B. introduce   C. introduced   D. to introduce

3) The crowd _____ are all his fans, they are crazy about him.
   A. waving to him   B. waved to him
   C. who waved to him   D. who waving to him

4) I have lost my interest _____.
   A. in my present job   B. of my present job
   C. from my present job   D. to my present job

5) I opened a _____ at a nearby bank.
   A. savings account   B. saving account
   C. savings' account   D. savings accounts

6) Spanish is the _____ language of Nicaragua (尼加拉瓜).
   A. office   B. officials'   C. official   D. office's

7) Julius Caesar was a brilliant general and a _____ writer.
   A. gifting   B. gifted   C. gift's   D. gift

8) As the secretary general of the United Nations between 1961 and 1971, U Thant (吴丹) had the job _____ among many warring countries.
   A. to work for peace   B. that worked for peace
   C. who worked for peace   D. when worked for peace

9) The French scientist Marie Curie became the first person _____ two times.
   A. wins the Nobel Prize   B. had won the Nobel Prize
   C. to win the Nobel Prize   D. won the Nobel Prize

10) English is one of the world's _____ languages.
    A. most widely spoken   B. most widely speaking
    C. most wide spoken   D. most wide speaking

Section D Sentence Writing

Chinese Papercut

1. What is Chinese Papercut?

    Tips: traditional, folk art, scissors…

    _____
    _____.

2. Do you know the origin of Chinese Papercut?

    Tips: originate, ancient, worship, ancestor, invention, dynasty...

    _____
    _____.

3. What are the themes of papercut / Chinese Papercut?

    Tips: theme, from…to…, dumb things (牲畜), surroundings...

    _____
    _____.

4. On what occasion do you usually see Chinese Papercut?

    Tips: merry atmosphere, ceremony, festival, decorate...

    _____
    _____.

Unit 8

Psychology

Section A Listening and Speaking

Task A General Pronunciation Rules

字母组合

1. ea

    [i:] 例词：beat, meat, feat, lead, bean, please

    　　　特例：great [greit], break [breik], steak [steik], forehead ['fɔrid; 'fɔ:hed]

    [e] 在 d, th, l, v, f 或 -sure 之前，经常读作 [e]

    　　　例词：head, weather, health, heavy, deaf, pleasure

    [iə] 在有些单词中读作 [iə]

    　　　例如：realize, realism, idea, ideal, theatre

2. ear

    [iə] 在词尾几乎总是读 [iə]

    　　　例词：ear, near, hear, clear, dear, appear

    [eə] 在少数单词的词尾读作 [eə]

    　　　例词：bear, pear, wear, tear (v.), swear

    [ə:] 在辅音之前

    　　　例词：learn, earn, heard, earth, research, rehearsal

    　　　特例：heart [hɑ:t], beard [biəd], weary ['wiəri], hearth [hɑ:θ]

3. ee

    [i:] 位于词尾或在除 r 之外的辅音字母之前

    　　　例词：bee, flee, feed, meet, sleep, keen, teenage

    　　　特例：coffee ['kɒfi], committee [kə'miti]

4. eer

    [iə] 例词：beer, deer, cheer, career, engineer, volunteer

Task B Conversations

Model Dialogue 1: Jogging and Smoking

1. Listen to the conversation and fill in the blanks with the expressions given below.

Daniel: Welcome back. You _____. Did you have a good run?

Renee: Yes. It was great. I jogged around the park twice. It was _____.

Daniel: That's a very long way. You probably ran five miles.

Renee: I've been jogging every day now _____.

Daniel: You _____. How about some ice cream?

Renee: Actually, I'd rather have a cigarette right now.

Daniel: What? A cigarette! Joggers aren't supposed to smoke.

Renee: It's OK. The doctor told me _____. But he didn't say I have to quit smoking.

Daniel: But your doctor is a smoker. He _____.

1. the longest run I've ever done
2. for the past three weeks
3. were gone for a long time
4. should get a reward
5. I have to exercise more
6. should have told you to quit

2. Role-play a conversation in pairs according to the given situation.

Daniel and Renee meet on the street again. They greet each other. Daniel wonders if Renee succeeds in quitting smoking. Renee says yes.

Model Dialogue 2: Traveling for Fun

1. Listen to the conversation and fill in the blanks with the expressions given below.

Nancy: Where do you want to go _____?

Ben: I can think of a lot of exciting places. We could go to Italy, Fiji, or China or maybe India.

Nancy: It seems we always _____ the world when we take our yearly trip. How about seeing our own country?

Ben: What do you mean? Rent a car and go to Las Vegas? That sounds like something my grandparents would do.

Nancy: I'm serious. We could rent a car and drive all over. We could see the Grand Canyon, Broadway and …

Ben: Well, now that you mention it. _____ within the US.

Nancy: Exactly. We've been to a dozen other countries, but we haven't seen our own.

Ben: Now _____. We could see a lot in a month.

1. go to the farthest corners of
2. for our vacation this summer
3. you've got me interested
4. I realize we've never taken a trip

2. Role-play a conversation in pairs according to the given situation.

Nancy and Ben decide to go to Las Vegas. Ben wants to travel first-class on the plane. Nancy says renting a car is better because of their budget. Ben tells Nancy they don't need to worry about the budget and he can manage it.

Task C Passage

Listen to the passage and choose the best answer to each question.

Word Tips: academic [ˌækəˈdemik] *adj.* 学院的，学术的

1) What was a typical student like in the past?

   A. They did not live on the campus.

   B. They attended classes every day.

   C. They went to college for three years.

   D. They ate breakfast at home.

2) What is a typical student like now?

   A. School is the center of their lives.

   B. They study part time.

   C. They don't work.

   D. All of them want to change their careers.

3) How will people study in the future?

   A. They are still some typical students.

   B. They do not need to study.

   C. They will study when they are old.

   D. Most people will take classes at some time.

Task D Spot Dictation

Listen to the passage three times and fill in the blanks.

Word Tips: disadvantage [ˌdisədˈvæntidʒ] *n.* 不利，劣势

"My daughter starts school in two weeks and I don't know 1) _____ to get her a computer or not," many parents say. "If I spend money for that, is she going to get something out of it? If I don't, is she going to be at a 2) _____? And if I'm going to get her a computer, what kind should I get? " The same questions are being asked 3)_____ in the 4) _____. Should the parent buy a computer for his child to use at home? Don't feel guilty if the 5) _____ is no. The child will 6) _____ far more from an hour spent with an 7) _____ parent.

Section B   Reading

Passage A

Pressure

Pre-reading Questions

1. Do you have any pressures in your school life?
2. How do you overcome your pressures?

Is it any wonder that many students fail to perform, not because they lack ability, but because of the unique pressure of the exam room?

We are **competitive** animals and we are sometimes going to get nervous. Removing pressure altogether from life is an impossible dream.

But how does it happen? Consider what happens when you are walking along the street. None of us actually think about the **mechanics** of how we walk. But now imagine that you are walking along narrow path with a 10 000-foot cliff on either side. Now, we might think about how we are moving our feet. And this, of course, is when we **are** most **likely to** fall.

Walking is, when you think about it, quite a **complex** set of movements and if we think too much about them, we are far more likely to get **confused**. This is why walking feels so strange when we are in front of a lot of people.

Instead of using the **subconscious** part of the brain, which is the most **efficient** way to **deliver** a familiar skill (skill like walking), we use the **conscious** part. And this is when it all goes wrong.

To put it another way, in order to **overcome nervousness** we must trust our subconscious ability. And, it turns out that we are far more likely to do so when we **are familiar with** the situation we are about to face. Of course, even when we are well prepared, we may still feel terribly nervous—but at least we will **be** more **equipped to deal with** our nerves.

Furthermore, we may also **benefit** from **reminding** ourselves that the big moment is, from a different **perspective**, not that big after all. Even a huge exam is not as important as a loving family, or good health. And even a huge job interview can be put into perspective by looking up at the stars and remembering that it is all rather little **in the grand scheme of things**. (332 words)

New Words

competitive	[kəm'petitiv]	adj. 竞争的，比赛的
mechanics	[mi'kæniks]	n. 机制，力学，机械学
complex	['kɔmpleks]	adj. 复杂的，难懂的；n. 建筑群，情结
confused	[kən'fjuzd]	adj. 糊涂的，迷乱的，混杂的
subconscious	[ˌsʌb'kɑːnʃəs]	adj. 下意识的，潜意识的
efficient	[i'fiʃənt]	adj. 有效率的，（直接）生效的
deliver	[di'livə]	vt. 发表，递送，使分娩；vi. 投递，传送
conscious	['kɑːnʃəs]	adj. 有意识的，神志清醒的
overcome	[ˌəuvər'kʌm]	vt. & vi. 战胜，克服
nervousness	['nɜːvəsnis]	n. 神经质，焦躁，胆小
furthermore	[ˌfɜːrðər'mɔːr]	adv. 此外，而且
benefit	['benəfit]	n. 利益，好处；vt. 有益于，有助于
remind	[ri'maind]	vt. 使想起，使记起；提醒
perspective	[pər'spektiv]	n. 观点，看法；adj.（按）透视画法的，透视的
scheme	[skim]	vt. & vi. 策划，图谋；n. 计划，阴谋

Useful Expressions

be likely to 可能
be familiar with 熟悉，认识
equip sb. to do sth. 使某人准备好做某事，使某人能做某事
deal with 与……交易，应付，对待

in the grand scheme of things 从大局来看，从整体来看

After-reading Activity

Life can be stressful; sometimes you'll have to deal with pressures from variety of causes such as family problems, job problems, financial difficulties, poor health, or even the death of someone close to you. What is your way to deal with pressures?

Comprehension

1. Choose the best way to complete each of the following sentences.

1) We are _____ animals and we sometimes feel nervous.
   A. stressful   B. strong   C. competitive   D. evil

2) From a different _____, we will find some so-called big matters are not that big after all.
   A. person   B. country   C. pressure   D. perspective

2. Complete the following summary with the words from the passage. The first letter of each missing word is given for your reference.

Do you believe that many students fail to 1) p_____ just because of the 2) u_____ pressure of the exam room? We live in a 3) c_____ world and we are sometimes going to get nervous. Instead of using the 4) s_____ part of the brain, which is the most 5) e_____ way to deliver a familiar skill, we use the conscious part. In order to 6) o_____ nervousness we must trust our subconscious ability. 7) F_____, we may also 8) b_____ from 9) r_____ ourselves that the big moment is, from a different 10) p_____, not that big after all.

Vocabulary

1. Complete the following sentences with the words given below. Change the form if necessary.

| benefit | competitive | remind | deliver | efficient |

1) A(n) _____ transport system is important to the long-term future of London.
2) As long as I _____ the goods, my boss is very happy.
3) Both sides have _____ from the talks.
4) The company say they're able to keep pricing _____.
5) I'm sorry, I've forgotten your name. Can you _____ me?

2. Complete the following sentences with proper prepositions or adverbs.

1) They believed there were likely _____ be further attacks.

2) Instead _____ moving at his usual pace, he was almost running.

3) Everyone is familiar _____ the TV screen's hypnotic (引人着迷的) power.

4) People usually complain about having to deal _____ too much bureaucracy (繁文缛节).

Sentence Structure

Combine the following sentences using the structure "instead of …".

Sample:

The price doesn't sink every day. The price rises.

The price rises every day instead of sinks.

1) He plans to do some work. He will not watch television.

2) He didn't give Bill the money. He gave it to me.

3) In warm weather he will not read in the library. He often reads under a tree.

4) She doesn't study. She plays tennis all day.

5) He did not do it himself. He got a man to do it.

Translation

1. Translate the following English sentences from the text into Chinese.

1) We are competitive animals and we are sometimes going to get nervous.

2) None of us actually think about the mechanics of how we walk.

3) This is why walking feels so strange when we are in front of a lot of people.

4) It turns out that we are far more likely to do so when we are familiar with the situation we are about to face.

5) Even a huge exam is not as important as a loving family, or good health.

2. Translate the following Chinese sentences into English with the words given in brackets.

1) 我们与那家公司有多年的生意往来。（deal with）

　_____ that firm for many years.

2) 这些人做事效率很高，井井有条，并且十分善于管理时间。（efficient）

　_____, very organized and excellent time managers.

3) 他是一位锐意进取、竞争意识很强的主管，颇受尊敬。（competitive）

　He is respected as a _____.

4) 这些火灾很可能会毁掉这片土地上的森林。（be likely to）

　_____ deforest the land.

5) 她熟悉现代爵士乐。（be familiar with）

　_____ modern jazz.

Passage B

Three Instant Mood Lifters

If you're feeling down, here are three mood lifters to keep you smiling!

1. Don't ask for too much

Why do we sometimes feel so **disappointed** at our own birthday party? The trouble is the **expectation**. The one **leads to** too much **focus** on the end point **rather than** simply **engaging in** the activities that make us happy. Actually we should have **socialized** with friends and families in a **pleasant atmosphere**.

When people have too high expectations, it can lead them to becoming **frustrated** when their current **emotional state** doesn't match their happiness ideal. It's **critically** important to try to **liberate** oneself of those expectations, especially the one who focused on happiness. And instead, he or she should accept his or her current happiness state.

2. Set personal goals and go after them

When people who **strive to** reach personal goals engage in more **purposeful leisure**, and they are, therefore, happier. In fact "purposeful leisure" is any activity that involves **self-improvement** and reflects a sense of choice, for example, learning a language, **pursuing** a hobby or trying a new sport. It may seem **obvious**, but happiness indeed comes from those goals.

*3. **Nurture** relationships with people you care about*

One of the important points of happiness is enjoying meaningful relationships with friends and families. But how do you define "meaningful"? To begin with, it involves being with the actual person rather than just their online figure. Beyond this, a meaningful relationship with a partner or a friend is one that's **authentic**. Furthermore, you are willing to understand what the person is thinking and experiencing.

A meaningful social **bond** is, at least in part, to benefit the other person rather than **solely** benefiting yourself.

(282 words)

Unit 8 Psychology

🌀 New Words

instant	['instənt]	*adj.* 立即的，迫切的；*n.* 瞬间，速食食品
lifter	['liftə]	*n.* 提升器，升降机
disappointed	[ˌdisə'pɔintid]	*adj.* 失望的，沮丧的
expectation	[ˌekspek'teʃən]	*n.* 期待，预期，前程
focus	['fəukəs]	*vt. & vi.* （使）集中，（使）聚集，调整；*n.* 焦点；（活动、注意力、兴趣等的）中心
pleasant	['pleznt]	*adj.* 可爱的，令人愉快的，晴朗的
socialize	['səuʃəlaiz]	*vi.* 与……交往，联谊；*vt.* 使社会化
atmosphere	['ætməsfir]	*n.* 大气，风格，气氛
frustrated	['frʌstreitid]	*adj.* 挫败的，失意的，泄气的
emotional	['iməuʃənl]	*adj.* 令人动情的，易动感情的
state	[steit]	*n.* 状况，国家，州
critically	['kritikli]	*adv.* 批判性地，危急地
liberate	['libəˌret]	*vt.* 解放，释放
strive	[straiv]	*vi.* 努力奋斗，斗争
purposeful	['pɜːrpəsfl]	*adj.* 有目的的，故意的
leisure	['liːʒər]	*n.* 空闲时间，闲暇；*adj.* 空闲的，闲暇的
self-improvement	['selfim'pruːvmənt]	*n.* 自我改善，自我修养，自强
pursue	[pər'suː]	*vt.* 继续，追求；*vi.* 追，追赶
obvious	['ɑːbviəs]	*adj.* 明显的，显著的
nurture	['nɜːrtʃə(r)]	*vt.* 养育，培育；*n.* 教养，培育
authentic	[ɔː'θentik]	*adj.* 真的，真正的，可信的
bond	[bɔnd]	*n.* 纽带，债券；*v.* 使结合，与……紧密联系
solely	['səuli]	*adv.* 唯一地，仅仅，纯粹

🌀 Useful Expressions

lead to 导致
rather than （要）……而不……，与其……倒不如……
engage in 参与
strive to 力图，力求

🔍 Comprehension

1. Mark the following statements *T* (*true*) or *F* (*false*) according to the text.

☐ 1) We sometimes feel so disappointed at our own birthday party because we have no expectations.

☐ 2) When people have too high expectations, they may become frustrated.

☐ 3) People who strive to reach personal goals are happier.

☐ 4) Happiness comes from leisure.

☐ 5) A meaningful social bond is to benefit both the other person and yourself.

2. Complete the following statements.

1) If you're feeling sad, there are _____ mood lifters to keep you smiling in this passage.

2) _____ leads to too much focus on the final result.

3) It's very important to try to _____ oneself of those expectations.

4) "Purposeful leisure" is any activity that involves _____ .

5) One of the important points of happiness is enjoying meaningful relationships with _____ .

Vocabulary and Structure

1. Put the following words under the corresponding pictures.

> expectation   critically   disappointed   happiness

1) _____   2) _____   3) _____   4) _____

2. Compare each pair of words and complete the following sentences with the right one. Change the form if necessary.

1) instant, convenient

   Would this evening be _____ for you?

   This _____ coffee are nice!

2) disappointed, disappear

   A Japanese woman _____ thirteen years ago.

   I was _____ that Kluge was not there.

3) expect, expectation

   He has little _____ of passing the exam.

   Don't _____ me to come and visit you there.

4) socialize, social

He never _____ with his colleagues.

We ought to organize more _____ events.

3. Complete the following sentences with the words given below. Change the form if necessary.

| atmosphere | disappointed | obvious | critically |
| liberate | strive | pursue | nurture |

1) _____ for the best, prepare for the worst.

2) The _____ at the test event was really good.

3) They did their best to _____ slaves.

4) He began to _____ an easy and comfortable life.

5) When things go wrong, all of us naturally feel _____.

6) It's _____ that you need more time to think.

7) Parents want to know the best way to _____ their child.

8) Moscow is running _____ low on food supplies.

4. Complete the following sentences with the expressions given below. Change the form if necessary.

| strive to | rather than | lead to | engage in |

1) I have never _____ the trade.

2) He _____ hard _____ keep himself very fit.

3) We'll have the meeting in the classroom _____ in the auditorium.

4) In given conditions, a bad thing can _____ good results.

Activity

The Fun Personality Quizzes

You're going to do several short personality quizzes that are intended to analyze your personality. You will be amazed by the accuracy of the results!

1. Which picture appeals to you the most? Consider both form and color.

2. Take a trip to the seaside and learn something more about yourself.

1) You awake one morning and find yourself in an odd yet familiar room.

   Describe the room and how it makes you feel.

   What kind of furnishings and decorations are there?

   Do you feel like you would like to leave the room?

2) Now imagine that you are walking towards the seaside.

   How many people do you see?

   A. Hundreds. B. A few dozen.

   C. One or two. D. None.

3) How far are the nearest people?

   A. Close by. B. Not very far off.

   C. Way off in the distance. D. The beach is deserted.

Passage C Fast Reading

The Meanings of Red, Yellow and Blue

A) We give meanings for colors. So when we mention the meanings of colors, we mean the things in our heart. And now let's look at the three primary colors.

B) Red is a very strong color. It is a noticeable color that is often used on caution and warning signs. It is often associated with stop or "beware". It's a hot color that evokes a powerful emotion of passion, *lust* (欲望), sex, energy, blood and war. Red is a good color to use for *accents* (关注) that need to take notice over other colors. Red is often used in flags for nations, as it is a symbol of pride and strength. It is also a *sporty* (有动感的) color that many car manufactures choose to *showcase* (使展示) their signature vehicles.

C) Yellow is the brightest color to the human eye. It represents youth, fun, happiness, sunshine and other light playful feelings. It is a cheerful energetic color. Yellow is often used for children's toys and clothes. Yellow is often hard to read when placed on a white background so designers must be careful when using yellow, that it isn't too difficult to read or notice. Though yellow is a bright cheerful color, as it starts to darken, it, however, quickly becomes a dirty and unpleasant color. Yellow can also be associated with being scared and, cowards. The term "yellow *belly*" (胆小鬼) is proof of that.

D) Blue is a cool calming color that shows creativity and intelligence. It is a popular color among large corporations, hospitals and airlines. It is a color of loyalty, strength, wisdom and trust. Blue has a calming effect on the *psyche* (心灵，精神). Blue is the color of the sky and the sea and is often used to represent those images. Blue is a color that generally looks good in almost any shade and is a popular color among males. Blue is not a good color when used for food as there are few blue foods found in nature and it suppresses the appetite.

Information Match

Please identify the paragraph from which the following information is derived. Each paragraph is marked with a letter.

_____ 1) Red can be used in a dangerous place.

_____ 2) If you want to calm down you can use blue color.

_____ 3) You hardly see yellow color sometimes because of the white background.

_____ 4) Most of men like the color.

_____ 5) You often see yellow color from children's toys.

Section C Grammar

定语（二）(Attribute Ⅱ)

九、从句作定语

在句子中做定语的从句，修饰一个名词或代词，被修饰的名词或代词就是先行词。定语从句常出现在先行词之后，由关系代词或关系副词引出。

（一）关系代词引导的定语从句

1. 指代人的代词有 who，whom，that。例如：

He *who laughs last* laughs best.

笑到最后的人，笑得最开心。

I'm planning to visit Steve and his wife, *whom I haven't seen for nearly one year*.

我打算去拜访史蒂夫和他的妻子。我将近一年没有见到他们了。

2. 指代事物的代词有 which，that，as。例如：

Most of us have been to museums *that display art by famous painters*.

我们当中的大多数人都去过展览知名画家艺术品的博物馆。

The art style *that Picasso and fellow artist Georges Braque invented* is called Cubism.

毕加索和他的合作者乔治·布拉克所创建的艺术风格称作是立体主义。

Kill not the goose *that lays the golden eggs*.

杀鸡取蛋，愚蠢荒唐。

3. 指代所属关系的代词有 whose，of which。例如：

The girl *whose hair is golden* is from England.

金色头发的那个女孩是英国人。

In Beijing, there are many places of historic interest, *of which I love the Forbidden City most*.

北京有很多历史古迹，我最喜欢紫禁城。

（二）关系副词引导的定语从句

1. 指代地点的副词有 where。例如：

Wanchai boasts the Academy of Performing Arts, *where everything from Chinese Opera to Shakespeare is performed.*

湾仔拥有演艺学院，从京剧到莎士比亚的各种剧目都在这里上演。

Finally, I have reached the point, *where I am enjoying my work*.

最后，我终于达到了享受工作的程度。

2. 指代时间的副词有 when。例如：

I still remember the time *when I lived in the countryside.*

我仍然记得住在农村的时光。

There are always some days *when everything seems to go wrong.*

总是有事不顺心的时候。

3. 指代原因的副词有 why。例如：

I can only think of one reason *why frank gave me the cold shoulder*.

弗兰克为什么对我很冷淡，我只能想到一个原因。

I can figure out the reason *why you put all your eggs in one basket*.

我理解你为什么会孤注一掷。

注意：1. 关系代词 that 和 which 在很多情况下可以互换，但先行词被 any，some，no，much，few，little，every，all，very，only，last 修饰时，引导定语从句用 that。例如：

No service that we have received is satisfactory.

我们受到的服务完全不能令人满意。

All that can be done has been done.

尽力而为。

Is there *anything that* you need my help？

有没有我能帮上忙的？

There is *little that* can be talked about on this issue.

关于这个问题，没什么可谈论的。

2. 先行词被形容词最高级或序数词修饰时，引导定语从句用 that。例如：

Switzerland is *the most* beautiful country *that* I've ever seen.

瑞士是我见过的最美丽的国家。

The *first* museum *that* he visited in China was the History Museum.

他到中国参观的第一个博物馆是历史博物馆。

3. 先行词中既有人又有事物时，引导定语从句用 that。

The famous director and his works that were televised have received great attention.

电视播出的那位著名导演及其作品引起了很大关注。

The local people and their handcrafts that aroused the tourists' interest are shot into a documentary film.

引起游客兴趣的当地人及手工艺品被拍成了纪录片。

4. 在非限制性定语从句中,指事物用which,指人用who或whom。例如:

He won the lottery, **which** makes his friends and neighbors green with envy.

他中了奖,他的朋友和邻居都羡慕不已。

My sister has come back from abroad, **whom** I haven't met for three years.

我姐姐从国外回来了,我已经三年没有见到她了。

(三)后置定语

1. 短语(含介词短语,分词短语)作定语一般后置。例如:

He gave me a basket **full of eggs**.

他给我一个装满鸡蛋的篮子。

English is a language **easy to learn but hard to master**.

英语是一门容易学但是难精通的语言。

2. 修饰 some,any,no,every 等词构成的不定代词的定语都后置。例如:

There is **nothing new** in today's newspaper.

今天报纸上没有什么新东西。

Someone important will give the students a speech on studying abroad.

一位重要的人物将给学生们做一场有关留学的演讲。

3. 动词不定式作定语要后置。例如:

Does he have the ability **to lead this group**?

他有能力领导这个团队吗?

I don't have the courage **to tell you the truth**.

我没有勇气告诉你真相。

4. 现在分词短语和过去分词短语做定语要后置。例如:

The girl **sitting by my side** is my cousin.

坐在我旁边的是我表妹。

Here is a map **showing you how to get to the airport**.

这儿有一张地图,告诉你怎样去飞机场。

Exercises

1. Complete the following sentences based on the given Chinese.

1) The story is about a girl _____.

故事讲的是一个被父母遗弃了的小女孩。

2) Eason Chan will hold a personal concert in London, _____.
陈奕迅将在伦敦举办个人演唱会，这是他第三次在英国演出了。

3) Sir Run Run Shaw, _____, has died at the age of 107.
邵逸夫，创建了巨大的亚洲影视帝国，在107岁时辞世。

4) National parks are important to us for many reasons, _____.
国家公园对我们很重要，原因其中之一就是它们有助于保护野生动物。

5) _____, money doesn't grow on trees.
正如大家所知，钱不是容易赚的。

6) I have come to explain the reason _____.
我要解释一下我昨天缺席的原因。

7) _____ is waiting.
我们所能做的只有等待。

8) This is the most romantic movie _____.
这是我看过的最浪漫的电影。

2. Choose the best way to complete each of the following sentences.

1) The matter _____ you were arguing about last night has been settled.
   A. that   B. what   C. why   D. for which

2) They talked about an hour of things and persons _____ they remembered in the childhood.
   A. which   B. that   C. who   D. whom

3) Who _____ has common sense (常识) will do such a thing?
   A. which   B. who   C. whom   D. that

4) All the apples _____ fell down were eaten by the pigs.
   A. that   B. those   C. which   D. what

5) They asked him to tell them everything _____ he saw at the spot.
   A. what   B. that   C. which   D. where

6) —How do you like the smartphone?
   —It's quite different from _____ I bought three years ago.
   A. that   B. which   C. the one   D. the one what

7) The universe _____ we know very little is filled with dark matters.
   A. which   B. where   C. that   D. about which

8) The rich businessman at last got a chance to visit the village _____ he grew up, _____ he had been dreaming of for years.
   A. that ... which   B. where ... that   C. in which ... what   D. where ... which

9) I gave the rule-breaker a warning, _____ he turned a deaf ear.

A. of which B. for which C. to that D. to which

10) China is the birthplace of kites, _____ kiteflying (放风筝) spread to Japan, Korea, Thailand and India.

A. from there B. where C. from where D. there

Section D Sentence Writing

What Is Your Personality Type?

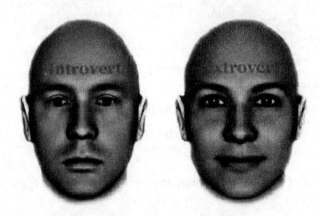

1. Can you describe your personality trait?

   Tips: open-minded, energetic, enthusiastic, quiet, prefer… to…

   _____
   _____.

2. Are you extroverted or introverted?

   Tips: extroverted, rather than, introverted, be concerned with…

   _____
   _____.

3. How do you get along with others?

   Tips: outgoing, interact with, have trouble in doing…, anxious, communicate with…

   _____
   _____.

4. When facing a problem, how do you solve it?

   Tips: tend to, think out aloud (把想的说出来), discuss with, make a list…

   _____
   _____.

Unit 9

Life Beyond the Earth

Section A Listening and Speaking

Task A General Pronunciation Rules

字母组合

1. ei

   [ei] 位于 n 或 l 之前时常读作 [ei]

   　　例词：r*ei*n, v*ei*n, s*ei*ner, r*ei*ndeer, v*ei*l

   [i:] 位于 c 或 s 之后

   　　例词：c*ei*ling, s*ei*ze, rec*ei*ve, conc*ei*ve, perc*ei*ve, rec*ei*ve

   [ai] 在有些单词中读 [ai]

   　　例词：*ei*ther, n*ei*ther, s*ei*smic, s*ei*smology

2. eig(h)

   [ei] 例词：r*eig*n, f*eig*n, *eig*ht, w*eig*ht, n*eig*hbor

   　　特例：h*eig*ht [hait], sl*eig*ht [slait]

3. er

   　　在重读音节中的发音：

   [ə:] 位于词尾或除了 r 以外的辅音之前

   　　例词：h*er*, pref*er*, f*er*tile, n*er*ve, s*er*ge, v*er*satile

   　　特例：cl*er*k [klɑ:k], s*er*geant ['sɑ:dʒənt]

   [e] 在双音节或多音节单词中位于 r 之前

   　　例词：ch*er*ry, m*er*ry, t*er*ror, t*er*rible, *er*ror

   [iər] 位于元音之前

   　　例词：*er*a, h*er*o, z*er*o, p*er*iod, s*er*ious, exp*er*ience

   　　在非重读音节中的发音：

   [ə] 例词：clev*er*, fev*er*, east*er*n, feath*er*, read*er*, tall*er*, small*er*, short*er*, thinn*er*

Task B Conversations

Model Dialogue 1: Talking About Campus Life

1. Listen to the conversation and fill in the blanks with the expressions given below.

> **Word Tips:**
> 1. campus ['kæmpəs] *n.*（大学）校园，大学
> 2. dorm [dɔ:m] *n.*（等于 dormitory）宿舍
> 3. canteen [kæn'ti:n] *n.* 食堂
> 4. eat out 下馆子
> 5. once in a while 偶尔，有时

Jack: Hey, David, is that you? _____!

David: Oh, hello, Jack, it seems I haven't seen you for ages! So _____?

Jack: Well, not so bad. Pretty good, in fact.

David: Really? Do you like living on campus?

Jack: Yeah, of course. There are so many young people coming from different places and you can always _____. What about you? Don't you enjoy it?

David: Not really. After all, _____ living in a dorm.

Jack: I think you just need some time to get used to it. Maybe you will soon find it convenient to live on campus.

David: Yeah, I hope so. But I don't like the food in the canteen. I really _____ cooked by my mother.

Jack: Well, I think the food here is all right. But if you want a change, you can _____.

David: That's true.

> 1. miss the food at home   4. make new friends
> 2. how is life on campus   5. long time no see
> 3. eat out once in a while   6. this is my first time

2. Role-play a conversation in pairs according to the given situation.

　　David and Jack meet again one month later. They greet each other. Jack asks David whether he has got used to campus life or not.

Model Dialogue 2: Choose an Elective Course

1. Listen to the conversation and fill in the blanks with the expressions given below.

> **Word Tips:**
> 1. choose [tʃuːz] *vt. & vi.* (chose, chosen) 选择，决定
> 2. elective [i'lektiv] *adj.* 选修的，选举的；*n.* 选修课
> 3. elective course 选修课
> 4. semester [si'mestə] *n.* 学期，学年
> 5. hesitate ['heziteit] *vt. & vi.* 踟蹰，犹豫，不愿意
> 6. as long as 只要

David: Hello, Sophia. Have you chosen your elective courses for this semester?

Sophia: Not yet, _____. What about you?

David: In fact, I really want to learn something about Art Design. But I heard that _____.

Sophia: If you are really interested in the course, I think you should choose it.

David: Well, _____ in the end.

Sophia: Come on, you can do it _____ you try your best. Besides, if you can learn some real skills, _____.

David: Yes, you've really _____. Thanks a lot!

Sophia: My pleasure!

1. it's worth your effort	4. the teacher is pretty strict
2. got your point	5. I am still hesitating
3. I am afraid I can't pass it	6. as long as

2. Role-play a conversation in pairs according to the given situation.

    David meets Sophia after class. They talk about their elective courses and teachers.

Task C Passage

Listen to the passage and choose the best answer to each question.

> **Word Tips:**
> 1. universe ['juːnivəːs] *n.* 宇宙，世界，领域
> 2. planet ['plænit] *n.* 行星
> 3. atmosphere ['ætməsfir] *n.* 气氛，大气，空气
> 4. extraterrestrial [ˌekstrətə'restriəl] *adj.* 地球外的，宇宙的；*n.* 外星生物
> 5. immense [i'mens] *adj.* 巨大的，广大的，无边无际的
> 6. signal ['signəl] *n.* 信号，暗号，导火线；*v.* 发信号；*adj.* 显著的，作为信号的

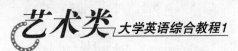

1) For a planet to have life on it, it must have _____

   A. air, heat, water and light.   B. atmosphere, food and water.

   C. atmosphere, water and plants.   D. air, water, food and plants.

2) Why is it difficult to find extraterrestrial life?

   A. Because it lives too far away from us.

   B. Because the universe is a very big place to search.

   C. Because it doesn't know how to send radio signals.

   D. Because there are millions of stars like our Earth.

3) If there is intelligent life elsewhere, how may it contact us?

   A. It may send radio signals to us.

   B. It may pay us a visit in person.

   C. It may drop into our backyard at night.

   D. It may contact us through computers.

Task D Spot Dictation

Listen to the passage three times and fill in the blanks.

Word Tips:
1. Mars [mɑːz] *n.* 火星，战神
2. microscopic [ˌmaikrə'skɔpik] *adj.* 微小的，微观的，用显微镜的
3. spacecraft ['speiskrɑːft] *n.* 宇宙飞船，航天器
4. explorer [ik'splɔːrə(r)] *n.* 探险家，勘探者，探测器

Earth seems to be a special place for life. There is 1) _____ of liquid water, and living things can get the 2) _____ they need from the warm 3) _____, or from the heat inside the Earth. We are now sure that none of the other planets in the 4) _____ system have large plants or animals. **Mars**, the 5) _____ most like the Earth, is one place that might have **microscopic** life. In the past, Mars was warmer and 6) _____ than it is now. If life started and died out, **spacecraft** or human **explorers** might one day find such 7) _____ somewhere under its ground.

Section B Reading

Are We Alone?

Pre-reading Questions

1. What are the three possibilities of finding life in the universe?
2. Why do scientists believe we are not alone?

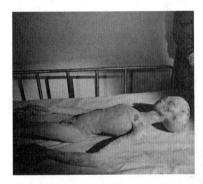

Humans **for the most part** have always believed that we are not alone, but in recent **decades** scientists have been more active **in** their **search for alien** life, and **thanks to** a lot of new **discoveries**, that possibility now seems much higher than ever.

According to the famous American *astronomer* **Carl Sagan**, the Universe is so big that if it's just for us, it seems like an **awful** waste of space. So scientists are **on the hunt for** life **beyond** Earth. In a talk **titled** "Current **Approaches** to Finding Life Beyond Earth, and What Happens If We Do," **SETI** (Search for Extraterrestrial Intelligence) astronomer **Seth Shostak talks of** three possible situations in which we could find life in the universe.

One *likelihood* is that we find it close to home, in our own **solar** system. **NASA**'s **Curiosity Rover** at this very moment is **searching** Mars for **signs** of past or present life. Ancient soils, **for instance**, with **cracked** surfaces and containing **hollows** suggest water was once present on the **Red Planet**.

Second, Shostak says, is that certain **telescopes**—like the **James Webb Space Telescope** to be **launched** in 2018—could "**sniff out**" gases such as *methane* and **oxygen located** in an *exoplanet*'s atmosphere simply by observing the **reflection** of light.

The last and final possibility is that scientists could continue the SETI work and keep one ear open for radio signals coming from other planets.

Regardless of how we find alien life, Shostak is confident that it will happen sooner rather than later. At least a half-dozen other worlds (besides Earth) that might have life are in our solar system. Shostak believes the chances of finding it are good, and if that happens, it'll happen in the next 20 years.

(286 words)

New Words

decade	['dekeɪd]	n. 十年，十个一组
search	[sɜːtʃ]	v. 搜寻，调查；n. 搜索，调查
alien	['eɪliən]	adj. 外国的，相异的；n. 外国人，外星人
discovery	[dɪ'skʌvəri]	n. 发现，被发现的事物
astronomer ★	[ə'strɒnəmə(r)]	n. 天文学者，天文学家
awful	['ɔːfl]	adj. 糟糕的，非常的；adv. 非常，极
hunt	[hʌnt]	vt. & vi. 打猎，追捕，搜索；n. 打猎，狩猎旅行
beyond	[bɪ'jɒnd]	prep. 超过，越过；adv. 在远处
title	['taɪtl]	n. 标题，头衔；vt. 加标题，赋予头衔
approach	[ə'prəʊtʃ]	vt. & vi. 接近，处理；n. 方法，接近
likelihood ★	['laɪklihʊd]	n. 可能，可能性
solar	['səʊlə(r)]	adj. 太阳的，日光的
curiosity	[ˌkjʊəri'ɒsəti]	n. 好奇心，奇特性
rover ★	['rəʊvə(r)]	n. 流浪者，漫游者
sign	[saɪn]	n. 符号，迹象，指示牌；vt. & vi. 签名，打手势
instance	['ɪnstəns]	n. 例子，实例，情况
crack	[kræk]	n. 裂缝，破裂声；vi. 破裂，打，撞
hollow	['hɒləʊ]	adj. 空的，虚伪的；n. 洞，山谷
telescope	['telɪskəʊp]	n. 望远镜
launch	[lɔːntʃ]	vt. 发射，发动，开展；vi. 投入，着手进行

sniff	[snif]	vt.& vi. 嗅，鄙视地说；n. 吸气，一股气味
methane ★	['mi:θein]	n. [化] 甲烷，沼气
oxygen	['ɔksidʒən]	n. [化] 氧，氧气
locate	[ləu'keit]	vt. 位于，确定……的位置；vi. 定位，定居
exoplanet ★	[ek'sɔpleinit]	n. 外星球
reflection	[ri'flekʃən]	n. 反映，（声、光、热等的）反射，映像
regardless	[ri'ga:dlis]	adv. 不顾后果地，无论如何；adj. 不重视的，不顾虑的

Useful Expressions

for the most part 多半，就绝大部分而言；大多
in search for 寻求，寻找
thanks to 多亏，幸亏，由于
on the hunt for 正在搜索
talk of 谈到，说到
for instance 例如，比如，拿……来说
sniff out 嗅出，发现，察觉
regardless of 不管，不顾，无

Proper Names

Carl Sagan ['ka:l 'seigən] 卡尔·萨根（美国天文学家、天体物理学家、宇宙学家、科幻作家）
SETI (Search for Extraterrestrial Intelligence) 搜寻地外文明计划
Seth Shostak [seθ 'ʃɔsteik] 赛思·肖斯塔克（美国 SETI 活动的资深天文学家）
NASA ['næsə] (National Aeronautics and Space Administration) 美国国家航空和宇宙航行局
Curiosity Rover [ˌkjuəri'ɔsəti 'rəuvə(r)] 好奇号火星探测车
Red Planet [red 'plænit] [口语] 火星，红色星球
James Webb Space Telescope [dʒeimz web speis 'teliskəup] 詹姆斯·韦伯太空望远镜

After-reading Activity

Have you ever thought that there would be a good chance of your meeting an alien? What would it look like? And what would happen then? Tell your classmates the kind of aliens in your imagination.

Background Information

Extraterrestrial Intelligence（地外文明）

地外文明一般指存在于地球以外，并发展到一定文明程度的智慧生命体，在地球以外的领域所建立的文明。它们尚没有被目前地球上的生命所观测到，倒是它们时常出现在许多虚构作品中。它们时常被作为人类文艺节目讨论或展示的对象。当然始终有人相信有外星人存在，但是目前没有确凿的证据来证实这一点。

Comprehension

1. **Choose the best way to complete each of the following sentences.**

    1) Scientists believe there might be life on Mars because some evidence shows that there used to be _____ on the planet.

        A. air   B. water   C. light   D. oxygen

    2) According to Shostak, certain telescopes might find such gases as methane and oxygen in an exoplanet's air through _____.

        A. sniffing out the air   B. observing the atmosphere

        C. observing the light reflection   D. sniffing out the light

2. **Complete the following summary with the words from the passage. The first letter of each missing word is given for your reference.**

    Scientists have been making great efforts to search for 1) a_____ life in recent 2) d_____. SETI astronomer Shostak believes there might be life on certain planets in our own 3) s_____ system, such as Mars. He also mentions two other possibilities of finding life in the 4) u_____. One is that certain 5) t_____ like the James Webb Space Telescope which is to be 6) l_____ in 2018 could find gases like methane and 7) o_____ in an exoplanet's atmosphere simply by observing the 8) r_____ of light. The last possibility is that scientists would be ready to receive radio 9) s_____ from other planets. 10) R_____ of the methods, Shostak is confident that it will be found sooner rather than later.

Vocabulary

1. Complete the following sentences with the words given below. Change the form if necessary.

   | beyond | approach | crack | locate | discovery |

   1) The beggar used a _____ bowl to collect money.

   2) We have made an important scientific _____ .

   3) The situation is completely _____ her control.

   4) It is very difficult for the rescue teams to _____ the survivors of the earthquake.

   5) We have different _____ to dealing with problems.

2. Complete the following sentences with proper prepositions or adverbs.

   1) The robbers turned out all the drawers in the house in search _____ jewels.

   2) The students are, _____ the most part, from the villages.

   3) Regardless _____ danger, he rushed into the burning house to save his mother.

   4) This is only my suggestion rather _____ an order for you.

   5) Some police dogs are trained to sniff _____ explosives (炸药).

Sentence Structure

Combine the following sentences using the structure "so...that...".

Sample:

John is very shy. He cannot talk to girls.

John is so shy that he cannot talk to girls.

1) It rained heavily outside. We had to stay at home.

2) The teacher was quite angry. He was unable to speak.

3) The novel is pretty popular nowadays. Almost everybody has read it.

4) She has prepared well for the exam. She is not nervous at all.

5) The speaker spoke loudly. Everyone could hear him in the room.

Translation

1. Translate the following English sentences from the text into Chinese.

   1) Humans for the most part have always believed that we are not alone, but in recent decades scientists have been more active in their search for alien life.

2) In a talk titled "Current Approaches to Finding Life Beyond Earth, and What Happens If We Do," SETI (Search for Extraterrestrial Intelligence) astronomer Seth Shostak talks of three possible situations in which we could find life in the universe.

3) Ancient soils, for instance, with cracked surfaces and containing hollows suggest water was once present on the Red Planet.

4) Second, Shostak says, is that certain telescopes—like the James Webb Space Telescope to be launched in 2018—could "sniff out" gases such as methane and oxygen located in an exoplanet's atmosphere simply by observing the reflection of light.

5) The last and final possibility is that scientists could continue the SETI work and keep one ear open for radio signals coming from other planets.

2. Translate the following Chinese sentences into English with the words given in brackets.

1) 多亏了他们帮忙，我们才按时完成了任务。（thanks to）

 _____, we have completed the task on time.

2) 警方进一步寻找线索。（on the hunt for）

 _____ further clues.

3) 现在再谈那件事也没用了。（talk of）

 There is no use _____.

4) 他不顾自己的安危，跳下水救了那个孩子。（regardless of）

 _____, he jumped into the water to save the child.

5) 她是职业女性而不是家庭主妇。（rather than）

 She is a career woman _____.

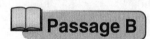

Close Encounters

Earth—our home planet—is the only place in the universe known to support life. Yet could life forms from outer space already have **paid** us **a visit**? Could they even be ***abducting*** members of the human race? It may seem like science **fiction**, but has Planet Earth already had a Close Encounter?

Unit 9 Life Beyond the Earth

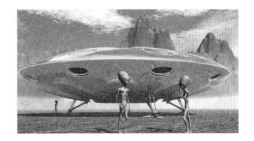

Stories of "Close Encounters" with alien life are part of our culture. Every year in the US there are thousands of reported **sightings** of **UFOs—unidentified** flying **objects**, and some people even **claim** to have been abducted by aliens. Natural **phenomena** or even **military** activities can explain most of the UFO **incidents**, but some still keep people guessing. *Skeptics* argue that such sightings and "Close Encounters" are only products of our imagination, perhaps **inspired** by science-fiction movies and popular culture.

Dr. Michael Shermer, **publisher** of **Skeptic Magazine**, **highlights** the difficulty of judging the truth about UFOs. Shermer has been writing about "the unexplained" for over 10 years. He questions not only the quality of the **evidence** but also the **reliability** of human *testimonies*, because people usually **tend to** make wild guesses about what they saw. These wild guesses include **mistaking** military **aircraft**, weather balloons and even the planet **Venus as** alien craft. Yet such sightings lead many people to believe in the existence of UFOs despite **logical** explanations from scientists and the US government. However, **official denials** of UFO landings may actually encourage a popular belief in their existence because of a **fascination** with *conspiracy* theories and a fear of government *cover-ups*.

Actually, **so far** there have been many supposed sightings of UFOs but no *definitive* evidence of a visit. All UFO sightings **may well** be **no more than** a simple *misinterpretation* of what we are seeing, and alien visitations a product of our over-active imaginations.

But whether or not aliens have **dropped into** our own backyard, many scientists do believe that they could exist. "I would be shocked if we are alone. It would be an **incredible** waste of space considering how many **galaxies** there are. There should be lots of planets like ours with life on." Shermer remarked.

(353 words)

New Words

encounter	[in'kauntə]	vt. 不期而遇，遭遇；vi. 碰见（尤指不期而遇）；n. 相遇，碰见
abduct ★	[æb'dʌkt]	vt. 劫持，诱拐
fiction	['fikʃən]	n. 小说，编造，虚构
sighting	['saitiŋ]	n. 瞄准，观察，视线

183

unidentified	[ˌʌnaiˈdentifaid]	adj. 不能辨认的，未经确认的
object	[ˈɔbdʒikt]	n. 物体，目标，对象
	[əbˈdʒekt]	vt. & vi. 反对，抱反感
claim	[kleim]	vt. 声称，要求，认领；n. 要求，认领物，索赔
phenomenon	[fiˈnɔminən]	n. 现象，事件
military	[ˈmilitəri]	adj. 军事的，军人的
incident	[ˈinsidənt]	n. 事件，小插曲，骚乱
skeptic ★	[ˈskeptik]	n. 怀疑论者，无神论者
inspire	[inˈspaiə]	vt. 鼓舞，激励，启迪
publisher	[ˈpʌbliʃə]	n. 出版商，公布者
highlight	[ˈhailait]	n.（图画或照片的）强光部分，最重要的事情，最精彩的部分；vt. 强调，突出，把……照亮
evidence	[ˈevidəns]	n. 证词，证据，迹象
reliability	[riˌlaiəˈbiləti]	n. 可靠，可信度
testimony ★	[ˈtestiməni]	n. 证词，证明，证据
mistake	[miˈsteik]	n. 错误；vi. 误解，弄错
aircraft	[ˈeəkrɑːft]	n. 飞机，航空器
logical	[ˈlɔdʒikl]	adj. 合逻辑的，合理的
official	[əˈfiʃl]	adj. 官方的，正式的，公务的；n. 官员，公务员
denial	[diˈnaiəl]	n. 否认，拒绝，背弃
fascination	[ˌfæsiˈneiʃn]	n. 魅力，魔力，入迷
conspiracy ★	[kənˈspirəsi]	n. 阴谋，共谋
cover-up ★	[ˈkʌvəˌʌp]	n. 掩饰，隐蔽
definitive ★	[diˈfinətiv]	adj. 决定性的，限定的
misinterpretation ★	[ˌmisintəːpriˈteiʃən]	n. 误解，曲解
incredible	[inˈkredəbl]	adj. 难以置信的，惊人的
galaxy	[ˈgæləksi]	n. [天] 星系，银河系

Useful Expressions

pay sb. a visit 登门拜访

tend to 趋向于，往往，朝某方向

mistake … as … 把……误认为……，搞错

so far 迄今为止，到目前为止

may well 很可能

no more than 至多，只不过，仅仅

drop into 顺便去某地，掉进

Proper Names

Close Encounter [kləuz in'kauntə] 近距离接触，亲密接触

UFO [ˌjuːefˈəu] (Unidentified Flying Object) 不明飞行物

Dr. Michael Shermer ['dɔktə 'maikl 'ʃəːmə] 迈克尔·舍默博士（美国"怀疑论者学会"的创始人）

Skeptic Magazine ['skeptik mægə'ziːn]《怀疑论者》杂志

Venus ['viːnəs] n.［天］金星，维纳斯（爱与美的女神）

Background Information

UFO（不明飞行物）

UFO 是指不明来历、不明性质，飘浮及飞行在天空中的物体。只要在目击者眼睛看不清或无法辨识确认的空中物体（例如胶袋、风筝之类）都称为 UFO。一些人相信它是来自其他星球的太空船，有些人则认为 UFO 属于自然现象。20 世纪 40 年代开始，美国上空发现碟状飞行物，当时的报纸把它称为"飞碟"，这是当代对不明飞行物的兴趣的开端，后来人们着眼于世界各地的不明飞行物报告，但至今尚未发现能让科学界普遍接受的说明它们来自地外文明的证据。一些不明飞行物照片经专家鉴定为骗局，有的则被认为是球状闪电或其他自然现象，但始终有部分发现根据现存科学知识无法解释，可能是未来新的科学知识才能解释的现象。

Comprehension

1. Mark the following statements *T* (*true*) or *F* (*false*) according to the text.

☐ 1) Some people have really been kidnapped by aliens.

☐ 2) All of the UFO incidents can be explained some way.

☐ 3) Dr. Michael Shermer suspects those people who claimed to have seen UFOs.

☐ 4) People tend to believe in the existence of UFOs more firmly due to the government denials.

☐ 5) There is not reliable evidence of aliens visiting us.

2. Complete the following statements.

1) Earth seems to be the only place in the universe to be able to _____ life.

2) Every year in the US, thousands of UFO incidents are reported and some people even _____ to have been abducted by aliens.

3) Skeptics believe that UFO sightings and close encounters are simply produced by our _____, which may be _____ by science fiction movies and popular culture.

4) Michael Shermer also questions the _____ of human witnesses who claimed to have seen UFOs.

5) People may _____ things like military aircraft weather balloons, flares as alien craft.

6) Many scientists do believe that aliens could exist, or else it would be an _____ waste of space.

Vocabulary and Structure

1. Put the following words under the corresponding pictures.

aircraft   galaxy   alien   backyard

1) _____ 2) _____ 3) _____ 4) _____

2. Compare each pair of words and complete the following sentences with the right one. Change the form if necessary.

1) object, objection

   Their parents have no _____ to their marriage.

   There seems to be an _____ under the water.

2) inspire, inspiring

   Their success has _____ more people to join their cause.

   The president's speech is very _____ .

3) evidence, evident

   It was _____ that someone had broken into my room.

   There was not enough _____ against him.

4) denial, deny

Nobody can _____ Bill Gate's influence on the whole world.

Despite official _____ , the rumors are still widespread.

5) fascination, fascinate

He has a deep _____ with the sea.

I am extremely _____ by the story.

3. Complete the following sentences with the words given below. Change the form if necessary.

| encounter | claim | official | phenomenon |
| incident | military | mistake | sighting |

1) The public refused to accept the _____ explanation for the accident.

2) We have _____ every kind of difficulty.

3) There were many reported _____ of the Loch Ness monster (尼斯湖水怪).

4) They _____ to have discovered a cure for the disease.

5) This disease is often _____ for a summer cold at the beginning.

6) The voting went ahead without _____.

7) Many interesting _____ still can't be explained by science.

8) All the freshmen had a _____ training last week.

4. Complete the following sentences with the expressions given below. Change the form if necessary.

| tend to | may well | no more than | so far | drop into |

1) He is _____ an ordinary English teacher.

2) Men _____ put on weight in middle age.

3) The film has made a profit of more than $590 million _____ .

4) The murderer _____ come from Britain.

5) They will _____ the office for a visit.

 Activity

Shooting a Movie about Aliens

There have been a lot of novels as well as movies about aliens. Some of them are cute and friendly to humans while others look frightening and aim to destroy us in order to occupy our

Earth. So what do you think they would be like? What would happen if we really find them one day? Shoot a movie in groups and show it to your fellow students.

1. Get familiar with some special English terms about movies.

director 导演
producer 制片人
leading actor/actress 男 / 女主角
supporting actor/actress 男 / 女配角
title 片名
screenplay/script 剧本
dialogue 对白
subtitle 字幕
recording 录音
editing 剪辑
trailer 宣传片

2. Match the sentences in A with the Chinese equivalents in B.

A

1) Find the proper script (　　)
2) Prepare the necessary equipment and costumes (　　)
3) Assign your roles (　　)
4) Fix the scenes and shoot (　　)
5) Go through the post production (　　)
6) Design the movie poster and trailer (　　)
7) Promote the movie (　　)

B

a) 准备必要的器材和服装
b) 进行后期制作

c) 分配角色

d) 找到合适的剧本

e) 设计电影海报及宣传片

f) 为电影做宣传

g) 确定场景并拍摄

3. Think about what you should pay attention to in order to shoot a great movie.

1) What kind of movie can be considered as a great movie?

2) Where can you find the proper script?

3) How to prepare the necessary equipment and costumes?

4) How can you assign the roles?

5) What are the effective ways to publicize your movie?

6) When and where are you going to show your movie?

Passage C Fast Reading

Do Aliens Exist? If So, Will They Kill Us?

A) In a new Discovery Channel *documentary* (纪录片) "Into the Universe with Stephen Hawking", the world's most famous *physicist* (物理学家) assumes about different forms of alien life and makes efforts under way to search and communicate with intelligent extraterrestrial civilizations. However, he warns that perhaps we shouldn't be advertising our location; perhaps we should just sit back and listen instead.

B) In an effort to find intelligent civilizations, we have to assume that they're a bit like us, so the first thing we look for are radio waves. The Search for Extraterrestrial Intelligence (SETI) has been doing this for 50 years, carefully listening for any ET call home. If humans communicate though radio waves, there's a good chance that another intelligent civilization has done the same.

C) Okay, so what if we start sending out signals advertising our presence. To assume alien civilizations will be friendly and welcome us with open arms seems extremely *naive* (天真的). As Hawking points out, if there's one thing we've learned from our human progress, although we might have the best of *intention*s (意图), we've *rarely* (很少地) "come in peace".

D) Mankind is all about resources; imagine if a more advanced civilization sees Earth as a rich supply of resources and sees our civilization as nothing more than ants *crawling* (爬行) over a big juicy apple. Wouldn't they just *wash* us *off* (洗掉)?

E) And so this is where Hawking leaves us, thinking about our fascination with broadcasting our presence into space. Wouldn't it just be better for us to stay as quiet as we can, listening rather than shouting from the rooftops? Personally, I think Hawking has a point. Although it might take hundreds, thousands or even millions of years for our signal to reach an intelligent "ear", if that ear isn't a friendly one, we've basically decided our future-Earth's destiny. So let's be careful about how we advertise ourselves, shall we? (306 words)

Information Match

Please identify the paragraph from which the following information is derived. Each paragraph is marked with a letter.

_____ 1) The advanced extraterrestrial civilization may consider our earth as a planet full of resources and view us human beings as merely a group of ants crawling over a big juicy apple.

_____ 2) It is quite probable that another intelligent civilization also communicate through radio signals.

_____ 3) The world-renowned physicist Stephen Hawking once talked about the possible forms of extraterrestrial intelligence and ways of finding and communicating with them.

_____ 4) The author personally agrees with Hawking in that we had better listen into the space instead of broadcasting our existence.

_____ 5) We can learn a lesson from our evolutionary history that we have seldom come in peace when arriving at a new place.

Background Information

Stephen Hawking（斯蒂芬·霍金）

斯蒂芬·霍金（1942年1月8日— ），英国剑桥大学著名物理学家，被誉为继爱因斯坦之后最杰出的理论物理学家之一。肌肉萎缩性侧索硬化症患者，全身瘫痪，不能发音。1979年至2009年，任卢卡斯数学教授，这是英国最崇高的教授职位。

霍金是当代最重要的广义相对论和宇宙论家,是当今享有国际盛誉的伟人之一,被称为在世的最伟大的科学家之一,还被称为"宇宙之王"。

 ## Section C Grammar

状语(一)(Adverbials I)

英语中,修饰动词、形容词、副词等的句子成分叫状语。

一、副词作状语

1. 地点(方位)副词和方式副词

I've got a feeling I've seen him before *somewhere*.

我有种感觉,我以前曾在哪里见过他。

He is a wolf in sheep's clothing, *outwardly* kind but *inwardly* vicious!

他是个披着羊皮的狼,外貌仁慈,内心狠毒!

2. 时间副词

The bank *recently* opened a branch in Germany.

这家银行最近在德国开设了分行。

Ingrid answered Peter's letter *immediately*.

英格丽德立即给彼得回了信。

3. 频度副词

Even Homer *sometimes* nods.

智者千虑,必有一失。

She is *seldom* ill.

她很少生病。

4. 程度副词

Going *too* far is as bad as not going far *enough*.

过犹不及。

It *really* gets my goat.

这真叫我发火。

二、不定式作状语

1. 表示目的

To join the American army, Deborah Sampson dressed up like a man.

为了参加美国军队，黛博拉·桑普森男扮女装。

The pyramids were built *to keep the mummies safe*.

修建金字塔是为了保证木乃伊的安全。

2. 表示原因

My parents were wild with joy *to hear of my success*.

我的父母听到我成功的消息欣喜若狂。

She burst into tears *to gain the first prize.*

得知自己获得了一等奖，她的泪水夺眶而出。

3. 表示结果

He hurried to the booking office *only to be told that all the tickets had been sold out*.

他匆忙赶到售票处，却被告知所有的票都卖光了。

He shut himself in his room *so as not to be disturbed*.

他把自己关在屋子里免受打扰。

三、介词短语作状语

1. 介词短语作状语，用来修饰动词。

Such a chance comes *once in a blue moon*. (频度)

这样的机会极其难得。

We save money *for rainy days*. (目的)

我们攒钱以备不时之需。

Without bread, love will fly out of the window. (条件)

没有面包，爱情飞窗外。

With all your faults, I still like you. (让步)

尽管你有很多缺点，我仍然喜欢你。

With time passing by, he grew into a mature man. (伴随状语)

随着时间的流逝，他成长为一个成熟的男人。

2. 介词短语作状语，用来修饰形容词。

   He was successful *in teaching children*.

   他教孩子很有一套。

   All of us want to be good *at our jobs*.

   我们都想在工作上表现优秀。

3. 介词短语作状语，修饰副词（比较少用）。

   Maybe someday *in the future*, we'll meet again.

   也许在未来的某一天，我们会再见面的。

   Our ancestors are stars, they are looking at us there *in the sky*.

   我们的祖先就像星星，他们在天空的那边望着我们。

4. 介词短语作状语，修饰整个句子。

   On the whole, my opinion is the same as yours.

   大体上，我的意见同你的差不多。

   In the long run, prices are bound to rise.

   从长远看，物价肯定要涨。

Exercises

1. **Complete the following sentences based on the given Chinese.**

   1) I felt as fit as a fiddle _____.

      洗完热水澡感到全身舒畅。

   2) It is just like looking for a needle _____.

      大海捞针。

   3) Many people are nice _____.

      很多人为了受人喜爱而行善。

   4) A young woman came in _____.

      一名年轻女子端着一杯咖啡走进来。

   5) People have used large quantities of natural resources _____.

      人们使用了大量的自然资源，结果产生了大批的废物。

   6) _____, the image of the sweet girl would appear to him in moments of sadness.

      从那天起，每当悲伤的时候，那个女孩甜美的形象就会浮现在眼前。

   7) Dad had risen from his chair and was standing _____.

      爸爸从椅子上直起身来，就站在旁边。

   8) _____, exercise is the best way to keep fit.

      毫无疑问，锻炼是保持身材最好的方法。

2. Choose the best way to complete each of the following sentences.

1) He speaks English _____.
   A. very good   B. fine   C. excellent   D. very well

2) Children are playing _____.
   A. in the amusement park   B. by the amusement park
   C. under the amusement park   D. the amusement park

3) She fell in love with him _____.
   A. at fist seeing   B. at first sight
   C. in first seeing   D. in first sight

4) He is too excited _____.
   A. to speak   B. speaking
   C. spoken   D. to speaking

5) His face was purple _____.
   A. in rage   B. being rage   C. with rage   D. to rage

6) He ran _____.
   A. to shelter from the rain   B. to shelter against the rain
   C. to shelter for the rain   D. sheltering from the rain

7) A bird in hand is worth two _____.
   A. in the tree   B. in the woods
   C. in the bush   D. in the garden

8) I'm starving _____.
   A. dying   B. to die   C. dead   D. to death

9) _____ she cast in a bone (离间) between the wife and husband.
   A. Under this means   B. By this means
   C. Through this means   D. In this means

10) _____, I'm not satisfied with his performance.
    A. To be honest   B. Be honest
    C. To be honestly   D. As honesty

Section D Sentence Writing

What Happens Once We Find Aliens

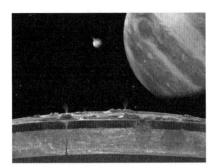 

1. Do aliens exist?

   Tips: universe, wonder, evidence, suspect, planet...

   _____
   _____.

2. If aliens exist, what do you think they would look like?

   Tips: look like, in my vision, skinny, figure, typical image, come into one's mind…

   _____
   _____.

3. Do aliens drive spacecraft? Do you believe in the existence of UFO?

   Tips: thousands of, unidentified flying objects (不明飞行物), only if...

   _____
   _____.

4. What would happen if aliens came to earth?

   Tips: discovery, change life, panic, declare, planet

   _____
   _____.

Unit 10

Architecture

Section A Listening and Speaking

Task A General Pronunciation Rules

字母组合：

1. ere

   [iə] 在重读音节中读 [iə]

   例词：h*ere*, m*ere*, sinc*ere*, coh*ere*, persev*ere*

   特例：th*ere* [ðeə(r)], w*ere* [wə:, wə], wh*ere* [weə]

2. ew

   [ju:] 位于除了 l, r, j, ch 以外的辅音之后

   例词：n*ew*, f*ew*, kn*ew*, h*ew*, m*ew*, y*ew*

   [u:] 位于 l, r, j, ch 之后

   例词：bl*ew*, fl*ew*, gr*ew*, thr*ew*, j*ew*el, j*ew*ellery, ch*ew*

3. ey

   [ei] 在重读音节中

   例词：th*ey*, pr*ey*, gr*ey*, surv*ey*, ob*ey*, conv*ey*

   特例：k*ey* [ki:], *ey*e [ai], g*ey*ser [gi:zə]

   [i] 在非重读的词尾中

   例词：monk*ey*, donk*ey*, hon*ey*, mon*ey*, vall*ey*, chimn*ey*

Task B Conversations

Model Dialogue 1: Eating out with Your Friends

1. Listen to the conversation and fill in the blanks with the expressions given below.

Steve: Hi, Lily! Nice to meet you here. I was thinking about you. _____ this Saturday?

Lily: _____ What about you?

Steve: I heard that there is a new Chinese restaurant located outside the school gate. The noodles with chicken soup are super tasty.

Lily: Oh, Steve, you know I am a big fan of noodles.

Steve: Well, I'm fed up with the same thing in our canteen and intend to have a bite at the new restaurant this Saturday. Would you like to _____?

Lily: _____. But I'm afraid _____, as I have little money left this weekend.

Steve: You don't need to worry about money. Be my guest and it will be my treat.

Lily: _____, Steve. I really have to get myself away from the heavy school work and enjoy something new other than canteen meals.

1. eat out with me for a change	4. What are you planning to do
2. It sounds like a great idea	5. Thank you for your kindness
3. Nothing special	6. I can't make it

2. Role-play a conversation in pairs according to the given situation.

Steve and Lily meet on the school shuttle bus. They are going over the menu of a newly-opened Chinese restaurant and plan to eat out again. But this time it will be Lily's treat.

Model Dialogue 2: Go Dutch

1. Listen to the conversation and fill in the blanks with the expressions given below.

Lily: Hello, Jimmy. Haven't seen you for a long time. How are things going these days?

Jimmy: Hello, Lily. Things are going well and _____ on my term paper.

Lily: I heard that you rent a new apartment at the south corner of Zhongshan Street.

Jimmy: Yes, it has been two months.

Lily: Well, I guess you are _____ by the various yummy foods on that street.

Jimmy: You're right. I _____ almost every meal since I moved there. My favorite food is Sichuan food, especially Kung Pao Chicken.

Lily: Sichuan food is also my one and only favorite!

Jimmy: Since Professor Smith's lecture on computer science has been shifted to next week. I'm free the whole day! _____.

Lily: Sounds great! But I have to go back to my dorm and get my purse.

Jimmy: Oh, Lily, _____.

Lily: You've always been so kind. But let's _____ this time. Please wait here for a while.

Jimmy: OK. See you then.

1. go Dutch	4. I've been working really hard
2. eat out	5. Would you like to go for lunch with me
3. attracted	6. it has to be my treat

2. Role-play a conversation in pairs according to the given situation.

Lily meets her classmates Dave and Jimmy on the way to the library. They talk about having dinner together at a Sichuan Restaurant to try Mapo Tofu. But Jimmy has no time and no money for it. Then they fix the problem by inviting Jimmy for dinner on Saturday night.

 Task C Passage

Listen to the passage and choose the best answer to each question.

Word Tips:
1. famous [feiməs] *adj.* 著名的
2. significant [sig'nifikənt] *adj.* 重大的，有意义的
3. private ['praivit] *adj.* 私人的
4. necessity [nə'sesiti] *n.* 必要性，必需品

1) Which of the following aspect was not mentioned about the influence of New York City ?
   A. Commerce.   B. Fashion.
   C. Education.   D. Location.

2) Why do New Yorkers often eat out ?
   A. Because they have no interest in cooking.
   B. Because they are busing working and the city is filled with a lot of restaurants.
   C. Because it is a tradition in American history.
   D. Because they have many friends.

3) What makes New Yorkers so special?
   A. They love to throw dinner parties at restaurants.
   B. They always invite special guests at home.
   C. They can taste different foods at different restaurants.
   D. They never cook at home.

Task D Spot Dictation

Listen to the passage three times and fill in the blanks.

> **Word Tips:**
> 1. amount [ə'maunt] *n.* 数量，总额
> 2. extra ['ekstrə] *adj.* 额外的
> 3. calorie ['kæləri] *n.* 卡路里（热量单位）
> 4. provide [prə'vaid] *vt.& vi.* 提供，供给
> 5. trend [trend] *n.* 趋势，走向

  Many Chinese modern families love to 1) _____ a large **amount** of money to eat out other than cook at home. Though it 2) _____ them time and 3) _____, every time we choose to eat a meal 4) _____ home, we add **extra calories** more than we need a day. And only a few restaurants **provide** clean and 5) _____ food with low 6) _____. As time goes by, too much eating out will 7) _____ our body system. In this case, making 8) _____ at home has now become a new **trend** and it can totally be 9) _____ and help you 10) _____.

Section B Reading

The Art of Building

Pre-reading Questions

1. Where did early human beings probably live? Can you give some examples?

2. Could you please tell us the architecture design that impresses you most? And why do you like it?

Unit 10 Architecture

Thousands of years ago, human beings are often **referred** to as cavemen, for they lived in caves or other **natural structures**. As time goes by, people began to learn new skills, develop new **tools**, and were able to build simple **shelters**.

As societies developed, they needed more kinds of buildings. Soon *forts*, *barns*, schools, bridges, **tombs**, and **temples** were being built, using **a variety of** materials. **Gradually**, creating buildings became an activity for experts which came to **be known as** "architecture."

Today architecture is a **refined** art requiring a lot of training, planning, and plenty of **talent**. In history, civilizations **are** often **related to** the surviving architectural achievements. An architect's work is to imagine and plan a building and then to keep an eye on its **construction**. For example, what is the building going to be used for and by whom? Where will it be built? What would be the most economical material to use? How much money will it cost? What's more, *documentation* produced by architects, typically drawings, sets the structure and the style of a building.

Architects also try to create buildings that people like to look at as well as to live, work, and play in. And changing styles **affect** architecture just as happens in other arts. The next time you see or walk around a city, notice the **various** styles of buildings. You'll find many differences between those designed recently and those of even 50 or 100 years ago. Different countries and cultures also produce different styles of architecture.

People today **are** still **amazed at** the buildings created by age long architects. The Great Wall of China and the temple at **Angkor Wat** in **Cambodia** are some of the architectural **wonders** you can study and visit.

Architecture is both the **process** and the product of human wisdom. The surviving architectural achievements have stood the test of war and time. This form of art and the people who keep **chasing** their architectural dreams should be **appreciated** by everyone on our planet.

New Words

refer	[ri'fəː(r)]	vt. 归因于……，送交；vi. 提到，关系到
natural	['nætʃərəl]	adj. 自然的，天生的
structure	['strʌktʃə]	n. 结构，构造，建筑物；vt. 构成，排列，安排
tool	[tuːl]	n. 工具，器具
shelter	['ʃeltə]	n. 居所，遮蔽
fort ★	[fɔːt]	n. 堡垒，要塞
barn ★	[baːn]	n. 谷仓，粮仓，牲口棚
tomb	[tuːm]	n. 坟墓，墓穴

temple	['templ]	n. 庙，寺
variety	[və'raiəti]	n. 多样化，种类
gradually	['grædjuəli]	adv. 逐步地，渐渐地
architecture	['a:kitektʃə]	n. 建筑学，建筑风格
refine	[ri'fain]	vt. 提炼，改善
talent	['tælənt]	n. 天资，才能，人才
construction	[kən'strʌkʃən]	n. 建筑物，建造
documentation ★	[dɔkjumen'teiʃn]	n. 文件材料
affect	[ə'fekt]	vt. 影响；n. 感情，心情
various	['veəriəs]	adj. 各种各样的；多方面的
amaze	[ə'meiz]	vt. 使大为吃惊，使惊奇；n. 吃惊，好奇
wonder	['wʌndə]	n. 奇观，奇迹；vt. 对……感到好奇；vi. 怀疑，想知道
process	['prəuses]	n. 过程，工序，做事方法；vt. 加工，处理；vi. 列队行进
chase	[tʃeis]	n. 追捕，打猎；vt. & vi. 追捕，追寻，追求（常与 after 连用）
appreciate	[ə'pri:ʃieit]	vt. 感激，欣赏

Useful Expressions

a variety of 种种，各种各样的
be known as 被称为，被认为是，以……著称
be related to 与……有关
be amazed at 对……感到惊讶

Proper Names

Angkor Wat ['æŋkɔ:r wɔt] n. 吴哥窟（柬埔寨的古都和游览胜地）
Cambodia [kæm'bəudiə] n. 柬埔寨（亚洲国名）

After-reading Activity

If you were given an assignment to build a restaurant outside the campus, what kind of style would you choose for the outlook and inside decoration? What would be the best material to use?

Background Information

1. Angkor Wat（吴哥窟）

吴哥窟又称吴哥寺，位于柬埔寨。它是吴哥古迹中保存得最完好的庙宇，以石头建筑与浮雕细致闻名于世，是柬埔寨吴哥王朝的都城遗址。现存古迹主要包括吴哥王城（大吴哥）和吴哥窟（小吴哥）。

吴哥窟是高棉古典建筑艺术的高峰，它结合了高棉寺庙建筑学的两个基本的布局：祭坛和回廊。其建筑可分东西南北四廊，每廊都各有城门。寺庙外围环绕一道护城河，象征环绕须弥山的咸海。它与中国万里长城、印度的泰姬陵和印度尼西亚的千佛坛一起，被誉为古代东方的四大奇迹。1992年，联合国将吴哥古迹列入世界文化遗产。此后吴哥窟作为吴哥古迹的重中之重，成为每一位到柬埔寨的游客不容错过的地方。吴哥窟的造型，已经成为柬埔寨国家的标志，展现在柬埔寨的国旗上。

2. Khmer Empire（吴哥王朝）

吴哥王朝（公元802—1431年）历史上共有25位国王，其势力范围远远超过今天柬埔寨的领土，版图包括现今整个柬埔寨、部分泰国、老挝、缅甸及越南。在吴哥王朝期间，建造王城及大小寺庙600余座，景象极为壮观，充分表现出吴哥民族的艺术成就。此外，吴哥王朝更积极兴建大规模的灌溉系统，有利耕作，可谓国泰民安，于12世纪前半叶达到全盛时期。但是由于连年大规模的寺庙营建和对外征服，安逸的生活变得战乱纷纷，苛捐杂税引发了人民起义和被征服地区持续不断的反抗。1431年，暹罗人首次攻陷首都吴哥通。为避免泰人的威胁，1434年索里约波王时迁都金边，柬埔寨逐渐走向衰落。

Comprehension

1. Choose the best way to complete each of the following sentences.

1) Creating buildings become _____ for experts since our society developed.

   A. structure   B. bridge

   C. architecture   D. tools

2) Many differences can be found out between those designed recently and those of _____ .

   A. 100 or 200 years ago B. 50 or 100 years ago

   C. 100 or 150 years ago D. 50 or 100 years later

2. Complete the following summary with the words from the passage. The first letter of each missing word is given for your reference.

   Once upon a time, human beings used to live in caves or natural 1) s_____. After they mastered some basic skills, they began to build simple 2) s_____ by using new tools. As societies developed, a 3) v_____ of materials were needed to create more buildings. For experts, this activity has been known as 4) "a_____". And the people who are working on this 5) r_____ art have been called 6) " a_____" . They not only imagine and plan a building, find a suitable location, but also have to keep an eye on its 7) c_____ and decide which is the best material to use. The next time you see or walk around a city, you will notice that the changing styles also 8) a_____ the buildings we live, work, and play in. You will be amazed at different styles from different countries and cultures, even those created long time ago. The art of building is both the process and the product of human 9) w_____ . Therefore, it should be 10) a_____ by everyone on our planet.

Vocabulary

1. Complete the following sentences with the words given below. Change the form if necessary.

   | natural | gradually | talent | process | chase |

   1) China is rich in _____ resources.

   2) The world is _____ filled up with electronic products.

   3) The increasingly serious competition for _____ in the labor market has become a heated topic.

   4) Be patient! To improve your health condition is a slow _____.

   5) It is human nature to _____ maximum profits.

2. Complete the following sentences with proper prepositions or adverbs.

   1) Hong Kong is known _____ the pearl of the Orient and Shopping Heaven.

   2) You will be amazed _____ how much this cookbook will help you balance your diet.

   3) Could you please keep an eye _____ the little kid before I come back from work?

   4) A variety _____ foods is sold at the department store.

   5) The information you provide may be related _____ this case.

Sentence Structure

Combine the following sentences using the structure "as well as"

Sample:

Architects try to create buildings that people like to look at.

Architects try to create buildings that people like to live in.

Architects try to create buildings that people like to look at as well as to live in.

1) Electric energy can be changed into light energy. Electric energy can be changed into sound energy.

2) He plays the guitar well. You play the guitar well.

3) Your wife is friendly to me. You are friendly to me.

4) They travel at full speed by day. They travel at full speed by night.

5) Tom is going to the bus station on foot. Dave is going to the bus station on foot.

 **Translation**

1. Translate the following English sentences from the text into Chinese.

1) As time passed, people learned new skills, developed new tools, and were able to build simple shelters.

2) An architect's work requires plenty of talent to imagine and plan a building and then to keep an eye on its construction.

3) Different countries and cultures also produce different styles of architecture.

4) The Great Wall of China and the temple at Angkor Wat in Cambodia, are some of the architectural wonders you can study and visit.

5) The surviving architectural achievements should be appreciated by everyone, because they have stood the test of war and time.

2. Translate the following Chinese sentences into English with the words given in brackets.

1) 在公共场合吸烟通常被认为是个坏习惯。(refer to... as...)

    _____ is usually _____ a bad habit.

2) 他出版了各种各样的书。(a variety of)

    _____ his books have been _____.

3) 这种巧克力棒在美国有别的叫法，但是我记不起来了。(be known as)

    This chocolate bars _____ in the United States, but I can't remember.

4) 我外出度假时，请帮我照看一下房子。(keep an eye on)

    Please _____ when I am out on holiday.

5) 他专业的游泳技能让我们惊讶不已。(be amazed at)
We _____ his expertise on _____.

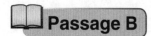

Grand Architect

Ieoh Ming Pei, commonly known as I.M. Pei, is one of the most important modern architects. He has created many **major** buildings throughout the world. And his style and ideas have strongly influenced the work of many other architects. He has **specialized in** building **multistory** structures in cities.

I.M. Pei was born in **Canton**, China on April 26, 1917. His father was a famous banker. In 1935, He went to America to study but couldn't return to China when World War II broke out. So most of his works have been in North America and Europe. In the 1940s Pei began working as a **professional** architect. He **worked on** such important projects as the **Mile High** Center in **Denver, Colorado**.

In 1955, Pei **formed** his own architectural company, I. M. Pei & **Associates**. The company's early work included a museum in New York, which was actually four buildings joined by bridges. He also created a design for a new type of airport **control tower** that **was widely used**.

Pei's buildings are often tall, with lots of glass and **steel**. The designs combine all kinds of *geometric* shapes. But his buildings are not dull or simple. In many of them, you can see the buidings' supports or building materials, and these are their only **decoration**. The way that *concrete*, glass, and steel look together creates interesting designs **on the sides of** Pei's buildings. Special **reflective** glass also **adds to** the designs. He often combines different shapes and **emphasizes** the picture these shapes make in the **skyline**.

In 1964, Jacqueline Kennedy selected Pei to design the Kennedy library. After that he became well-known all of the world. Some of Pei's most famous work includes the East Wing of the **National Gallery of Art** in Washington, D.C., and the glass pyramid at the **Louvre Museum** in Paris, a new historic **landmark** for Paris.

Pei has won a wide variety of prizes and awards in the field of architecture. In 1983, he won the **Pritzker Prize**, sometimes called the Nobel Prize of architecture.

Unit 10 Architecture

New Words

major	['meidʒə]	adj. 主要的，重要的；n. 主修科目；vi. 主修，专攻（常与 in 连用）
specialize	['speʃəlaiz]	vi. 专门从事，专攻，详细说明
multistory	[mʌlti'stɔ:ri]	adj. 多层的
professional	[prə'feʃənəl]	adj. 专业的，专业性的；n. 专业人士
form	[fɔ:m]	n. 形状，形式；vt. 形成，构成；vi. 形成，产生
associate	[ə'səuʃieit]	vt. 使发生联系，联想；vi. 交往，结交
steel	[sti:l]	n. 钢，钢铁
geometric ★	[ˌdʒi:ə'metrik]	adj. 几何学的
decoration	[ˌdekə'reiʃən]	n. 装饰，装潢，装饰品
concrete ★	['kɔnkri:t]	n. 混凝土
reflective	[ri'flektiv]	adj.（指物体表面）反光的，（指人、心情等）深思熟虑的
emphasize	['emfəsaiz]	vt. 强调，使突出
skyline	['skailain]	n. 地平线，天际线
landmark	['lændma:k]	n. 地标，里程碑；adj. 有重大意义或影响的

Useful Expressions

specialize in 专门研究
control tower （机场）指挥塔台
work on 从事……
be widely used 被广泛应用
on the sides of 在……周边
add to 加入，增加

Proper Names

Ieoh Ming Pei ['iəu miŋ 'pei] 贝聿铭（美籍华人建筑师）

Canton ['kæn'tɔn] 广东
Mile High [mail hai] 英里高（位于丹佛）
Denver ['denvə] n. 丹佛（美国城市）
Colorado [ˌkɔlə'rɑːdəu] 美国科罗拉多州（位于美国西部）
Jacqueline Kennedy ['dʒækliːn 'kenidiː] 杰奎琳·肯尼迪（美国前第一夫人）
Kennedy Library ['kenidiː 'laibrəri] 肯尼迪图书馆
National Gallery of Art ['næʃnəl 'gæləri əv ɑːt] 美国国家艺术馆
Louvre Museum ['luːvə(r) mjuˈziːəm] 卢浮宫
Pritzker Prize ['pritsə praiz] 普利兹克建筑奖

Comprehension

1. Mark the following statements *T (true)* or *F (false)* according to the text.

☐ 1) I. M. Pei is one of the most important ancient architects.

☐ 2) I. M. Pei was born in America.

☐ 3) I. M. Pei began working as a professional architect since 1930s.

☐ 4) I. M. Pei formed his own architectural company when he was 38.

☐ 5) I. M. Pei became well-known all of the world after he designed the Kennedy library.

2 Complete the following statements.

1) A building which is having more than one can be called _____.

2) Ieoh Ming Pei has created many major buildings _____ the world.

3) Ieoh Ming Pei also created a design for a new type of airport control tower that was _____ used.

4) You can see the buildings' supports or building materials, and these are their only _____.

5) Ieoh Ming Pei often combines different shapes and _____ the picture these shapes make in the skyline.

Vocabulary and Structure

1. Put the following words under the corresponding pictures.

| multistory | steel | rectangles | geometry |

Unit 10 Architecture

1) _____ 2) _____ 3) _____ 4) _____

2. Compare each pair of words and complete the following sentences with the right one. Change the form if necessary.

1) special, specialize

   The Halloween costume you wear is really _____.

   Professor Li _____ in chemistry.

2) profession, professional

   Women in the medical _____ had risen to 17.5%.

   His _____ career started at Peking University.

3) associate, association

   I have never been _____ with this project.

   The _____ of the two companies dates from the 18th century.

4) decorate, decoration

   The new apartment will be _____ by a famous designer.

   The _____ and furnishings should be practical for a family home.

3. Complete the following sentences with the words given below. Change the form if necessary.

| major | throughout | form | geometric |
| concrete | reflective | emphasize | associate |

1) We have to think twice before we choose our _____ .

2) They tried to _____ a study group on physics.

3) Do not sleep on _____ floor.

4) His problems are _____ with heavy drinking.

5) The story is so impressive that it could be used to _____ human rights.

6) A _____ surface or material can send back light or heat.

7) New Year's Day is a public holiday _____ China.

8) _____ designs were popular wall decorations in the 14th century.

4. Complete the following sentences with the expressions given below. Change the form if necessary.

> work on   be widely used   on the sides of   add to

1) The computer technology has _____ in our daily life.
2) We have been _____ putting the food together the whole morning.
3) Do you have anything to _____ the shopping list?
4) Tea plants are grown _____ the mountains.

 **Activity**

Planning for an Architectural Design

You've been appointed as the chief architect by a local land agent to design a residential building. What factors will you consider essential for the project?

1. Get familiar with some special English terms about architectural design.

constructing assignment 建设任务
design drawing 设计图纸
design criterion 设定标准
investment budge 投资预算

2. Match the sentences in A with the Chinese equivalents in B.

A

1) Choose a location.   (   )

2) Choose a qualified construction crew. (   )

3) Draw up criteria and calculate the budget. (   )

4) Do researches on how to work out the difficulties and problems that you might encounter in the process of construction . (   )

5) Find construction materials from a reliable supplier. (   )

6) Last minute details. (   )

B

a) 从可靠的供应商处寻找建筑材料

b) 选择恰当的位置

c) 制定建筑标准并做好预算

d) 最后的细节

e) 研究在施工过程中可能遇到的困难和问题的解决办法

f) 选择合格的施工队

3. Think about what you should pay attention to in order to have a full preparation.

1) When choosing a location for a commercial residential building, what should you put into consideration?

2) How to choose a qualified construction crew?

3) How to precisely (精确地) make a budget?

4) How to figure out the problems during the whole process of architectural design?

5) How to build mutual trust (相互信任) between you and your construction partner?

6) After your design has been completed and ready to carry out, what else should you pay attention to?

 Passage C Fast Reading

Wonder of the World: the Taj Mahal

A) The **Taj Mahal** (泰姬陵) was built by the fifth **Mughal Emperor Shah Jahan** (莫卧儿王朝皇帝沙贾汗) in 1631 in memory of his third but the most favourite wife. It is thought as a legend of eternal love and a poem-in-*marble* (大理石). The awesome structure stands as a proof of Shah Jahan's intense love for his wife Mumtaz Mahal (姬蔓·芭奴), in fact a soul-mate.

B) Several hundred years ago, when the emperor **Jahangir** (贾汗季) ruled over northern India, his son, **Prince Khurram** (库拉姆亲王), married Mumtaz Mahal. The two were almost always together, and together they had 14 children. Prince Khurram became emperor in 1628 and was called Emperor Shah Jahan.

C) But three years later Mumtaz Mahal died after giving birth to their 14th child. The death so crushed the emperor that all his hair and beard were said to have grown snow white in a few months. He decided to build the most beautiful monument to his wife. Beginning in about 1632, over 20,000 workers labored for 22 years to create what was to become one of the wonders of the world.

D) The great *monument* was called the Taj Mahal. It was built in the city of Agra, India, the capital of Shah Jahan's empire. Its several buildings sit on the south bank of the **Yamuna River** (亚穆纳河). The dome is made of white marble, but the tomb is set against the plain across the river and it is this background that works its magic of colours that, through their reflection, changes the view of the Taj. The colours change at different hours of the day and during different seasons. Many of its walls and *pillars* (柱子) shine with *precious stones* (宝石).

E) Different people have different views of the Taj but it would be enough to say that the Taj has a life of its own. It's a masterpiece of the art and science of architecture, a representative of an era called the period of Mughal Empire. It was made a *World Heritage Site* (世界文化遗址) in 1983.

Proper Names

Taj Mahal [tɑːdʒ məˈhɑːl] 印度泰姬陵
Shah Jahan [ʃɑː dʒəˈhɑːn] 沙贾汗（印度莫卧儿帝国皇帝）
Prince Khnrram 库拉姆亲王
Yamuna River 亚穆纳河

Information Match

Please identify the paragraph from which the following information is derived. Each paragraph is marked with a letter.

_____ 1) Prince Khurram became Emperor Shah Jahan in 1628.

_____ 2) It is the Taj Mahal's background that works its magic of colours.

_____ 3) Taj Mahal was made a World Heritage Site in 1983.

_____ 4) It took 22 years to create the world wonder Taj Mahal.

_____ 5) Taj Mahal is a symbol of Shah Jahan's eternal love for his wife.

Background Information

Shah Jahan（沙贾汗）

Shah Jahan（1592—1666），是印度莫卧儿帝国第五代皇帝，原名库拉姆（Khrram），即位后称沙贾汗，波斯语意为"世界之王"。沙贾汗在位期间，他的第三个妻子 Mumtaz Mahal 获得皇宫中最高头衔——泰姬·马哈尔。泰姬难产死后，这位痴情的国王为纪念亡妻，历经 22 年，修筑了举世闻名的泰姬陵。泰姬陵位于北方邦西南部的阿格拉布市郊区，距离新德里 195 公里，是世界七大建筑奇迹之一。泰姬陵建筑集中了印度、中东及波斯的艺术特点，是一件集伊斯兰和印度建筑艺术于一体的古代经典作品。在世人眼中，泰姬陵是爱情绵长的象征。

Section C Grammar

状语（二）(Adverbials Ⅱ)

四、分词作状语

注意：选择现在分词还是过去分词，关键看主句的主语。如分词的动作与主句的主语是主动关系，分词就用现在分词；如果是被动关系就用过去分词。

1. 表示时间、地点

   When feeling upset, I will listen to classical music to calm down.

   当我生气的时候，我会听古典音乐使自己平静下来。

   He is always ready to help **wherever needed**.

   无论哪里需要他，他都愿意给予帮助。

2. 表示原因

   Feeling sorry for his own behavior, he apologized to me sincerely.

   对他自己的行为感到抱歉，他真诚地向我道了歉。

   Scolded by the teacher, the girl felt unfair.

   受到老师的责备，这个女孩感到很不公平。

3. 表示条件

   Coated with sugar, strawberries will taste better.

   如果洒上糖，草莓尝起来味道会更好。

   Given one more month, I will promise to hand in a piece of more creative work.

   如果再给我一个月的时间，我保证会交上一幅更有创意的作品。

4. 表示让步

   Even if failing ten times, I wouldn't lose courage.

   即使要失败十次，我也绝不灰心。

   His achievements, **though hardly exciting**, were widely admired.

   尽管他的成就不怎么激动人心，可依然备受赞赏。

5. 表示伴随

   He was caught **cheating in the exam** on the spot.

   他被当场抓住考试作弊。

   He stared at me, **astonished**.

   他瞪着我，惊呆了。

五、从句作状语（状语从句）

状语从句指句子用作状语，起副词作用的句子。它可以修饰谓语、非谓语动词、定语、状语或整个句子。

1. 时间状语从句：通常由 when, as, while, as soon as, before, after, since, till, until 等引导。

   特殊引导词：every time, no sooner ... than, hardly ... when, scarcely... when, etc.

   We had **scarcely** driven a mile **when** the car broke down.

   我们刚开了一英里，车就抛锚了。

2. 地点状语从句：通常由 where 引导。

   特殊引导词：wherever, anywhere, everywhere etc.

Some people enjoy themselves *wherever* they are.

有些人能够随遇而安。

3. 原因状语从句：通常由 because，since，as，for 引导。

   特殊引导词：seeing that, now that, considering that, given that, etc.

   Now that everybody has come, let's begin our discussion.

   既然大家都来了，我们开始讨论吧。

4. 目的状语从句：通常由 so that，in order that 引导。

   特殊引导词：lest, in case, in the hope that, etc.

   I will give you all the facts *so that* you can judge for yourself.

   我会把事实都告诉你，以便你可以自己判断。

5. 结果状语从句：通常由 so ... that，such ... that 引导。

   特殊引导词：to the extent that, to such a degree that, etc.

   Everyone lent a hand, *so that* the work was finished ahead of schedule.

   每个人都过来帮忙，所以工作提前完成了。

6. 条件状语从句：通常由 if, unless 引导。

   特殊引导词：as/so long as，only if，providing/provided that，in case that，etc.

   Provided they are fit, they should go on playing for another four or five years.

   只要他们身体强健，他们应该继续再打四五年比赛。

7. 让步状语从句：通常由 though, although, even if, even though 引导。

   特殊引导词：as（句子要倒装），while，no matter...，in spite of the fact that，whatever, whoever，wherever，whenever，however，whichever

   Much *as* I respect him, I can't agree to his proposal.

   尽管我很尊敬他，但我却不同意他的建议。

8. 比较状语从句：通常由 as, than 引导。

   特殊引导词：the more ... the more ...，no ... more than，not so much as ...

   She is *as* bad-tempered *as* her mother.

   她跟她妈妈一样脾气坏。

9. 方式状语从句：通常由 as，as if (though)，how 引导。

   特殊引导词：the way

   When in Rome, do *as* the Romans do.

   入乡随俗。

Exercises

1. Complete the following sentences based on the given Chinese.

   1) _____ in the door than the phone rang.

我一进门，电话铃就响了。

2) I was afraid to open the door _____.

我不敢开门，唯恐他还跟着我。

3) You will do all right _____.

只要你听我的建议，你一定会做好的。

4) I'll call you _____.

我一下班回家就给你打电话。

5) I sent an e-mail to the university I was applying for, _____.

我给申请的大学发了电子邮件，希望获得更详细的信息。

6) _____ all day long, he failed the final English exam.

他整天都在校园里闲逛，结果期末英语考试没及格。

7) When _____, you should choose your words carefully.

当讨论敏感话题的时候，你应该小心措辞。

8) He was sitting under the tree, _____.

他坐在树下，陷入沉思中。

2. Choose the best way to complete each of the following sentences.

1) A cook will be immediately fired if he is found _____ in the kitchen.

 A. smoke   B. smoking   C. to smoke   D. smoked

2) Though _____ money, his parents managed to send him abroad.

 A. lacked   B. lacking of   C. lacking   D. lacked in

3) _____ such heavy pollution already, it's time for the government to take some actions.

 A. Having suffered   B. Suffering

 C. To suffer   D. Suffered

4) "Our picnic is ruined again," said Bob, _____ at the heavy rain out of the window.

 A. looking   B. to look

 C. looked   D. having looked

5) _____ the child to bed, she began to continue writing her novel.

 A. Sending   B. Being sent

 C. Sent   D. To send

6) When _____, water changes into steam.

 A. to heat   B. heating

 C. heated   D. they are heated

7) _____, we had to walk home.

 A. There was no bus   B. We couldn't find a bus

 C. There being no bus   D. There no bus

8) _____ to the party, Mary was greatly hurt.

   A. Having not been invited   B. Not having been invited

   C. Having not invited   D. Not having invited

9) There was a terrible noise _____ the sudden burst of light.

   A. followed   B. following

   C. to be followed   D. being followed

10) Leave your key with a neighbor _____ you lock yourself out one day.

   A. ever since   B. even if

   C. soon after   D. in case

Section D   Sentence Writing

My House Paint Color!

1. What is the paint color of the house?

   Tips: body, roof, trim, front door…

   _____
   _____.

2. What are your favorite colors for a house?

   Tips: love/like, perfect, stand out …

   _____
   _____.

3. What is the impact of a certain color on a house as well as on its local environment?

   Tips: exterior color (外墙颜色), choose, affect, not only…but also, highlight …

_____
_____.

4. What will be the right color if you paint your classroom?

   Tips: first of all, then, finally, emphasize, avoid, extreme contrast, strive, balance …

   _____
   _____.

Glossary

Unit 1

New Words

refine [ri'fain] *vt.* 精制，改善，使高雅
cave [keiv] *n.* 洞穴
mountainside ['mauntənsaid] *n.* 山腰，山坡
painting ['peintiŋ] *n.* 绘画，油画
elaborated ★ [i'læbərətid] *adj.* 复杂的，精心制作的，精巧的
imagine [i'mædʒin] *vt.* 设想，想象；*vi.* 想象，猜想，推测
ancient ['einʃənt] *adj.* 古代的，古老的；*n.* 古代人
obtain [əb'tein] *vt.* 获得，得到，达到（目的）；*vi.* 通行，流行，存在
buffalo ['bʌfələu] *n.* 水牛
strength [streŋθ] *n.* 力量，优点
abstract ['æbstrækt] *adj.* 抽象的，难解的，抽象派的，茫然的
symbol ['simbl] *n.* 象征，标志，符号
amazing [ə'meiziŋ] *adj.* 令人惊异的
work [wə:k] *n.* （艺术家、作家、作曲家等的）作品，著作
Egyptian ★ [i'dʒipʃn] *n.* 埃及人；*adj.* 埃及的，埃及人的
religion [ri'lidʒən] *n.* 宗教
pyramid ★ ['pirəmid] *n.* 金字塔
creativity [ˌkri:ei'tivəti] *n.* 创造性，创造力
religious [ri'lidʒəs] *adj.* 宗教的，虔诚的
classical ['klæsikl] *adj.* 古典的，经典的
gain [gein] *vt./vi.* 获得，赢得
favor ['feivə] *n.* 好感，宠爱，欢心
portrait ['pɔ:treit] *n.* 肖像，肖像画

photograph ['fəutəgra:f] *n.* 相片
Dutch [dʌtʃ] *adj.* 荷兰的 *n.* 荷兰人
lifetime ['laiftaim] *n.* 一生，寿命，使用期限
characterize ['kærəktəraiz] *vt.* 表示……的典型，赋予……特色
intense [in'tens] *adj.* 紧张的，激烈的，深刻的
contrast ['kɔntra:st] *n.* 对比，对照物；*v.* 对比，成对照
intensify [in'tensifai] *vt.* 强化，加剧
calm [ka:m] *adj.* 平静的，冷静的；*v.* （使）平静，（使）镇静；*n.* 镇定，平静
seldom ['seldəm] *adv.* 很少，难得；*adj.* 很少的，难得的，稀少的
distorted [dis'tɔ:tid] *adj.* 扭曲的，变形的
unique [ju'ni:k] *adj.* 独特的，独一无二的
fade [feid] *vi.* 褪去，逐渐消逝；*vt.* 使褪色；*adj.* 乏味的，平淡的
mental ['mentl] *adj.* 内心的，精神的，思想的
develop [di'veləp] *v.* 发展，开发，冲洗（照片）
reflect [ri'flekt] *v.* 反映，反射，反省

Useful Expressions

come upon 偶遇，突然发现或遇到
a variety of 多种的，种种
make the most of 充分利用
fade from 从……中消逝
as well 也，又
whether…or… 是……还是……
curved lines ★ 曲线

Proper Nouns

the Great Sphinx [sfiŋks] 狮身人面像
Vincent van Gogh ['vinsənt væn'gəu] 文森特·梵高（荷兰画家）

Unit 2

New Words

define [di'fain] *vt.* 定义，界定

root [ruːt] *n.* 根，根源

folk [fəuk] *n.* 民族，人们；*adj.* 民间的，普通平民的

tradition [trə'diʃn] *n.* 传统，惯例

slave [sleiv] *n.* 奴隶

audience ['ɔːdiəns] *n.* 观众，读者，听众

recording [ri'kɔːdiŋ] *n.* 记录，录音，唱片

original [ə'ridʒənl] *adj.* 原始的，独创的，最初的

feature ['fiːtʃə(r)] *n.* 特征，容貌，（期刊的）特辑，故事片；*vt.* 使有特色；描写……的特征；*vi.* 起主要作用，作重要角色

pianist ['piənist] *n.* 钢琴家，钢琴师

composition [ˌkɔmpə'ziʃn] *n.* 作文，作曲，创作

pioneer [ˌpaiə'niə(r)] *n.* 拓荒者，先驱者；*vt.* 开拓，做……的先锋

contribution [ˌkɔntri'bjuːʃn] *n.* 贡献，捐赠

entertainer [ˌentə'teinə(r)] *n.* 表演者，艺人

swing [swiŋ] *n.* 摇摆乐，摇摆舞

surpass [sə'paːs] *vt.* 超过，胜过

rhythm ['riðəm] *n.* ［诗］节奏，韵律；［乐］节拍

melody ['melədi] *n.* 旋律，曲调

smooth [smuːð] *adj.* 光滑的，流畅的

era ['iərə] *n.* 纪元，年代，时代

classics ['klæsiks] *n.* 文学名著，优秀的典范

varied ['veərid] *adj.* 各种各样的

musician [mju'ziʃn] *n.* 音乐家

continent ['kɔntinənt] *n.* 大陆，陆地

close-knit [ˌkləus'nit] *adj.* 紧密的，组织严密的

tour [tuə(r)] *vi.* 观光，巡回

infant ['infənt] *n.* 婴儿，幼儿

demo ['deməu] *n.* 演示，样本唱片

producer [prə'djuːsə(r)] *n.* 生产者，制作人

sign [sain] *vt. & vi.* 签名；*n.* 符号，指示牌

mortgage★ ['mɔːgidʒ] *n. & vt.* 抵押贷款

album ['ælbəm] *n.* 唱片，相册，集邮簿

numerous ['njuːmərəs] *adj.* 很多的，许多的

performance [pə'fɔːməns] *n.* 表演，演技，表现

broadcast ['brɔːdkaːst] *vt.* 广播；*n.* 电台, 电视节目

live [laiv] *adj.* 活着的，生动的，现场直播的

throughout [θruː'aut] *prep.* （表示时间）自始至终，在……期间；（表示空间）遍及……地域

breakthrough ['breikθruː] *n.* 突破

theme [θi:m] n. [乐] 主题，主旋律
hit [hit] n. 成功而轰动（或风行）一时的事物（如唱片、电影或戏剧）
billboard ['bilbɔ:d] n. 广告牌，告示牌
award [ə'wɔ:d] n. 奖品；vt. 授予，奖给奖品
genre ★ ['ʒɔnrə] n. 种类，体裁，流派
gospel ★ ['gɔspl] n. 福音（书），福音音乐（尤流行于美国南部黑人基督徒中）

Useful Expressions

have its root in 植根于
borrow from 借用
in particular 尤其是，特别
in addition to 除此之外
cross over 横过（河等），穿过
be richly influenced by 受到……很大的影响
to the delight of sb. 使某人感到开心
in person 亲自，亲身
under the condition 在某种条件下

Proper Nouns

New Orleans [nju: 'ɔ:liənz] n. 新奥尔良（美国港口城市）
Diexieland ['diksilænd] 迪克西兰
Original Dixieland Jazz Band 迪克西兰爵士乐队
Jelly Roll Morton ['dʒeli rəu 'mɔ:tən] 杰利·罗尔·莫顿（美国爵士乐作曲家、钢琴家）
Louis Armstrong ['lu(:)is 'a:mstrɔŋ] 路易斯·阿姆斯特朗（爵士乐之父）
Benny Goodman ['beni: 'gudmæn] 本尼·古德曼（美国单簧管演奏家、爵士乐音乐家）
Carnegie Hall [ka:'negi 'hɔ:l] 卡内基音乐厅
Billie Holiday ['bili 'hɔlədei] 比莉·霍利戴（20世纪爵士歌坛三大天后之一）
Sarah Vaughan ['seərə vɔ:n] 莎拉·沃恩（20世纪爵士歌坛三大天后之一）
Ella Fitzgerald ['elə fits'dʒerəld] 埃拉·菲茨杰拉德（20世纪爵士歌坛三大天后之一）
Celine Marie Claudette Dion [sei'li:n mə'ri: klɔ:'det 'daiən] 席琳·玛丽·克劳德特·迪翁
Rene Angelil ['renei 'eindʒilil] 雷尼·安杰利（席琳·迪翁的丈夫和经纪人）
Juno Awards ['dʒu:nəu ə'wɔ:d] 朱诺奖（授予加拿大音乐艺术家以及团体的奖项）
Eurovision Song Contest ['juərəviʒn sɔŋ 'kɔntest] 欧洲电视网歌唱大赛
Ireland ['aiələnd] 爱尔兰（岛）
Dublin ['dʌblin] 都柏林（爱尔兰首都）
Europe ['juərəp] n. 欧洲

Grammy Award ['græmi ə'wɔːd] 格莱美奖
Academy Award [ə'kædəmi ə'wɔːd] 学院奖（奥斯卡奖）

Unit 3

New Words

flu [fluː] *n.* 流行性感冒，流感
last [laːst] *vi.* 持续；*vt.* 够用，足够维持（某段时间）；*adj.* 最近的，最后的，最不想要的
secretary ['sekrətri] *n.* 秘书，干事
church [tʃəːtʃ] *n.* [宗] 教堂，教会
hand [hænd] *n.* 手，协助，帮助；*vt.* 传递，交给
special ['speʃl] *adj.* 特殊的，特别的；*n.* 特色菜，特产
envelope ['envələup] *n.* 信封，封皮
worth [wəːθ] *adj.* 值……钱，值得的；*n.* 财富，财产，价值
hug [hʌg] *vt.* 热烈地拥抱，抱紧（某物）；*n.* 拥抱
store [stɔː(r)] *n.* 商店
much-needed★ *adj.* 急需的
item ['aitəm] *n.* 条款，项目，物品
cashier [kæ'ʃiə(r)] *n.* 收银员，出纳员
blessing★ ['blesiŋ] *n.* 福气，恩赐
reply [ri'plai] *n. & vt.* 回复，答复
giant ['dʒaiənt] *adj.* 巨大的，特大的；*n.* 巨人，卓越人物
loving ['lʌviŋ] *adj.* 充满爱意的，慈爱的，关爱的
turkey ['təːki] *n.* 火鸡
change [tʃeindʒ] *n. & vt.* 改变，变化；*n.* 零钱，找头
awkward ['ɔːkwəd] *adj.* 棘手的，使人尴尬的，笨拙的
pray [prei] *vt.* 祈祷，祷求
counter ['kauntə(r)] *n.* （商店或酒吧的）柜台；*adj.* 相反的
purse [pəːs] *n.* 钱包，女用手提包
bless [bles] *vt.* 保佑，为……祈求上帝保佑
move [muːv] *vt. & vi.* 移动，搬家；*vt.* 使感动
realize ['riːəlaiz] *vt. & vi.* 认识，领会，实现
deed [diːd] *n.* 行为，行动，事迹
celebrate ['selibreit] *vt.* 庆祝，庆贺
mark [maːk] *vt.* 标示，为……做标记；*n.* 成绩，分数，记号
gift [gift] *n.* 礼物，天赋

223

beloved [bi'lʌvd] *adj.* 心爱的，钟爱的；*n.* 心爱的人
symbol ['simbl] *n.* 象征，标志，符号
arrow ['ærəu] *n.* 箭，箭头
cause [kɔːz] *vt.* 引起，导致；*n.* 原因，动机，事业
target ['tɑːgit] *n.* 目标，对象
emperor★ ['emp(ə)rə] *n.* 君主，帝王
rule [ruːl] *vt.* 统治，控制，支配；*n.* 规则，规定
warlike★ ['wɔːlaik] *adj.* 好战的，尚武的
solve [sɔlv] *vt.* 解决（问题）
ban [bæn] *n.* 禁止，取缔；*vt.* 禁令
priest★ [priːst] *n.* 牧师，神父
marry ['mæri] *vt. & vi.* （使）结婚，娶，嫁；*vt.* 为……主持婚礼
prison ['prizn] *n.* 监狱
heal [hiːl] *vt.* 治愈，愈合
jailer★ ['dʒeilə(r)] *n.* 监狱看守
sign [sain] *vt. & vi.* 签名，署名，打手势；*n.* 符号，手势，指示牌
farewell [ˌfeə'wel] *n.* 告别，欢送；*adj.* 告别的，送行的
involve [in'vɔlv] *vt.* 涉及，牵涉，参与
replace [ri'pleis] *vt.* 代替，替换，把……放回原处
commercial [kə'məːʃl] *adj.* 商业的，贸易的，盈利的

Useful Expressions

be sick with 患……病
grocery certificates ★ 杂货购物券
seem like 看上去像，看起来像
turn around 转身，使调整方向，（使）好转
reach for... 伸手去拿，伸手去够
due to 因为，由于
fall in love (with sb.) 爱上（某人）
have difficulty (in) doing 做某事有困难
believe in 相信，信奉，信仰
in secret 偷偷地，私下地

Proper Nouns

Cupid ['kjuːpid] 丘比特（罗马神话中的爱神）

Unit 4

New Words

necktie ['nektai] *n.* 领带
request [ri'kwest] *n.* 要求，需要
purchase ['pə:tʃəs] *n.* 购买，购买行为，购置物
solution [sə'lu:ʃn] *n.* 解决，溶解
target ['ta:git] *n.* 目标
appeal [ə'pi:l] *vi.* 有吸引力，提请注意
grab [græb] *v.* 抓住，夺取
advertisement [əd'və:tismənt] *n.* 广告，宣传
successful [sək'sesfl] *adj.* 成功的，有成就的
advertising ['ædvətaiz] *adj.* 广告的，广告业的；*n.* 广告，做广告
provide [prə'vaid] *vt. & vi.* 提供，供给，供应
promote [prə'məut] *vt.* 促进，提升，促销
advertise ['ædvətaiz] *vt. & vi.* 做广告，做宣传
consumer [kən'sju:mə] *n.* 消费者
design [di'zain] *vt.* 设计，绘制
image ['imidʒ] *n.* 形象，影像
improve [im'pru:v] *vt. & vi.* 提高，改善，改良
diet ['daiət] *n.* 日常饮食，规定饮食；*vt. & vi.* （使）节制饮食
attractive [ə'træktiv] *adj.* 引人注目的，有吸引力的
encourage [in'kʌridʒ] *vt.* 鼓励，鼓舞
pursue [pə'sju:] *vt.* 继续，追求
engineer [ˌendʒi'niə(r)] *n.* 工程师
negative ['negətiv] *adj.* 负面的，消极的，否认的
impact ['impækt] *n.* 影响，冲击，碰撞
persuade [pə'sweid] *vt.* 说服，使信服
sugary ['ʃugəri] *adj.* 含糖的，甜的
overweight [ˌəuvə'weit] *adj.* 超重的，过重的
overall [ˌəuvər'ɔ:l] *adj.* 全面的，综合的
socialize ['səuʃəlaiz] *vi.* 参与社交，联谊
talked-about★ [tɔ:kət'əbaut] *adj.* 谈论的
ad-filmmaker ★ [æd' film meikə] *n.* 广告片制作人
hug [hʌg] *n. & vt.* 拥抱，紧抱

vending ['vendiŋ] *n.* （尤指在公共场所）贩卖
install [in'stɔːl] *vt.* 安装，安顿，任命
respond [ri'spɔnd] *vt. & vi.* 回答，响应 *vi.* 作出反应，回报或回复
currency ['kʌrənsi] *n.* 货币，通用，流通
specifically [spə'sifikli] *adv.* 特有地，明确地
dispenser [di'spensə(r)] *n.* 自动售卖机，配药师，自动取款机（或饮水机等）
specific [spə'sifik] *adj.* 明确的，特种的，具体的；*n.* 特性，细节
bold [bəuld] *adj.* 醒目的，勇敢的，无畏的；*n.* 粗体字，黑体字
innovative ['inəveitiv] *adj.* 革新的，创新的
unexpected [ˌʌnik'spektid] *adj.* 想不到的，意外的
engage [in'geidʒ] *vt.* 吸引住，聘用；*vi.* 与……建立密切关系，从事
position [pə'ziʃn] *n.* 位置，地位，职位；*vt.* 安置，把……放在适当位置
stunt★ [stʌnt] *n.* 惊险动作，特技，噱头
affection [ə'fekʃn] *n.* 喜爱，慈爱，情感或感情
discourage [dis'kʌridʒ] *vt.* 使气馁，使沮丧
threatening ['θretniŋ] *adj.* 胁迫的，险恶的
demonstrate ['demənstreit] *vt.* 证明，展示，演示；*vi.* 示威游行
favour ['feivə] *n.* 好感，宠爱，关切；*vt.* 支持，赞成
campaign [kæm'pein] *n.* 运动，活动
influence ['influəns] *n.* 影响力，影响；*vt.* 影响，感染
instill [in'stil] *vt.* 逐步灌输
belief [bi'liːf] *n.* 信念，信条

Useful Expressions

tend to 倾向，易于
at least 至少
focus on 集中于
have an impact on 对……有影响
respond to 对……作出回应
be rewarded with 拿……作为奖励
on the rise 在增加，在上涨
at large 总体地，（囚犯）在逃，逍遥法外
roll out 推出，铺开

Proper Nouns

Tom Bernardin [tɔm bə'nɑːdjən] 汤姆·贝尔纳丁（人名）（美国李奥贝纳全球主席及行政总裁）
Coca-Cola [ˌkəukə 'kəulə] 可口可乐
National University of Singapore ['næʃnəl ˌjuːni'vəːsəti əvˌsiŋə'pɔː] 新加坡国立大学
Singapore [ˌsiŋə'pɔː] *n.* 新加坡（东南亚国家）
Ogilvy & Mather [ˌɔːdʒil'viː 'mæðə(r)] 奥美广告公司

Unit 5

New Words

rusty ['rʌsti] *adj.* 迟钝的，生锈的
rhythm ['riðəm] *n.* 节奏，韵律
quarterfinal [kwɔːtə'fainəl] *n.* 四分之一决赛
tournament ['tuənəmənt] *n.* 锦标赛，联赛
indoors ['indɔːz] *adv.* 在室内
immediately [i'miːdiətli] *adv.* 立即，立刻
throughout [θruː'aut] *prep.* 贯穿，遍及
professional [prə'feʃənəl] *adj.* 专业的，职业的
weird [wiəd] *adj.* 怪诞的，超自然的，奇异的
prime [praim] *n.* 精华，全盛
late [leit] *adj.* 已故的，迟到的
leap [liːp] *vi.* 跳，冲动的行动 *vt.* 跳过，使跳跃
rookie ['ruki] *n.* 新手，新人（俗称"菜鸟"）
champion ['tʃæmpiən] *n.* 冠军
defensive [di'fensiv] *adj.* 防御的，防守的，辩护的，自卫的
outstanding [aut'stændiŋ] *adj.* 杰出的，显著的
athlete ['æθliːt] *n.* 运动员，体育家
soundness ['saundnis] *n.* 健康，稳固
artistry ['ɑːtistri] *n.* 艺术性，工艺
competitive [kəm'petətiv] *adj.* 竞争的，比赛的，有竞争力的
single-handedly ['siŋgl-'hændidli] *adv.* 单手的，单枪匹马的
redefine [ˌriːdi'fain] *v.* 重新定义，再定义
comparison [kəm'pærisn] *n.* 比较，对照

contrived★ [kən'traivd] adj. 人为的，做作的
undergo [ˌʌndə'gəu] v. 经历
radical ['rædikəl] adj. 激进的，根本的
circle ['sə:kl] n. 圆，圈子；vt. 圈出，包围，绕……运转；vi. 环绕，盘旋
unending [ʌn'endiŋ] adj. 不断的，无止境的
announce [ə'nauns] vt. 宣布，播报
retirement [ri'taiəmənt] n. 退休，退役
reflect [ri'flekt] vt. & vi. 反射（光、热、声或影像），反映，考虑，反省
cynic★ ['sinik] n. 愤世嫉俗者，犬儒学派的人
limitation [ˌlimi'teiʃn] n. 限制，限度
diligent ['dilidʒənt] adj. 勤奋的，勤勉的，用功的
latterly ['lætəli] adv. 近来，最近，后来
counter ['kauntə] vt. 反击，还击
league [li:g] n. 联盟；社团
obvious ['ɔbviəs] adj. 明显的，显著的
accomplish [ə'kʌmpliʃ] vt. 完成，达到（目的）
elevate ['eliveit] vt. 提升，举起
saviour★ ['seivjə] n. 救世主，救星
draw [drɔ:] n. 平局，抽签
secure [si'kjuə] vt. 保护，争取到
imperfection [ˌimpə'fekʃn] n. 不完美，瑕疵

Useful Expressions

one-on-one 一对一的
to be frank 坦白地说
much less 更不用说，不及
beyond doubt 毫无疑问
turn back the clock 时光逆转
reflect (with pride) on （自豪地）回想……
CV (Curriculum Vitae) 简历
a roll of 一卷
be regarded as 被当作是……，被认为是……
send off 寄出，罚出场
have regret about 为……感到遗憾
win back 重获，赢回
free kick （足球）任意球
in the manner 以某种方式

Proper Nouns

Michael Jordan ['maikəl 'dʒɔːdən] *n.* 迈克尔·乔丹（人名）
LeBron James [lə 'brɔn 'dʒæmz] *n.* 勒布朗·詹姆斯（人名）
Bruce Lee [bruːs 'liː] *n.* 李小龙（人名）
Mike Tyson [maik taisən] *n.* 迈克·泰森（人名）
NBA (National Basketball Association) 美国职业篮球协会
MVP (Most Valuable Player) 最有价值球员
David Beckham [deivid 'bekhæm] 大卫·贝克汉姆（人名）
PSG 巴黎圣日耳曼（Paris Saint Garment 的简称）
Manchester United ['mæntʃistə juˈnaitid] 曼彻斯特联队（简称"曼联"）
Nou Camp [njuː kæmp] 诺坎普球场（西班牙巴塞罗那队主场馆）
FA Cups [faː kʌps] 英格兰足总杯（The Football Association Challenge Cup 的简称）
Real Madrid [riːl məˈdrid] 皇家马德里队（简称"皇马"）
AC Milan ['ei 'siː miˈlæn] AC 米兰
Paris St-Germain ['pæris seint dʒəˈmein] 巴黎圣日耳曼（简称为"PSG"）
LA Galaxy [ˌelˈei ˈgæləksi] 洛杉矶银河队
Argentina [ˌaːdʒənˈtiːnə] 阿根廷
Diego Simeone [diˈeigəu ˈsimiən] 迭戈·西蒙尼（人名）
Old Trafford [əuld ˈtræfəd] 老特拉福德球场（位于英格兰）

Unit 6

New Words

imagery [ˈimidʒəri] *n.* 形象，意象
historical [hisˈtɔrikl] *adj.* 历史的，史学的
literature [ˈlitrətʃə] *n.* 文学，文艺，著作
character [ˈkærəktə(r)] *n.* 角色，性格
appear [əˈpiə(r)] *vi.* 出现，显得，似乎
irrational★ [iˈræʃənl] *adj.* 非理性的
inspiration [ˌinspəˈreiʃn] *n.* 灵感，鼓舞
vision [ˈviʒn] *n.* 幻想，远见，视力
represent [ˌrepriˈzent] *vt.* 代表，表现
symbolism★ [ˈsimbəlizəm] *n.* 象征主义
expressionism★ [ikˈspreʃənizəm] *n.* 表现主义
playwright [ˈpleirait] *n.* 剧作家

coin [kɔin] *vi.* 杜撰，创造
narrative ['nærətiv] *adj.* 叙事的，叙事体的
distinguish [di'stiŋgwiʃ] *vi.* 区别，区分
fantasy ['fæntəsi] *n.* 幻想
animation [ˌæni'meiʃn] *n.* 动画片
depiction [di'pikʃn] *n.* 描写，描绘
remain [ri'mein] *vi.* 保持，依然
rarity ['reərəti] *n.* 罕见，珍贵
confessional★ [kən'feʃnl] *adj.* 忏悔的，自白的
identify [ai'dentifai] *vt.* 辨别出，识别
originate [ə'ridʒineit] *vi.* 发源，起源
contemporary [kən'temprəri] *adj.* 当代的，同时代的
psychological [ˌsaikə'lɔdʒikl] *adj.* 心理的，心理学的
discipline ['disəplin] *n.* 纪律，规章制度
desire [di'zaiə(r)] *n.* 渴望，欲望
boutique [bu'tik] *n.* 精品店，专卖流行衣服的小商店
magazine [ˌmægə'zi:n] *n.* 杂志
promote [prə'məut] *vt.* 提升，促进
reputation [ˌrepju'teiʃn] *n.* 名誉，声望
label ['leibl] *n.* 标签，商标
collaborator★ [kə'læbəreitə(r)] *n.* 合作者
graphics★ ['græfiks] *n.* 图像，图形
rank [ræŋk] *vt.* 评定等级，名列，位居
influential [ˌinflu'enʃl] *adj.* 有影响力的
stylist ['stailist] *n.* 设计师，造型师
prominent ['prɔminənt] *adj.* 杰出的，显著的
broker ['brəukə(r)] *n.* 经纪人，代理人
elitist [i'li:tist] *n.* 优秀人才，杰出人物

Useful Expressions

base on 基于，建立在……基础上
served as 充当，起……作用
consist of 由……组成，由……构成
comic strips 连环漫画
range from 从……到……范围
train as 受过……训练
get involved in 涉及，参加……活动

stick to 坚持做某事
along with 和……一起
take control of 控制
interpret as 把……看作，把……理解为
pop up stores （短期经营）时尚潮店

Proper Nouns

August Strindberg [ɔːgʌst 'strindbərg] 奥古斯特·斯特林堡（瑞典剧作家）
Winsor McCay ['winzə mai' kei] 温瑟·麦凯（美国著名漫画家和动画导演）
Jasper John ['dʒæspə dʒɔn] 贾斯珀·约翰（美国战后著名艺术家）
Jim Dine [dʒim dain] 吉姆·迪恩（美国波普艺术家）
Anne Rice [æn rais] 安妮·赖斯（美国当代著名小说家）
Stephen King ['stiːvən kiŋ] 史蒂芬·金（美国畅销书作家）
Robert Altman ['rɔbət 'ɔːltmən] 罗伯特·阿特曼（美国著名电影导演）
John Sayles [dʒɔn 'seilz] 约翰·赛尔斯（美国独立导演、编剧、作家）
Paul McCartney [pɔːl mək' kʌtni] 保罗·麦卡特尼（英国音乐家、创作歌手及作曲家）
Billy Joel ['bili 'dʒəuel] 比利·乔尔（美国天才歌手、钢琴家、作曲家、作词家）
Nicola Formichetti [ni'kɔː lʌ fɔrmi'keti] 尼克拉·弗米切提（著名造型师、设计师、时尚编辑）
Diesel [dizl] 迪赛（意大利著名时尚品牌）
Katy England ['keti 'iŋglənd] 凯蒂·英格兰（英国著名造型师、时尚编辑）
Lane Crawford ['lein 'krɔfəd] 连卡佛（亚洲最具影响力的时装及生活专门店）

Unit 7

New Words

philosopher [fə'lɔsəfə(r)] n. 哲学家，哲人
curiosity [kjuəri'ɔsiti] n. 好奇心，好奇
wisdom ['wizdəm] n. 智慧，才智
boost [buːst] vt. 促进，提高；vi. 宣扬；n. 提高，增加，吹捧
lecture ['lektʃə] n. & vt. 演讲，教训
challenge ['tʃæləndʒ] vt. 向……挑战；n. 挑战，怀疑
false [fɔːls] adj. 错误的，伪造的
courage ['kʌridʒ] n. 勇气，胆量
philosophy [fə'lɔsəfi] n. 哲学，哲理，人生观
spot [spɔt] n. 地点，斑点，污点；vt. 认出，发现

anger ['æŋgə(r)] vt. 触怒，激怒；n. 愤怒
embarrassed [im'bærəst] adj. 尴尬的，窘迫的
eventually [i'ventʃuəli] adv. 最终，终于
leader ['li:də(r)] n. 领导者，领袖
prison ['prizn] n. 监狱
misbehave [ˌmisbi'heiv] vi. & vt. 行为不礼貌，使行为不端
deadly ['dedli] adj. 极端的，非常的，致命的
punishment ['pʌniʃmənt] n. 惩罚，处罚，刑罚
poison ['pɔizn] n. 毒药，毒；vi. & vt. 下毒，使中毒
obey [ə'bei] vt. 遵守，服从
preserve [pri'zə:v] vt. 保存，保留，保护
generation [ˌdʒenə'reiʃn] n. 一代（约30年），一代人
civil ['sivl] adj. 公民的，国内的
arrest [ə'rest] vt. 逮捕，拘捕
certain ['sə:tn] adj. 某些，某一，确信的
spark [spa:k] vt. 引发，发出火花；n. 火花
protest ['prəutest] n. 抗议；vt. & vi. 反对，抗议
resident ['rezidənt] n. 居民
choose [tʃu:z] vt./vi. 选择，挑选，选出
minister ['ministə(r)] n. 牧师，部长
nonviolence ['nɔn'vaiələns] n. 非暴力，非暴力政策
powerful ['pauəfl] adj. 强大的，强有力的
demanding [di'ma:ndiŋ] adj. 强人所难的，强求的
peaceful ['pi:sfl] adj. 和平的，爱好和平的，安静的
strike [straik] n. 罢工；vt. 打击，撞击
organize ['ɔ:gənaiz] vt. 组织，安排，使有条理
march [ma:tʃ] n. 游行示威，行军；vi. 前进，行军
deliver [di'livə(r)] vt. 发表，递送
content ['kɔntent] n. 内容，（书等的）目录，满足
equal ['i:kwəl] adj. 平等的，相同的
reform [ri'fɔ:m] n. 改革，改良，改造；vt. & vi. 改善
award [ə'wɔ:d] vt. 授予，赠予；n. 奖
unfortunately [ʌn'fɔ:tʃənətli] adv. 不幸的是，遗憾的是
shoot [ʃu:t] vi. 射击，射杀
establish [i'stæbliʃ] vt. 建立，创立

Useful Expressions

figure out 计算出，弄明白，解决，想出
searched for 寻找，搜寻
break down 毁掉，分解，发生故障
pay for 为……而付钱，赔偿
put sb. in prison 把某人关进监狱，关押
Systematic Theology ★ [ˌsɪstə'mætɪk θɪ'ɔlədʒi] 系统神学
give up 放弃，交出
the same as 与……相同
such as 比如，诸如
because of 因为，由于
be regarded as 被认为是

Proper Nouns

Greece [griːs] 希腊
Socrates ['sɔkrətiːz] 苏格拉底（公元前 469?—前 399 古希腊哲学家）
Plato ['pleitəu] 柏拉图（约公元前 427—约前 347 古希腊哲学家）
Athens ['æθinz] 雅典（希腊首都）
Ph.D. 文学博士，哲学博士（Doctor of Philosophy 的缩写）
Boston University ['bɔʃtən ˌjuːni'vəːsəti] 波士顿大学
Rosa Parks ['rəuzə 'paːks] 罗莎·帕克斯
Martin Luther King, Jr. ['maːtin 'luθəkiŋ 'dʒuːniə(r)] 马丁·路德·金
Mahatma Gandhi [mə'hætmə 'gændi:] 圣雄甘地
Washington, D.C. ['wɔʃiŋtən 'diː'siː] 华盛顿特区（DC 是 District of Columbia 的缩写）

Unit 8

New Words

competitive [kəm'petitiv] *adj.* 竞争的，比赛的
mechanics [mi'kæniks] *n.* 机制，力学，机械学
complex ['kɔmpleks] *adj.* 复杂的，难懂的；*n.* 建筑群，情结
confused [kən'fjuzd] *adj.* 糊涂的，迷乱的，混杂的
subconscious [ˌsʌb'kɑːnʃəs] *adj.* 下意识的，潜意识的

233

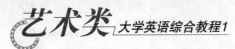

efficient [i'fiʃənt] *adj.* 有效率的，（直接）生效的
deliver [di'livə] *vt.* 发表，递送，使分娩；*vi.* 投递，传送
conscious ['kɑːnʃəs] *adj.* 有意识的，神志清醒的
overcome [ˌəuvər'kʌm] *vt. & vi.* 战胜，克服
nervousness ['nəːvəsnis] *n.* 神经质，焦躁，胆小
furthermore [ˌfəːrðər'mɔːr] *adv.* 此外，而且
benefit ['benəfit] *n.* 利益，好处；*vt.* 有益于，有助于
remind [ri'maind] *vt.* 使想起，使记起；提醒
perspective [pər'spektiv] *n.* 观点，看法；*adj.*（按）透视画法的，透视的
scheme [skiːm] *vt. & vi.* 策划，图谋；*n.* 计划，阴谋
instant ['instənt] *adj.* 立即的，迫切的；*n.* 瞬间，速食食品
lifter ['liftə] *n.* 提升器，升降机
disappointed [ˌdisə'pɔintid] *adj.* 失望的，沮丧的
expectation [ˌekspek'teʃən] *n.* 期待，预期，前程
focus ['fəukəs] *vt. & vi.*（使）集中，（使）聚集，调整；*n.* 焦点；（活动、注意力、兴等的）中心
socialize ['səuʃəlaiz] *vi.* 与……交往，联谊；*vt.* 使社会化
pleasant ['pleznt] *adj.* 可爱的，令人愉快的，晴朗的
atmosphere ['ætməsfir] *n.* 大气，风格，气氛
frustrated ['frʌstreitid] *adj.* 挫败的，失意的，泄气的
emotional ['iməuʃənl] *adj.* 令人动情的，易动感情的
state [steit] *n.* 状况，国家，州
critically ['kritikli] *adv.* 批判性地，危急地
liberate ['libəˌret] *vt.* 解放，释放
strive [straiv] *vi.* 努力奋斗，斗争
purposeful ['pəːrpəsfl] *adj.* 有目的的，故意的
leisure ['liːʒər] *n.* 空闲时间，闲暇；*adj.* 空闲的，闲暇的
self-improvement 自我改善，自我修养，自强
pursue [pər'suː] *vt.* 继续，追求；*vi.* 追，追赶
obvious ['ɑːbviəs] *adj.* 明显的，显著的
nurture ['nəːrtʃə(r)] *vt.* 养育，培育；*n.* 教养，培育
authentic [ɔː'θentik] *adj.* 真的，真正的，可信的
bond [bɔnd] *n.* 纽带，债券；*v.* 使结合，与……紧密联系
solely ['səuli] *adv.* 唯一地，仅仅，纯粹

Useful Expressions

be likely to 可能

be familiar with 熟悉，认识
equip sb. to do sth. 使某人准备好做某事，使某人能做某事
deal with 与……交易，应付，对待
in the grand scheme of things 从大局来看，从整体来看
lead to 导致
rather than （要）……而不……，与其……倒不如……
engage in 参与
strive to 力图，力求

Unit 9

New Words

decade ['dekeid] *n.* 十年，十个一组
search [sə:tʃ] *v.* 搜寻，调查；*n.* 搜索，调查
alien ['eiliən] *adj.* 外国的，相异的；*n.* 外国人，外星人
discovery [di'skʌvəri] *n.* 发现，被发现的事物
astronomer★ [ə'strɔnəmə(r)] *n.* 天文学者，天文学家
awful ['ɔ:fl] *adj.* 糟糕的，非常的；*adv.* 非常，极
hunt [hʌnt] *vt. & vi.* 打猎，追捕，搜索；*n.* 打猎，狩猎旅行
beyond [bi'jɔnd] *prep.* 超过，越过；*adv.* 在远处
title ['taitl] *n.* 标题，头衔；*vt.* 加标题，赋予头衔
approach [ə'prəutʃ] *vt. & vi.* 接近，处理；*n.* 方法，接近
likelihood★ ['laiklihud] *n.* 可能，可能性
solar ['səulə(r)] *adj.* 太阳的，日光的
curiosity [ˌkjuəri'ɔsəti] *n.* 好奇心，奇特性
rover★ ['rəuvə(r)] *n.* 流浪者，漫游者
sign [sain] *n.* 符号，迹象，指示牌；*vt. & vi.* 签名，打手势
instance ['instəns] *n.* 例子，实例，情况
crack [kræk] *n.* 裂缝，破裂声；*vi.* 破裂，打，撞
hollow ['hɔləu] *adj.* 空的，虚伪的；*n.* 洞，山谷
telescope ['teliskəup] *n.* 望远镜
launch [lɔ:ntʃ] *vt.* 发射，发动，开展；*vi.* 投入，着手进行
sniff [snif] *vt. & vi.* 嗅，鄙视地说；*n.* 吸气，一股气味
methane★ ['mi:θein] *n.* [化]甲烷，沼气
oxygen ['ɔksidʒən] *n.* [化]氧，氧气
locate [ləu'keit] *vt.* 位于，确定……的位置；*vi.* 定位，定居

exoplanet★ [ek'sɔpleinit] *n.* 外星球
reflection [ri'flekʃən] *n.* 反映，（声、光、热等的）反射，映像
regardless [ri'ɡɑːdlis] *adv.* 不顾后果地，无论如何；*adj.* 不重视的，不顾虑的
encounter [in'kauntə] *vt.* 不期而遇，遭遇；*vi.* 碰见（尤指不期而遇）；*n.* 相遇，碰见
abduct★ [æb'dʌkt] *vt.* 劫持，诱拐
fiction ['fikʃən] *n.* 小说，编造，虚构
sighting ['saitiŋ] *n.* 瞄准，观察，视线
unidentified [ˌʌnai'dentifaid] *adj.* 不能辨认的，未经确认的
object ['ɔbdʒikt] *n.* 物体，目标，对象
         [əb'dʒekt] *vt. & vi.* 反对，抱反感
claim [kleim] *vt.* 声称，要求，认领；*n.* 要求，认领物，索赔
phenomenon [fi'nɔminən] *n.* 现象，事件
military ['militəri] *adj.* 军事的，军人的
incident ['insidənt] *n.* 事件，小插曲，骚乱
skeptic★ ['skeptik] *n.* 怀疑论者，无神论者
inspire [in'spaiə] *vt.* 鼓舞，激励，启迪
publisher ['pʌbliʃə] *n.* 出版商，公布者
highlight ['hailait] *n.*（图画或照片的）强光部分，最重要的事情，最精彩的部分；*vt.* 强调，突出，把……照亮
evidence ['evidəns] *n.* 证词，证据，迹象
reliability [riˌlaiə'biləti] *n.* 可靠，可信度
testimony★ ['testiməni] *n.* 证词，证明，证据
mistake [mi'steik] *n.* 错误；*vi.* 误解，弄错
aircraft ['eəkrɑːft] *n.* 飞机，航空器
logical ['lɔdʒikl] *adj.* 合逻辑的，合理的
official [ə'fiʃl] *adj.* 官方的，正式的，公务的；*n.* 官员，公务员
denial [di'naiəl] *n.* 否认，拒绝，背弃
fascination [ˌfæsi'neiʃn] *n.* 魅力，魔力，入迷
conspiracy★ [kən'spirəsi] *n.* 阴谋，共谋
cover-up★ ['kʌvəˌʌp] *n.* 掩饰，隐蔽
definitive★ [di'finətiv] *adj.* 决定性的，限定的
misinterpretation★ [ˌmisintə:pri'teiʃən] *n.* 误解，曲解
incredible [in'kredəbl] *adj.* 难以置信的，惊人的
galaxy ['ɡæləksi] *n.*［天］星系，银河系

Useful Expressions

for the most part 多半，就绝大部分而言；大多

in search for 寻求，寻找
thanks to 多亏，幸亏，由于
on the hunt for 正在搜索
talk of 谈到，说到
for instance 例如，比如，拿……来说
sniff out 嗅出，发现，察觉
regardless of 不管，不顾，无
pay sb. a visit 登门拜访
tend to 趋向于，往往，朝某方向
mistake ... as ... 把……误认为……，搞错
so far 迄今为止，到目前为止
may well 很可能
no more than 至多，只不过，仅仅
drop into 顺便去某地，掉进

Proper Nouns

Carl Sagan [ˈkɑːl ˈseigən] 卡尔·萨根（美国天文学家、天体物理学家、宇宙学家、科幻作家）
SETI (Search for Extraterrestrial Intelligence) 搜寻地外文明计划
Seth Shostak [seθ ˈʃɔsteik] 赛思·肖斯塔克（美国 SETI 活动的资深天文学家）
NASA [ˈnæsə] (National Aeronautics and Space Administration) 美国国家航空和宇宙航行局
Curiosity Rover [ˌkjuəriˈɔsəti ˈrəuvə(r)] 好奇号火星探测车
Red Planet [red ˈplænit] [口语] 火星，红色星球
James Webb Space Telescope [dʒeimz web speis ˈteliskəup] 詹姆斯·韦伯太空望远镜
Close Encounter [kləuz inˈkauntə] 近距离接触，亲密接触
UFO [ˌjuːefˈəu] (Unidentified Flying Object) 不明飞行物
Dr. Michael Shermer [ˈdɔktə ˈmaikl ˈʃəːmə] 迈克尔·舍默博士（美国"怀疑论者学会"的创始人）
Skeptic Magazine [ˈskeptik mægəˈziːn]《怀疑论者》杂志
Venus [ˈviːnəs] *n*. [天] 金星，维纳斯（爱与美的女神）

Unit 10

New Words

refer [riˈfəː(r)] *vt*. 归因于……，送交；*vi*. 提到，关系到
natural [ˈnætʃərəl] *adj*. 自然的，天生的

structure ['strʌktʃə] *n.* 结构，构造，建筑物；*vt.* 构成，排列，安排
tool [tu:l] *n.* 工具，器具
shelter ['ʃeltə] *n.* 居所，遮蔽
fort★ [fɔ:t] *n.* 堡垒，要塞
barn★ [ba:n] *n.* 谷仓，粮仓，牲口棚
tomb [tu:m] *n.* 坟墓，墓穴
temple ['templ] *n.* 庙，寺
variety [və'raiəti] *n.* 多样化，种类
gradually ['grædjuəli] *adv.* 逐步地，渐渐地
architecture ['a:kitektʃə] *n.* 建筑学，建筑风格
refine [ri'fain] *vt.* 提炼，改善
talent ['tælənt] *n.* 天资，才能，人才
construction [kən'strʌkʃən] *n.* 建筑物，建造
documentation★ [dɔkjumen'teiʃn] *n.* 文件材料
affect [ə'fekt] *vt.* 影响；*n.* 感情，心情
various ['veəriəs] *adj.* 各种各样的；多方面的
amaze [ə'meiz] *vt.* 使大为吃惊，使惊奇；*n.* 吃惊，好奇
wonder ['wʌndə] *n.* 奇观，奇迹；*vt.* 对……感到好奇；*vi.* 怀疑，想知道
process ['prəuses] *n.* 过程，工序，做事方法；*vt.* 加工，处理；*vi.* 列队行进
chase [tʃeis] *n.* 追捕，打猎；*vt. & vi.* 追捕，追寻，追求（常与*after*连用）
appreciate [ə'pri:ʃieit] *vt.* 感激，欣赏
major ['meidʒə] *adj.* 主要的，重要的；*n.* 主修科目；*vi.* 主修，专攻（常与*in*连用）
specialize ['speʃəlaiz] *vi.* 专门从事，专攻，详细说明
multistory [mʌlti'stɔ:ri] *adj.* 多层的
professional [prə'feʃənəl] *adj.* 专业的，专业性的；*n.* 专业人士
form [fɔ:m] *n.* 形状，形式；*vt.* 形成，构成；*vi.* 形成，产生
associate [ə'səuʃieit] *vt.* 使发生联系，联想；*vi.* 交往，结交
steel [sti:l] *n.* 钢，钢铁
geometric★ [,dʒi:ə'metrik] *adj.* 几何学的
decoration [,dekə'reiʃən] *n.* 装饰，装潢，装饰品
concrete★ ['kɔnkri:t] *n.* 混凝土
reflective [ri'flektiv] *adj.* （指物体表面）反光的，（指人、心情等）深思熟虑的
emphasize ['emfəsaiz] *vt.* 强调，使突出
skyline ['skailain] *n.* 地平线，天际线
landmark ['lændma:k] *n.* 地标，里程碑；*adj.* 有重大意义或影响的

Useful Expressions

a variety of 种种，各种各样的
be known as 被称为，被认为是，以……著称
be related to 与……有关
be amazed at 对……感到惊讶
specialize in 专门研究
control tower （机场）指挥塔台
work on 从事……
be widely used 被广泛应用
on the sides of 在……周边
add to 加入，增加

Proper Nouns

Angkor Wat ['æŋkɔːr wɔt]] *n.* 吴哥窟（柬埔寨的古都和游览胜地）
Cambodia [kæm'bəudiə] *n.* 柬埔寨（亚洲国名）
Ieoh Ming Pei ['iəu miŋ 'pei] 贝聿铭（美籍华人建筑师）
Canton ['kæn'tɔn] 广东
Mile High [mail hai] 英里高（位于丹佛）
Denver ['denvə] *n.* 丹佛（美国城市）
Colorado [ˌkɔləˈraːdəu] 美国科罗拉多州（位于美国西部）
Jacqueline Kennedy ['dʒækliːn 'kenidiː] 杰奎琳·肯尼迪（美国前第一夫人）
Kennedy Library ['kenidiː 'laibrəri] 肯尼迪图书馆
National Gallery of Art ['næʃnəl 'gæləri əv aːt] 美国国家艺术馆
Louvre Museum ['luːvə(r) mjuˈziːəm] 卢浮宫
Pritzker Prize ['pritsə praiz] 普利兹克建筑奖
Taj Mahal [taːdʒ məˈhaːl] 印度泰姬陵
Shah Jahan [ʃaː dʒəˈhaːn] 沙贾汗（印度莫卧儿帝国皇帝）
Prince Khnrram 库拉姆亲王
Yamuna River 亚穆纳河